中国教师发展基金会教师出版专项基金资助

基于程序性记忆原理的口语产出研究
——从间接引语中宾语从句结构的角度

陈峥嵘 著

学苑出版社

图书在版编目（CIP）数据

基于程序性记忆原理的口语产出研究：从间接引语中宾语从句结构的角度 / 陈峥嵘著 .—北京：学苑出版社，2015.7

ISBN 978-7-5077-4807-9

Ⅰ. ①基… Ⅱ. ①陈… Ⅲ. ①英语—口语—研究 Ⅳ. ①H319.9

中国版本图书馆CIP数据核字（2015）第160991号

责任编辑：郑泽英　李点点
封面设计：陈四雄
出版发行：学苑出版社
社　　址：北京市丰台区南方庄2号院1号楼
邮政编码：100079
网　　址：www.book001.com
电子邮箱：xueyuanpress@163.com
销售电话：010-67601101（销售部）、67603091（总编室）
经　　销：全国新华书店
印　刷　厂：北京长阳汇文印刷厂
开本尺寸：880mm×1230mm　　1/32
印　　张：9.5
字　　数：250千字
版　　次：2015年11月北京第1版
印　　次：2015年11月北京第1次印刷
定　　价：35.00元

A Study of Oral Production Based on the Principles of Procedural Memory: A Perspective of the Object Clause Structure in Indirect Speech

by Chen Zhengrong

前　　言

　　本书是在我的博士论文《基于程序性记忆原理的口语产出研究——从间接引语中宾语从句结构的角度》的基础上修改而成的。全书共分九章，约30万字（英文）。本研究主要基于程序性记忆的原理及口语产出的特点，构建了信息处理模型作为理论框架，以间接引语中宾语从句结构使用情况为突破口，采用一系列的实证研究系统考察了中国英语学习者口语产出情况以及程序性记忆对第二语言口语产出的影响作用。

　　本研究从信息处理的角度引入程序性记忆和自动性的概念，重新定义了语言能力，将流利度、准确度和复杂度作为指标来考察被试者在口头产出间接引语中宾语从句的结构时的情况，有利于促进中国外语教学界和语言心理学界在程序性记忆及口语方面的理论研究。本研究还通过揭示程序性记忆与词汇学习的相关性，进一步丰富了Ullman的DP记忆模式。在研究方法上，本研究大量借助认知心理学、认知脑科学领域的理论和实验研究成果，设计了横断式研究、对比式个案研究、跟踪式个案研究、交叉式个案研究以及认知行为实验、反省式访谈和问卷，拓展了国内第二语言习得口语研究的视角和研究手段。在教学方面，本研究对语言能力提出新的内容，并将程序性记忆及自动性引入口语评价指标中，有利于口语教师和学生调整口语训练的方式。同时，本研究的研究成果将对英语口语的教育决策、教材编写和教学方法产生指导性的意义，并为许多行之有效的传统教法和学法（精讲多练原则以及背诵、复述等）提供理论依据和实践指导。

在此，衷心感谢我的博士生导师——南京解放军国际关系学院陈开顺教授在我读博期间对我的悉心指导和鼓励。本研究的完成得到了南京解放军国际关系学院、东南大学、南京大学、南京师范大学等高校老师、同行和学生的鼎力支持，在此一并表示感谢！特别感谢东南大学学习中心的李雪松老师、王晓芳同学在实验方法上给予我的指导和帮助。当然，我的研究工作离不开家人一贯默默的支持。他们的关爱是我前进的动力。感谢他们！

本书在出版过程中得到了2014年度教育部中国教师发展基金会教师出版基金项目、东南大学外国语学院博士启动基金项目及东南大学社科处的大力支持和资助，在此表示衷心的感谢！

由于本人水平及经验有限，书中难免存在诸多不足之处，诚望各位同行和读者提出批评和建议。谢谢！

ABSTRACT

As an essential part of the multiple memory system, procedural memory has been considered important in L1 and L2 learning. Drawing on the principles of procedural memory, this study explores L2 oral proficiency of Chinese university students by establishing an information-processing framework and specifically investigates the effects of procedural memory on L2 oral proficiency with empirical studies by focusing on the object clause structure in indirect speech.

The information-processing framework of the present study is influenced by the current cognitive models which are most closely related to procedural memory, including schema theory, Anderson's ACT models and Ullman's declarative/procedural model. It redefines linguistic competence by introducing procedural memory and automaticity from the perspective of information processing. According to this framework, this study proposes that to assess the subjects' oral proficiency, the major indices should include fluency, accuracy and complexity which have been redefined and investigated at various levels.

As to research methods, the current study consists of a cross-sectional study, a comparative case study, a longitudinal case study and a cross-comparative case study, accompanied by cognitive behavioral experiments, retrospective interviews and follow-up questionnaires to address the following research questions: (1) the characteristics of different groups of subjects (Chinese high-proficiency English speakers vs. Chinese low-proficiency English speakers and the native English speakers vs. Chinese high-proficiency English speakers) in the application of procedural memory in oral production of the object clause structure in indirect speech under the equivalent condition of the mastery of declarative knowledge; (2) the effects of the systematic oral training approaches in light of the principles of procedural memory on the improvement of oral production of the object clause structure in indirect speech; and (3) the factors influencing the application of procedural memory in oral production of the object clause structure in indirect speech as well as in oral production in general. To address the research questions mentioned above, the E-prime 1.0 software, Adobe Audition 3.0 software and SPSS 15.0 were applied in data collection and data analysis.

Major findings have been obtained as follows.

1. According to the procedural memory-based indices of L2 oral proficiency, the high-proficiency English speakers of Chinese tertiary non-English majors performed better than the low-proficiency ones in fluency, accuracy and complexity in the object clause structure in indirect speech. Compared with the low-proficiency peers, the Chinese high-proficiency English speakers used more chunks, thus demonstrating the importance of procedural memory for L2 oral proficiency. However, when the difficulty of the tasks increased to a certain degree, the performance of accuracy of the high-proficiency subjects was not satisfactory. This phenomenon occurred because they overstressed fluency. In addition, in some cases (for example, in Cognitive Behavioral

Experiment Two: Questions and Answers in **Chapter Five**), in order to ensure the correctness of the exercises, the high-proficiency subjects tended to use reduction strategies and choose less complex linguistic units, which makes the difference between the high-proficiency subjects and the low-proficiency subjects statistically insignificant.

    2. In use of object clause structure in indirect speech, Chinese high-proficiency English speakers performed as accurately as the native speakers, and used structures of similar or greater complexity. However, their performance was not as good as that of the native speakers in fluency (measured by response time). This indicates that under the conditions of sufficient practice, Chinese high-proficiency English speakers can perform well in accuracy or complexity when they have accumulated enough procedural knowledge, the skills of the application of procedural memory and the ability to restructure procedural knowledge, etc. Meanwhile, it is found that the native English speakers tended to use the type of procedural memory which is separately stored in the brain and has nothing to do with declarative memory. For the L2 speakers from China, they tended to use the type of procedural memory parasitizing in declarative memory and influencing the automatic processing of its retrieval and application. The linguistic units they produced have been analyzed and proceduralized and are therefore beneficial to the functioning of working memory in terms of speed and storage capacity.

    3. L2 oral proficiency can be improved to varying degrees by using the principles of procedural memory such as increasing the time and intensity of oral practice. Once the learner has formed procedural

memory of the object clause structure in indirect speech, it is hard for him to forget the knowledge he has learned by procedural memory. This indicates the enduring nature of procedural knowledge and the importance of practice in the proceduralization of procedural knowledge. Besides, it is found that in the longitudinal study the pronunciation of words of the subject was improved in fluency and accuracy, which develops Ullman's DP model as to the fact that procedural memory has the correlation to lexical processing as well. In addition, it is found that the development and functioning of schemata played an important part in the exploration of the effects of procedural memory in the oral production. Furthermore, orally training the subject by constantly changing the linguistic units within the sentence structure played an important role in the formation of procedural memory. This finding indicates that procedural memory exists and functions in the mental storage of linguistic units of different levels and sizes. It also stresses the importance of the syntagmatic relations in the formation of procedural memory.

4. Both implicit and explicit factors influence oral proficiency. The former include anxiety, confidence, the anti-interference of L1, the ability to restructure the sentence structures, familiarity to the grammatical structures and linguistic units, the frequency of oral practice, the use of reduction strategies, etc. The latter include the difficulty and the length of the sentences tested and their linguistic units. Nevertheless, with the emphasis on the principles of procedural memory, L2 oral proficiency can be improved by reducing anxiety and increasing speaking confidence.

The findings of the study are hopefully significant in theory, methodology and pedagogy.

Theoretically, the study may contribute to the understanding of oral production from the psycholinguistic perspective, and to the theoretical study of procedural memory in China. In addition, the study of procedural memory may ontribute to the development of the theories of linguistic competence. Moreover, the study may enrich the content of Ullman's DP model by demonstrating the correlation of procedural memory to lexical processing in L2 speaking through the experiments.

Methodologically, the study is significant in that it was conducted in a multi-disciplinary way which enriches the methods of language research. In addition, the research designed a series of studies such as the comparative study, the longitudinal study, etc. Each study consists of the quantitative and qualitative parts in which quantitative and qualitative analysis was also applied. By doing so, the current research ensures its reliability and validity in methodology.

Pedagogically, this study is of great instructive significance in the following aspects. First, by enriching the content of linguistic competence and adding automaticity into the indices of the assessment of one's L2 oral production, this study would help L2 teachers and learners take proper steps to reduce and eliminate the difficulties in oral production and adjust their ways of training L2 speaking abilities. Second, based on the findings of the quantitative and qualitative researches, this study is of great instructive significance to the reform of the teaching and learning methods, teaching material compilation and so on in China by probing the effects of procedural memory on L2 learning, especially on L2 speaking. Third, with the help of the survey of memory studies as well as the findings of the experiments, this study reveals that traditional skill training methods like recitation, retelling and rehearsal are still of great importance in improving L2 speaking abilities.

LIST OF ABBREVIATIONS

ALP	average length of pause
CBE I	Cognitive Behavioral Experiment One
CBE II	Cognitive Behavioral Experiment Two
CECR	College English Curriculum Requirements
CET-SET	College English Test-Spoken English Test
CF	chunk frequency
COLSEC	College Learners' Spoken English Corpus
DD	the degree of difficulties in pronunciation and use of linguistic units
DM	declarative memory
DS	direct speech
EEG	electroencephalogram
EK	encyclopedia knowledge
ERP	the event-related potential
fMRI	the Functional Magnetic Resonance Imaging
GA	Group A

基于程序性记忆原理的口语产出研究
——从间接引语中宾语从句结构的角度

GB	Group B
HPS	high-proficiency subject
InDS	indirect speech
L1	first language
L2	second language
LPS	low-proficiency subject
LTM	long-term memory
MALP	the mean value of average length of pause
Mean H	the mean value of high-proficiency subject
Mean L	the mean value of low-proficiency subject
MLR	the mean length of run
MMLR	the mean value of mean length of run
MNCF	the mean number of chunks
MPTR	the mean phonation time ratio
MREP	the mean ratio of errors in pronunciation
MREULU	the mean ratio of errors in use of linguistic units
MSR	the mean speech rate
MTRT	the mean total response time
N	the number of sentences tested
NC	the number of sentences which are correct in sentence builders and sentence patterns

LIST OF ABBREVIATIONS

NCF	the number of chunks in one sentence
NE	native English speakers
NNE	non-native English speakers
OCS	the object clause structure
ORT	oral production response time
PM	procedural memory
PRS	perceptual representation system
PTR	phonation time ratio
RCQ	Role Category Questionnaire
REP	ratio of errors in pronunciation
REULU	ratio of errors in use of linguistic units
RRT	recognition response time
RT	response time
SC	syntactic complexity
SLA	second language acquisition
SLL	second language learning
SM	sensory memory
spm	syllables per minute
spr	syllables per run
SR	speech rate

基于程序性记忆原理的口语产出研究
——从间接引语中宾语从句结构的角度

STM   short-term memory

SVLV   syntactic variety and lexical variety

TRT   total response time

TABLE OF CONTENTS

Chapter One INTRODUCTION ·· 1
  1.1   Introduction ·· 1
  1.2   Need for the Study ··· 3
  1.3   Significance of the Study ··· 6
  1.4   Organization of the Dissertation ·· 11

Chapter Two PROCEDURAL MEMORY AND LANGUAGE
                LEARNING ··· 13
  2.1   Introduction ·· 13
  2.2   Information Processing-Based Memory Research ······ 13
  2.3   Multiple Memory Systems ··· 16
  2.4   Procedural Memory ··· 23
  2.5   Studies of the Role of Procedural Memory
       in Language Learning ·· 35
  2.6   Drawbacks with Previous Studies ··· 51
  2.7   Summary ··· 53

Chapter Three FINDINGS ON ORAL PRODUCTION ······ 54
  3.1   Introduction ·· 54
  3.2   Physiological Mechanisms of Speech Production ········· 55
  3.3   Psychological Processes in Oral Production ················ 61
  3.4   Studies Related to Non-linguistic Factors Influencing
       Oral Production ··· 66

3.5　Studies Related to Indices of Oral Production Ability … 67
3.6　Problems with the Previous Studies …………………… 68
3.7　Summary ……………………………………………… 71

Chapter Four　A CONCEPTUAL FRAMEWORK FOR THE PRESENT STUDY …………………… 72

4.1　Introduction …………………………………………… 72
4.2　The Focus of the Present Study ……………………… 72
4.3　A General Information-Processing Framework ……… 75
4.4　A New Approach to Linguistic Competence ………… 78
4.5　Identification of Functioning of Procedural Memory … 80
4.6　Oral Proficiency in the Newly-developed Concept of Linguistic Competence ………………………………… 86
4.7　Summary ……………………………………………… 97

Chapter Five　RESEARCH DESIGN …………………… 98

5.1　Introduction …………………………………………… 98
5.2　Research Principles …………………………………… 99
5.3　Research Questions …………………………………… 103
5.4　The Pilot Study ………………………………………… 105
5.5　A Cross-sectional Study between High-proficiency and Low-proficiency L2 Speakers ……………………… 106
5.6　A Comparative Case Study between Native English Speakers and Non-native English Speakers ………… 135
5.7　A Longitudinal Case Study of a Low-proficiency Subject ………………………………………………… 144
5.8　A Cross-comparative Case Study between and within Subjects ………………………………………………… 149
5.9　Summary ……………………………………………… 151

TABLE OF CONTENTS

Chapter Six RESULTS AND DISCUSSION (1) : DIFFERENCES BETWEEN HIGH-PROFICIENCY AND LOW-PROFICIENCY L2 SPEAKERS ··············· **152**
6.1   Introduction ··· 152
6.2   Differences of Oral Production between High-proficiency and Low-proficiency L2 Speakers··························· 153
6.3   The Effects of Chunks ································· 168
6.4   Major Factors Influencing Oral Production ············· 170
6.5   Summary ··· 177

Chapter Seven RESULTS AND DISCUSSION (2): FEATURES OF NATIVE ENGLISH SPEAKERS AND HIGH-PROFICIENCY NON-NATIVE ENGLISH SPEAKERS ························ **178**
7.1   Introduction ·· 178
7.2   Similarities and Difficulties between Native English Speakers and High-proficiency Non-native English Speakers ··· 179
7.3   The Effects of Chunks ··································· 192
7.4   Major Factors Influencing Oral Production of the Object Clause Structure of Indirect Speech ·· 193
7.5   Summary ··· 194

Chapter Eight RESULTS AND DISCUSSION (3): THE EFFECTS OF THE PRINCIPLES OF PROCEDURAL MEMORY ON ORAL PRODUCTION ··· **195**
8.1   Introduction ·· 195
8.2   Major Results and Discussion for Fluency ············· 196
8.3   Major Results and Discussion for Accuracy ············· 209
8.4   Major Results and Discussion for Complexity ············ 214

8.5	Results and Discussion for the Interviews	218
8.6	Other Findings and Discussion	220
8.7	Summary	223

Chapter Nine   CONCLUSION ······ 224

9.1	Introduction	224
9.2	Major Findings	224
9.3	Implications	230
9.4	Limitations	236
9.5	Suggestions for Future Research	237
9.6	Summary	238

REFERENCES   APPENDICES ······ 267

Appendix 1	An Oral Task	267
Appendix 2	全国大学英语四六口语考试（CET-SET）大纲	268
Appendix 3	Multiple Choices	270
Appendix 4	CBE I: Listen, Judge and Speak & Listen and Repeat	274
Appendix 5	CBE II: Questions and Answers	276
Appendix 6	Questionnaire	278
Appendix 7	The E-prime Experiment: The Change of Sentence Patterns	281
Appendix 8	The Tests and Training Plans for Jun	282

Chapter One
INTRODUCTION

1.1 Introduction

The study was motivated by the problems in oral production of Chinese tertiary non-English major students in Southeast University, such as disfluency and inaccurate use of language units and grammar rules. According to the investigation made by the present researcher, many university students' speaking proficiency is still far from satisfactory though they have higher scores in CET 4, CET 6 and other important written exams.

Traditionally, to solve the problems mentioned above, language teachers tend to refer to the findings in the field of linguistics, especially in Second Language Acquisition (SLA) and pedagogy to analyze such problems in second language learning (SLL) (Wen & Wang, 2004). However, with the development of multi-disciplines, especially the development of cognitive science in the 1980s, the complexity of language learning has been gradually recognized. For example, the principles and ideas in psycholinguistics are useful for researchers to adopt a more scientific approach to language learning (Garman, 2003; Skehan, 1998; Steinberg & Sciarini, 2007). Peter Skehan (1998, p.1) in his book *A Cognitive Approach to Language Learning* points out that 'Psycholinguistics, the study of the psychological processes underlying language learning and use, has been insufficiently influential on our profession as a foundation discipline, losing out in importance to linguistics and sociolinguistics. Aiming at the problems in SLA and SLL, he offers a cognitive approach to language learning and research from a processing perspective and emphasizes that it will have a beneficial influence on the way research concerns and pedagogic practice come together more closely if such a perspective gathers pace.

Besides psycholinguistics, some other newly developing disciplines such as cognitive psychology, cognitive linguistics, cognitive neuroscience and neurolinguistics include language learning as part of their research areas (Carroll, 2000; Gazzaniga et al., 2002; Jensen, 2000; Squire, 1982; Solso et al., 2005; Sternberg, 2006; Stilling et al., 1995). In these disciplines, language processing and production are considered continuous and highly complex which involve multiple levels of analysis (Yang & Zhang, 2007).

As a basic component of cognitive processes, memory has been widely concerned with and the findings of the research on memory have been considered very fruitful (Anderson, 1983b, 1983c, 1995; Gazzaniga et al., 2002; Jensen, 2000; Solso et al., 2005; Squire, 1982; Ullman, 2001a; Zhou et al., 2008). Among these findings, the role of memory in language learning has been put forward and stressed (Squire, 1994; Solso et al., 2005).

In consideration of the relevance of memory to language learning and SLA research, the current study probed the problems mentioned above, selecting the object clause structure in indirect speech as the starting point of this study and falling back on the idea of procedural memory from the perspective of cross-disciplines.

Specifically, the present study addresses the following questions.

1. What are the distinctive features of high-proficiency and low-proficiency L2 speakers in the application of procedural memory in the oral production of the object clause structure in indirect speech?

2. Concerning the oral production of the object clause structure in indirect speech, what are the distinctive features of native English speakers and non-native English speakers with high oral proficiency in the application of procedural memory?

3. What are the effects of the systematic oral training approaches in the light of the principles of procedural memory on the improvement of oral production of the object clause structure in indirect speech?

4. What are the major implicit and explicit factors influencing the application of procedural memory in oral production of the object clause structure in indirect speech and in oral production in general?

1.2 Need for the Study

The following are the major reasons for undertaking the present study of oral production on the basis of the findings of procedural memory from the perspective of object clause structure in indirect speech.

1.2.1 Understanding the role of procedural memory in L2 speaking

The development of cognitive science boomed in the late 1980s, which contributed to the research on the multiple memory system (Atkinson & Shiffrin, 1968; Baddeley & Hitch, 1974; Chen, 2009; Graf & Schacter, 1985; Schacter, 1987; Tulving, 1972). Among the various types of memory in this system, procedural memory is an important component and has become a new research topic in Western countries (Ullman, 2004). Many findings of the studies of procedural memory have been obtained from across disciplines such as psychology, cognitive neuroscience and cognitive psychology (Anderson, 1976; Corkin, 1968; Ullman et al., 1997; Ullman, 2001a, 2001c). Among these findings, Ullman's DP model has been considered comparatively mature (Ullman,

2001a, 2001c; Ullman et al., 1997). The basic premise of the DP model is that important aspects of the distinction between the mental lexicon and the mental grammar in language are tied to the distinction between declarative and procedural memory. Lexical memory depends largely on the declarative memory system, whereas aspects of grammar depend on the procedural memory system.

So far, however, there have been comparatively few studies on procedural memory in China (Zhou et al., 2008). Furthermore, fewer studies have been carried out to test the correlation between procedural memory and L2 learning, especially from the perspective of L2 speaking proficiency. For the researchers and educators in linguistics, the neural and psychological mechanism of procedural memory needs to be better understood in order to develop hypotheses about its roles in L2 speaking. As a result, it deserves due attention to the present study concerning the relationship between procedural memory and L2 oral production.

1.2.2 Investigating new indices of L2 oral proficiency from a multi-disciplinary perspective

Fluency, accuracy and complexity are the main indices of oral production discussed by the linguists in China (Yang, 1999; Zhang, 1999a, 1999b, 2000; Zhang & Wu, 2001) while few multi-dimensional studies in China or abroad explore the indices of L2 oral proficiency by combining with the nature of language processing and cognitive mechanism (Xu, 2009). Only after understanding the nature of oral production and the cognitive mechanisms involved in the process of oral production could one explore the indices of L2 oral production better. Meanwhile, the theories related to language competence from across disciplines are needed with the purpose of enriching the indices of L2 oral proficiency in China.

1.2.3 Contributing to the syntactical research

In China, research on syntax has been mostly influenced by the theories of Saussure, Chomsky and Halliday (Hu & Jiang, 2003; Yong, 1992). However, some drawbacks in such aspects as follows still exist. (1) Limited research areas. Most research areas are limited in a single point of syntax such as tense, voice, inversion, etc. Few researches have been carried out on complex and typical syntactical structures such as direct speech and indirect speech. (2) Lack of the combination of multi-disciplinary and multi-dimensional research methods. This viewpoint can be revealed in the following aspects. First, much research on syntax is about theoretical issues rather than about applied research. Second, empirical studies are much fewer than documentary researches or surveys. Third, cross-sectional studies are more frequently undertaken than longitudinal ones. Fourth, compared to the exploration of the syntactical structures of Chinese, few studies of English syntax have been conducted in multidisciplinary methods due to lack of interdisciplinarity (Chang, 2009). (3) Lack of value in application. The theoretical research findings concerning syntax have seldom been applied to the field of pedagogy of the English language.

The present study is necessary to be conducted because it sets foot in the exploration of the object clause, one of the compelling topics for analysis in the research on syntax. The major reasons for the focus on the object clause lie in the following points. First, the object clause is complex to most English learners in China because such syntactical structure includes very complex semantic and syntactical processing such as the inflection of verbs and nouns for person, tense, voice, etc. as well as the shift of personal pronouns, word order, adverbials of time, etc. The grammatical items are among the most difficult ones in the process of English learning for learners in China (Li, 2008). As a result, the structure is very typical in grammar. Meanwhile, it is the feature of the structure that helps with the exploration of the effects of procedural memory in the current study because this feature accords with procedural memory which is mainly related to the use of grammatical units. Second, the researches on the object clause are mostly limited to the teaching level. In other words, many English teachers in China tend to stress the grammatical knowledge and the usage of object clause structure in indirect speech rather than paying attention to exploring the causes of the problems existing in use of such structure. Third, so far, few researches in China have been conducted on the processing of the object clause structure from the perspective of oral production and procedural memory.

It is also worth mentioning that the present study attempts to apply the principle of syntagmatic relations in the oral training of the low-proficiency subject. The reason for this is that the object clause in indirect speech is involved with the change of subjects, verbs, adverbials and so on, which is closely related to the principle of syntagmatic relations (Lyons, 2002, p.96). In the oral training, the application of change the words in the same word category may be beneficial to the flexible use of sentence patterns.

1.3 Significance of the Study

1.3.1 Theoretical significance

The study is theoretically significant because of the following three reasons.

(1) Firstly, this study may contribute to the development and perfection of the theories of linguistic competence as well as the further understanding of the processes of oral production from the

psycholinguistic and cognitive perspective.

There are some imperfections in the present theories of linguistic competence. For example, the present theories of linguistic competence do not define the concept of knowledge from the perspective of psycholinguistics in which knowledge should contain all that the long-term memory stores (Skehan, 1998). Since procedural memory is a type of long-term memory, the concept of knowledge should contain what procedural memory stores. For another example, from the perspective of cognitive psychology, the skills that a person has grasped are not simply isolated muscular activities but closely related to advanced mental activities (Neisser, 1967, p.292, p.293). In this sense, the importance of skills should be emphasized. Therefore, language theories should contain contents concerning both proficiency and performance. Also, it is worth noticing that the rate of retrieving knowledge (for example, fluency or automaticity) should deserve more attention because it could be an element to differentiate high-proficiency and low-proficiency language learners (Chen, 2002a, 2002c; Zhang, 1999a, 1999b). According to Chen's proposal of a more embracing view of linguistic competence from the cognitive perspective, the proficiency of oral production is influenced by the concept of linguistic competence (Chen, 2002a, 2002b, 2002c, 2009). Therefore, as an important component in the information processing models and the new concept of linguistic competence, procedural memory should be closely related to oral production. The current study may theoretically support Chen's proposal with detailed illustrations and enrich the concept of linguistic competence by emphasizing the importance of procedural memory and automaticity.

Oral production is always considered very complex in language processing and production (Levelt, 1989). The reasons mainly lie in the following two aspects. First, the processes of oral production are implicit and invisible activities involving speakers' speech organs and relevant regions in the brain. Second, the processes of oral production work almost simultaneously and cannot be separated from each other. On the basis of the previous researches on oral production and experimental findings, the current study may contribute to a better understanding of oral production in its physiological mechanism and psychological processing. In addition, the information processing models such as Anderson's ACT models and Levelt's model presented in the present study mainly concern the role of the linguistic units in the psychological processes of oral production, which has some relevance to the study on procedural memory. Hence, the theoretical exploration of oral production may result in more fruitful findings with the support and evidence from psycholinguistics and cognitive science.

(2) Secondly, this study may contribute to the study of procedural memory, especially in China.

According to the literature review, so far few researches have been conducted on procedural memory and its relevant issues in China (Zhou et al., 2008). In this study, different memory models are introduced and theoretical and experimental findings from across disciplines are reanalyzed according to their roles in language learning. By doing so, the current study intends to sort out the theoretical and experimental foundations of the study on procedural memory and its role in L2 speaking proficiency.

In addition, the current study further explores procedural memory and its relevance to L2 learning, especially L2 oral production by two major experiments which will be introduced in greater detail in the section **"Research Design"**. With the help of the experiments, the present study attempts to investigate the effects of procedural memory on L2 oral proficiency.

(3) Thirdly, this study may enrich the content of Ullman's DP model by exploring the correlation of procedural memory to lexical

processing in L2 speaking.

Ullman's declarative/procedural (DP) model claims that the mental lexicon of memorized word-specific knowledge depends on the largely declarative memory system, which underlies the storage and use of knowledge of facts and events while the mental grammar, which subserves the rule-governed combination of lexical items into complex representations, depends on the procedural memory system (Ullman, 2004). In the procedural memory system, procedural memory supports the learning and execution of motor and cognitive skills, especially those involving sequences.

However, through the review of the literature, it is found that procedural memory could also be related to lexical issues. If the findings of experimental studies in the present study proved the hypothesis of the researcher, it would be of great theoretical significance to the development of Ullman's DP model and, more broadly, to the study of procedural memory in cognitive psychology and psycholinguistics.

1.3.2　Methodological significance

The study is significant in methodology in that it was conducted with a multi-disciplinary and multi-dimensional method, which has its advantages over those merely adopting commonly used methods in linguistics. In the quantitative part of the study, the design and the implementation of the cognitive behavioral experiments were based on the previous studies in linguistics, psychology and cognitive neuroscience. In addition, the collection and the analysis of the data were carried out with the principles and approaches of psychology, cognitive neuroscience and acoustics, such as E-prime programs, Adobe Audition 3.0 software and SPSS 15.0. In the qualitative part of the study, a multi-dimensional approach was taken to investigate the differences in the effects of procedural memory on oral production, which is reflected in the following two aspects. (1) Various subjects are selected, including both high-proficiency and low-proficiency English speakers from Chinese tertiary non-English majors and native English speakers. (2) The application of instruments is multi-dimensional. The present study consists of a pilot study, two cognitive behavioral experiments, three different case studies, retrospective interviews and follow-up questionnaires, etc.

With the multi-disciplinary and multi-dimensional method, the study is consequently more systematic and scientific in exploring the effects of procedural memory on oral production and in making it possible for future studies to duplicate and modify the study.

1.3.3 Pedagogical significance

(1) Firstly, this study will be significant in L2 speaking training.

As far as the reform of teaching methods is concerned, to instruct L2 students to make good use of the principles of procedural memory may become a great task in L2 speaking training. L2 speaking teachers may help students realize the importance of procedural memory in L2 speaking and offer them strategies of how to accumulate and make good use of the principles of procedural memory. For example, the use of chunks, idioms and collocations may be encouraged in L2 speaking training.

Moreover, on the basis of the experimental study and the newly-proposed linguistic theory, this study adds automaticity as a factor into fluency, an index for evaluating one's L2 oral production, which may help L2 teachers and learners adjust their ways of training L2 speaking abilities. In addition, this study also establishes some approaches for the judgment of errors in L2 oral production, which may help the English teachers and learners take some appropriate steps to reduce and eliminate these errors.

(2) Secondly, this study is of great instructive significance to the reform of L2 learning methods and teaching material compilation in China.

As to the reform of L2 learning, the concept of proceduralization in L2 learning is advocated by the current study, which is based on the L2 Speaking Development Model proposed by Wu (1999). It can be said that practice has great impact on proceduralization and on L2 learning in reconstructuring procedural knowledge.

As to the teaching material compilation, this study also plays an important part. Because the skill-based training and procedural learning are advocated by the present study, the exercises which fit the concept of procedural memory and emphasize practice can be introduced in the course books or other exercise books to improve the learners' automaticity, accuracy and complexity in oral production.

(3) Thirdly, with the help of the survey of memory studies as well as the findings of the experiments carried out in the study, this study is significant in reproving that traditional skill training methods like recitation, rehearsal and retelling are still of great use in improving L2 speaking in spite of the fact that these traditional skill training methods are now believed to be out of date by too many linguistic researchers.

1.4 Organization of the Dissertation

Chapter One "Introduction" includes the need for the study, the significance of the study and the organization of the dissertation.

Chapter Two begins with the literature review of the researches on information processing models and the multiple memory system. It then accounts for the relationship between procedural memory and L2 learning by reviewing relevant studies. At the end of the first subsection, a summary is made about the problems existing in the previous studies including unexplored issues in procedural memory and L2 speaking proficiency and methodological issues.

Chapter Three deals with the findings of related studies of oral production including its physiological mechanism and psychological processes, the studies related to non-linguistic factors influencing oral production proficiency, indices of oral production proficiency, and solutions to problems in oral production. Problems with previous studies found out in the literature review are mentioned as well.

Chapter Four builds an information processing framework in which procedural memory, linguistic competence and the indices of oral production (fluency, accuracy and complexity) are included.

On the basis of the framework, **Chapter Five** introduces the research design of the present study, which consists of the research principles, the four research questions and the design of a cross-sectional study, a comparative case study, a longitudinal case study and a cross-comparative case study, accompanied by cognitive behavioral experiments, retrospective interviews and follow-up questionnaires. The data collection and data analysis are also introduced in this chapter.

Chapter Six, Chapter Seven and **Chapter Eight** are about the major results and discussion for the studies conducted in **Chapter Five**. In addition, some other findings obtained in the experiments are reported since they are connected to the research on procedural memory and language learning.

Chapter Nine is the **Conclusion,** which summarizes the major findings, implications and limitations of the present study. At the end of this part, suggestions for future research are made.

Chapter Two
PROCEDURAL MEMORY AND LANGUAGE LEARNING

2.1　Introduction

This chapter begins with the introduction of information processing models and the multiple memory system to help learn procedural memory better. Then it reviews the literature concerning the theoretical and empirical studies on procedural memory and its relevance to L2 learning. It also points out the drawbacks with the previous studies. By doing so, the chapter presents the need for the present research on the effects of procedural memory in L2 learning.

2.2　Information Processing–Based Memory Research

The study of memory has a long history. Traditional studies of memory began in the realms of philosophy, including the techniques of artificially enhancing the memory. So far, many metaphors have been adopted as to the explanations of memory process, such as the storehouse metaphor and the computer metaphor (Roediger, 1980). In the late nineteenth and early twentieth century, memory has been put within the paradigms of cognitive neuroscience, a combination between cognitive psychology and neuroscience. Schacter and Tulving (1994) defined a memory system in terms of its brain mechanisms, the kind of information it processes, and the principles of its operation. The definitions of memory (Eliasmith, 2001; Winn & Snyder, 2001) are different to some degree while these definitions still have something in common. For instance, they all have the same implication that memory is closely related to information processing.

In consideration of the close relationship between memory and information processing, the study begins with the introduction of information processing models.

2.2.1 General information processing system

From an information processing perspective, there are three main stages (Encoding/registration, Storage and Retrieval) in the formation and retrieval of memory as shown in Figure 2-1.

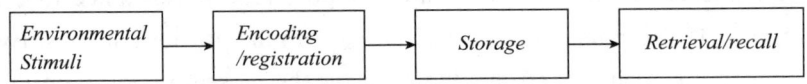

Figure 2-1　Information Processing System

In this system, encoding/registration refers to the processing and combining of the received information input by the environmental stimuli. Storage means the creation of a permanent record of the encoded information. Retrieval/recall refers to calling back the information stored in the previous stage in response to some cues for use in a process or activity. The simplified system is commonly accepted by many psychologists and other researchers. This emphasis is on the flow of information through the system which is used in a wide range of activities, including remembering lists of numbers, solving mathematical problems, and using languages as well (Carroll, 2000).

2.2.2 Multi-store model (or Atkinson-Shiffrin memory model, 1968)

As indicated in Figure 2-2, the multi-store model of Atkinson and Shiffrin categorizes the memory into three types according to time

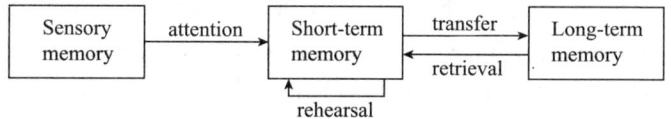

Figure 2-2 Atkinson-Shiffrin Memory Model, 1968

duration and stages of information flow.

This multi-store model provides an important framework for learning and memory theories to evolve from. However, it has been criticized for some problems. For example, it is too simplistic in its components. In other models of memory, long-term memory is believed to be actually made up of multiple subcomponents, such as episodic memory and semantic memory (Gazzaniga et al., 2002). For another example, the multi-store model also proposes that rehearsal is the only mechanism by which information eventually reaches long-term storage, however, evidence shows that we are also capable of remembering things without rehearsal (Craik & Lockhart, 1972).

In a word, the multi-store model presents a hypothetical layout of the function of memory systems while it is not in any way representative of a physical "picture" of memory systems.

2.2.3 Levels of processing model

Craik and Lockhart (1972) in their levels of processing model claimed that stimulus information is processed at multiple levels simultaneously (not serially) depending on characteristics, attention and meaningfulness. This model suggests that we can process information in two ways:

shallow processing and deep processing. According to this model, the level or depth of processing of a stimulus has a large effect on its memorability. The fundamental concept of the levels-of-processing effect is that different methods of encoding information into memory result in different types of memory codes. Memory codes differ in their strength. The strength of the memory code, in turn, determines speed of decay of the memory trace and success of recall from memory over time.

In some sense, Craik and Lockhart's Levels of Processing Model is relevant to memory and language learning. It considers that there is an infinite number of processing levels of memory being encoded. The levels are indistinct and boundaries between the levels are nonexistent. Under this model, storage is said to be determined by processing and deep processing takes longer than shallow processing. In the levels of processing model, the efficiency of learning can be theoretically improved by changing the method of processing or encoding information. Nevertheless, the levels-of-processing approach has been doubted by some researchers who deem that the approach only describes the levels of processing, rather than explains and in fact, it is hard to judge the level of processing being used by learners due to the lack of an independent measure of processing depth (Challis & Brodbeck, 1992; Gallo & Roediger, 2002).

The value of this model lies in "the greater emphasis on memory as processing in current theories though there exist doubts on the model(Craik, 2002)."

2.3 Multiple Memory Systems

The distinctions between different types of memory systems and memory processes have been drawn for a long time (Tulving, 1987). So far, a growing number of investigators in cognitive psychology, neuropsychology and neuroscience have argued for the existence of multiple memory systems. Considerable experimental evidence has been cited as support for the distinctions among three and even more memory systems (Cohen, 1984; Lashley, 1950; Oakley, 1983; Schacter, 1985; Schacter & Tulving, 1982; Sherry & Schacter, 1987; Squire, 1982; Tulving, 1983, 1984, 1985). In addition to providing neuroanatomical dissociations of the role of different brain structures in various memory tasks, an important goal of multiple-memory-systems research is an elucidation of the psychological operating principles that distinguish different types of memory (Baddeley & Hitch, 1974; Graf & Schacter, 1985; Schacter, 1987; Squire, 1982, 1987; Tulving, 1987; Zhu & Yang, 2003).

In this dissertation, the classification of memory is based on the multiple- memory-systems theory. The multiple memory systems consist of the sensory stores, the short-term memory, the working memory and long-term memory in which procedural memory is included.

2.3.1 Sensory stores

The sensory stores take in the variety of colors, tones, tastes and smells that people experience each day and retain them, for a brief, in a raw, unanalyzed form (Carroll, 2000, p.47). Traditionally, this sensory store is referred to as sensory memory. The examples of sensory memory include the ability to remember what the item looked like with just a second of observation of the item, or memorization. According to the partial report experiments conducted by George Sperling (1960), the capacity of sensory memory was approximately 12 items while it degraded very quickly (within a few hundred milliseconds). Then on the basis of further studies, it was inferred that information in the visual sensory store persisted for approximately 1 second. Comparable studies of auditory sensory store have found out the relatively longer duration

(Carroll, 2000, p.48).

As mentioned above, the sensory stores represent information in a literal, unanalyzed form. Though most of the information in these stores disappears very rapidly, the sensory stores perform the invaluable function of preserving new information long enough for more extensive processing to be initiated.

2.3.2　Short-term memory

Some of the information in sensory memory is then transferred to short-term memory (STM). Short-term memory allows one to recall something from several seconds to as long as a minute without rehearsal while the information drops out of memory if it is not rehearsed, it (Solso et al., 2005). As to its capacity, experiments show that the storage of short-term memory was 7 ± 2 units (Miller, 1956). Modern estimates of the capacity of short-term seven units while the density of information in a unit can vary enormously through a process called **chunking**. For example, if presented with the string: FBIPHDTWAIBM people are able to remember only a few items. However, if the same information is shown in the following way: FBI…PHD…TWA…IBM people can remember a great deal more letters (Solso et al., 2005). This is because they are able to chunk the information into meaningful groups of letters. Because of the limited capacity and duration of information, STM has not paid much attention in language research.

2.3.3　Working Memory

Baddeley and Hitch's working memory model further subdivides STM into a number of sub-stores and processes (Baddeley & Hitch,1974). This model consists of three basic stores: the central executive, the phonological loop and the visuo-spatial sketchpad. The central executive is a controlling attentional system that supervises and coordinates current cognitive processing. The phonological loop holds a couple of seconds of speech sounds and plays a part in reading. The visuospatial sketchpad is used in the creation of mental images and in the solution of visual and spatial problems. The model is shown in Figure 2-3.

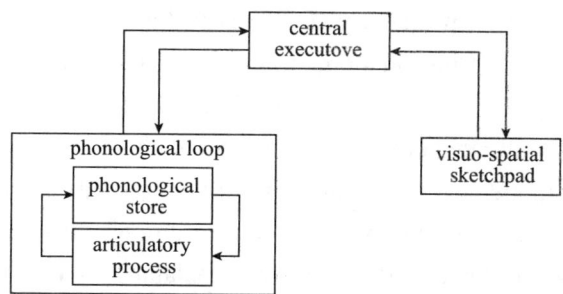

Figure 2-3   The Working Memory Model (Baddeley & Hitch, 1974)

In 2000, this model was expanded with the multimodal episodic buffer (Baddeley, 2000). The episodic buffer is dedicated to linking information across domains to form integrated units of visual, spatial, and verbal information and chronological ordering (e.g., the memory of a story or a movie scene). The episodic buffer is also assumed to have links to long-term memory and semantic meaning.

As mentioned above, this classification of working memory is based on different functions of elements in information processing. Working memory differs from STM in that STM has been viewed as passive repository of information while working memory has both storage and processing functions. The working memory model may explain some practical observations such as the reason why it is easier to do two different tasks (one verbal and one visual) than two similar tasks (e.g., two visual), and the word-length effect (Li et al., 2007). Meanwhile, the chunks at the highest level of the hierarchy can be retained in working memory, which helps with expanding the capacity of working memory.

2.3.4 Long-term memory

The storage in sensory memory and STM is generally limited in capacity and duration, which means that information is not retained indefinitely. By contrast, long-term memory (LTM) is featured by its diversity of codes, abstraction of information, structure, capacity, and permanence (Solso et al., 2005). LTM can store much larger quantities of information for potentially unlimited duration (sometimes a whole life span).

Long-term memories are maintained by more stable and permanent changes in neural connections widely spread throughout the brain. The hippocampus and the adjacent cortex and thalamus are essential to the consolidation of information from short-term to long-term memory. The simplified notion of LTM is that information in STM is converted in LTM if it remains in STM long enough (Hebb, 1949). However, information in STM should be combined with other existing, meaningful memories and then long-term memorability can be enhanced (Solso et al., 2005).

The complexity of LTM results in various views and classifications of it. The studies of patients with certain brain injuries (such as damage to the hippocampus) suggest that different memories work with the different parts of the brain and they have different tasks in cognitive processes (Corkin, 1968; Milner, Corkin & Teuber, 1968). With the development of cognitive science, the dichotomous classifications of memory have been widely accepted, among which the explicit (declarative) memory system and the implicit (nondeclarative/ procedural) memory system are representative (Cohen & Squire, 1980; Gazzaniga et al., 2002; Squire, 1992; Tulving & Schacter, 1990).

Declarative memory requires conscious recall, in that some conscious processes must call back the information. It is sometimes called explicit memory since it consists of information that is explicitly stored and retrieved. It can be further sub-divided into **semantic memory** and **episodic memory**. Semantic memory allows the encoding of abstract knowledge about the world. Episodic memory, on the other hand, involves conscious awareness of past events, such as the sensations, emotions, and personal associations of a particular place or time. It is our personal, autobiographical memory.

In contrast, **nondeclarative memory** (or **implicit memory**) is not based on the conscious recall of information but on implicit learning. **Procedural memory** is one form of nondeclarative memory that involves the learning of variety of motor (e.g., the knowledge of how to ride a bike) and cognitive skills (e.g., the acquisition of reading skills). One form of nondeclarative memory that acts within the perceptual system is known as the **perceptual representation system** (PRS). In the PRS, the structure and form of objects and words can be primed by experience. Two other domains of nondeclarative memory include **classical conditioning** and **nonassociative learning**. Classical conditioning occurs when a conditioned stimulus (an otherwise neutral stimulus to the organism) is paired with an unconditioned stimulus (one that elicits some response from the organism). Following this paring, the conditioned stimulus can evoke a response similar to that typically evoked by the unconditioned stimulus. Nonassociative learning involves forms of simple learning such as habituation and sensitization. The components of long-term memory are shown as Figure 2-4.

In order to understand the neural, cognitive, and computational (i.e., neuron-cognitive) bases of second language acquisition and processing better and address the theoretical gaps, Ullman and his colleagues (Ullman, 2001a, 2001c; Ullman et al., 1997) proposed and explored the declarative/procedural (DP) memory model. In this model, the acquisition and processing of both first and second languages are closely connected to well-studied brain systems which are known to subserve the particular non-language functions. The introduction of the DP model will be expounded in **Section 2.4**.

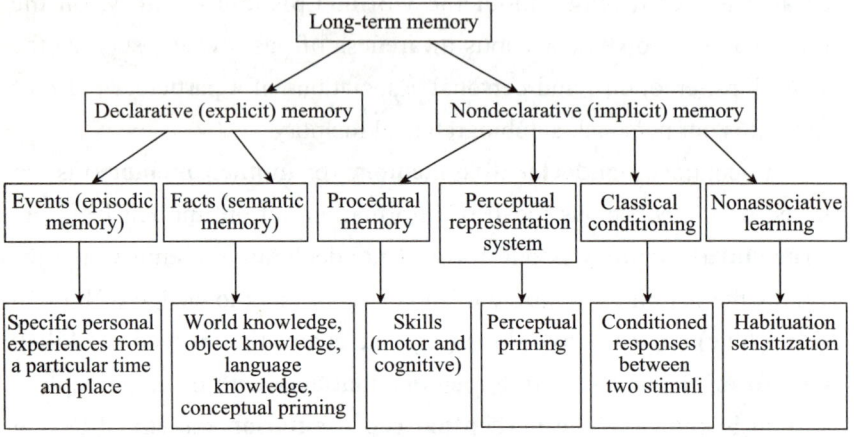

Figure 2-4   Models of Long-term Memory (Gazzaniga et al., 2002)

2.3.5   A summary and diagram indicating types of memory and information

To sum up, the classification of different types is mainly based on different principles such as the time duration and the functions of various types of memory. Meanwhile, it is worth noticing that the development of multiple disciplines such as cognitive science and psychology contributes to the development of the contents of the multiple memory system.

The review of different memory models helps us further understand the components of the multiple memory system. Based on Figure 2-4 "Models of Long-term Memory (Gazzaniga et al., 2002)" and Ullman's DP model, the following diagram will be of great help in the illustration of types of memory and information.

Table 2-1 The diagram of different types of memory and information

Memory	Sensory stores			
	Short-term memory			
	Working memory	The central executive		
		The visual-spatial sketchpad		
		The phonological loop		
	Long–term memory	Declarative (explicit) memory	Events (episodic memory)	
			Facts (semantic memory)	
		Procedural (implicit) memory	Motor and cognitive skills and habits	
			Perceptual priming	
			Simple casual conditioning	
			Others	

The current study will focus on procedural memory, its effects on L2 oral production and the correlation between procedural memory and L2 to speaking proficiency.

2.4 Procedural Memory

This section introduces the representative views, neural studies and definitions concerning procedural memory.

2.4.1 Views concerning procedural memory

Historically speaking, the concept "procedural memory" has been developed for a long time. Three influential views will be introduced in the research area of procedural memory. Among these views, the ACT models and Ullman's DP model will be expounded in great detail as they are the important theories applied in the present study.

2.4.1.1 Distinctions of declarative knowledge and procedural knowledge

The distinction between declarative and procedural knowledge is intuitive and ancient, and received an early formulation in the work of Piaget, who studied sensori-motor and representational knowledge, as well as the transition from the former to the latter (Piaget, 1945, p.51). According to Piaget, declarative knowledge is our fund of factual information about the world and procedural knowledge is our repertoire of rules and skills by which we navigate the world. Conceptually, the difference between procedural and declarative knowledge coincides with Ryle's (1949) classic distinction between knowing how (operating on the environment in ways difficult to verbalize) and knowing that (stating knowledge in the form of propositions).

Declarative knowledge is said to be knowledge of objects and events which is recorded during higher cognitive processes or consciousness and can be accessed by such processes while procedural knowledge is said to be knowledge of how to perform a cognitive skill and is inaccessible to conscious processes (Anderson, 1983b, 1983c, 1983d; Turban & Aronson, 1988).

Procedural knowledge can be highly efficient once it has been developed and can work independently without consciousness in many cases (Anderson, 1983b, 1983c, 1983d, 1993). Cognitive skills can be acquired without acquisition of new declarative knowledge. Declarative knowledge may be acquired later than procedural knowledge. In a dynamic control task, the development of declarative knowledge paralleled but lagged behind the development of procedural knowledge (Stanley et al., 1989). Even in high-proficiency cognitive skill acquisition such as learning to design psychological experiments, such learning often involves generalizing specific knowledge to form generic schemas in addition to specializing general knowledge to specific situations

(Schraagen, 1993; VanLehn, 1995). Conscious activations can record and access declarative knowledge while unconscious activations cannot (Coward & Sun, 2004). Both conscious and unconscious activations can generate behavior and lead to procedural knowledge. However, conscious activations may generate behaviors which are inconsistent with those generated by unconscious activations. A conscious activation will often be less effective in generating skilled behavior than an unconscious activation.

The distinction between these two kinds of knowledge can show us the features of procedural memory.

2.4.1.2 Anderson's views on declarative memory and procedural memory

The Adaptive Control of Thought (ACT) model as well as several versions of ACT including ACT*and ACT-R (Adaptive Control of Thought-Rational) system is notable in the information processing theories (Anderson, 1983; Anderson & Lebiere, 1998).

As Figure 2-5 shows, the ACT framework is a production system theory for both memory of facts and skills. The theory holds that during the development of automatic skills, conscious representations are gradually transformed into unconscious ones. It proposes that human cognition arose as an interaction between declarative and procedural knowledge structures.

The ACT and ACT* models can be applied to explain the processes of language acquisition and learning (Anderson, 1976; Anderson & Bower, 1973). Learning a language, like any other type of skill learning (for example, driving a car or playing tennis), involves the development of procedures that transform declarative knowledge into a form that makesfor easy and efficient performance. According to Anderson (2005), the transition of declarative to procedural knowledge takes place in three stages: (1) in the cognitive stage, the learner makes use of conscious

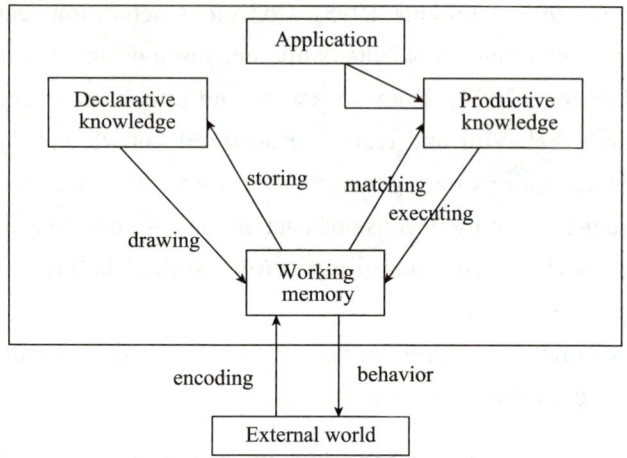

Figure 2-5　Anderson's ACT Model (1983)

activity. The knowledge acquired is typically declarative in nature and can often be described verbally by the learner; (2) in the associative stage, errors in the original declarative knowledge are detected and corrected, and the knowledge is also proceduralized. During this stage, condition-action pairs which are initially represented in declarative form are gradually converted into production sets. However, the initial declarative representation never vanishes; (3) finally, in the autonomous stage, performances become more or less totally automatic and errors disappear. The learner relies less on working memory and performance takes place below the threshold of consciousness.

O'malley, Chamot and Walker (1987) also supported the models by claiming that learning begins with declarative knowledge which slowly becomes proceduralized, and that the mechanism by which this takes place is practice.

The ACT model is only a cognitive model, thus in language teaching, we need to identify the goal structure of the problem space and provide instruction in the problem-solving context. Additionally, working memory load needs to be minimized for better quality of oral production.

The 1990s saw the development of the ACT-R theory. The ACT-R theory is the theory of the Production Rule Framework, which correctly captures cognitive skills using a set of rules (Anderson & Lebiere, 1998). The ACT-R theory emphasizes two types of knowledge-procedural and declarative-and two types of storage/access to knowledge-working memory and long-term memory. Declarative knowledge is defined by Anderson as knowledge that is accessible by introspection and represents conscious awareness of facts, whereas procedural knowledge is not available by introspection, and represents knowledge about performing a function. According to the ACT-R theory, procedural knowledge is not subject to any working memory limits while, instead, to an activation constraint by the storage of working memory.

It is the separation of long-term and working (short-term) memory that distinguishes ACT-R from other production rule systems and the differentiation between declarative and procedural knowledge is one of the main differences between production rule and other frameworks. The distinction between working memory and long-term memory is a representation of the psychological notion of long and short term memory.

2.4.1.3 Ullman's DP model

As a matter of fact, the studies of declarative and procedural memory have obtained fruitful findings in the field of neural science (Eichenbaum & Cohen, 2001; Mishkin, Malamut, & Bachevalier, 1984; Schacter & Tulving, 1994; Squire & Knowlton, 2000). Because of its relevance to language learning, the present study selected Ullman's declarative/procedural (DP) model to address these and related issues.

The declarative and procedural memory systems were proposed

and explored on the basis of the fact that multiple characteristics of these two memory systems, including their computational, neuroanatomical, physiological and biochemical substrates (Ullman et al., 1997; Ullman, 2001a, 2001b, 2001c; Ullman, 2004). The basic premise of the DP model is to distinguish between the mental lexicon and the mental grammar in language and between declarative memory and procedural memory which have been implicated in non-language functions in humans and other animals (Eichenbaum & Cohen, 2001; Mishkin, Malamut, & Bachevalier, 1984; Schacter & Tulving, 1994; Squire & Knowlton, 2000).

In the following part, the major views and findings of the DP model will be introduced by making a comparison between the two memory systems and then the claims and predictions of the DP model will be presented as they pertain to L1 and high-proficiency L2.

a. The declarative memory system has been viewed as a system contributing to the learning, representation and use of knowledge about facts (semantic knowledge) and events (episodic knowledge) while the procedural memory system is implicated in the learning of new and in the control of long-established motor and cognitive skills and habits, especially those involving sequences (Aldridge & Berridge, 1998; Eichenbaum & Cohen, 2001; Mishkin, Malamut, & Bachevalier, 1984; Schacter & Tulving, 1994; Squire & Knowlton, 2000; Willingham, 1998; Ullman, 2004). According to the DP model, in L1 and high-experience L2, the declarative memory system underlies the mental lexicon, whereas the procedural memory system subserves aspects of the mental grammar. In contrast, in lower-experience L2, rule-governed complex representations depend largely on declarative memory (Ullman, 2001a, 2001b, 2001c; Ullman et al., 1997).

b. The knowledge learned in the declarative memory system might be explicitly (consciously) recollected while learning and remembering the procedures in the procedural memory system is largely implicit.

c. Declarative memory is subserved by regions of the medial temporal lobe-in particular, the hippocampus-which are largely connected with temporal and temporoparietal neocortical regions while the procedural memory system is rooted in portions of the frontal cortex (including Broca's area and the supplementary motor area), the basal ganglia, parietal cortex and the dentate nucleus of the cerebellum.

d. The declarative memory system underlies the mental lexicon, whereas the procedural system subserves aspects of mental grammar (Pinker & Ullman, 2002).

e. The irregular forms are considered to be linked to lexical and non-linguistic semantic memory (i.e., declarative memory), and to temporal/temporoparietal cortex while regular forms are considered to be linked to syntax, motor skill, and left frontal cortex and the basal ganglia (i.e., procedural memory) (Pinker & Ullman, 2002).

Ullman's DP model does not assume that all parts of these two memory systems subserve language (Ullman, 2004). The model states that at least in the procedural system, and probably also in the declarative system, parallel circuits are posited to have analogous computational functions in language and in other domains.

Other findings and predictions of DP model are displayed as follows.

(1) At lower levels of L2 experience, declarative memory is posited to subserve the learning and use not only of idiosyncratic lexical knowledge but also of complex linguistic representations. During early adulthood, women should show an advantage at L2 acquisition as compared to men. Due to the attenuation of declarative memory, older learners (especially postmenopausal women) should have particular difficulty acquiring an L2 even to low proficiency.

(2) At higher levels of L2 experience, the procedural system should

be able to acquire knowledge (although this may be more difficult for older L2 learners), resulting in a neurocognitive pattern similar to that of L1. That is, with idiosyncratic lexical knowledge stored in declarative memory, while rule-governed complex forms are composed by the procedural system.

(3) Dissociations between simple and complex forms are expected in high-experience L2 and in L1 but less so or not at all in low-experience L2. In direct comparisons between L1 and L2 within subjects, the use of complex forms should depend more on declarative memory brain structures in low-experience L2 than in L1 or high-experience L2, in which complex forms should show a greater dependence on procedural memory brain structures. In contrast, idiosyncratic lexical knowledge should be stored in declarative memory in all individuals, and therefore no lexical dissociations between L1 and either low- or high-experience L2 are expected.

2.4.2　Neural studies of procedural memory

2.4.2.1　Brain region related to procedural memory

As an important part of LTM (long-term memory), procedural memory is thought of as a huge database where the information can be stored for a long time. The neural studies of procedural memory are closely related to that of LTM.

Figure 2-6 shows the specialized modules that LTM in humans is believed to be partitioned into.

Among these parts related to LTM, amygdala and cerebellum are considered closely relevant to procedural memory. The amygdala is located in the anterior and medial part of the limbic lobe and is a major component of the limbic pathway. It contains many connections to both the hypothalamus and prefrontal cortex that are responsible for visceral/autonomic responses and personality respectively (Nolte, 1999). Because of the connection of the amygdala to these structures, it can influence and affect the emotional feelings and related physiological responses to certain situations. The damage of the amygdala may result in the impairment of the ability to learn new emotions as well as react appropriately in different situations. The autonomic responses that are associated with a stimulus are also impaired. The cerebellum is located at the back of the brain, underlying the occipital and temporal lobes of the cerebral cortex. It is involved in movement planning objectives such as adjusting limb movement, postural balance and eye movements (Nolte, 1999). The cerebellum is mainly involved in the functions such as maintenance of balance and posture, coordination of voluntary movements, motor learning and cognitive functions. If the right hemisphere of the cerebellum is damaged then the right parts of the body are affected. The cerebellum also has many limbic associations that suggest that cerebellar damage can cause some cognitive disturbances. The learning and acquisition of new complex skills may be greatly reduced as a result as well as the quality of life.

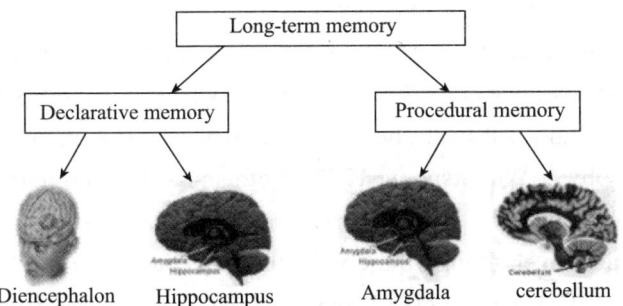

Figure 2-6   Long-term Memory

So far, the neural studies of procedural memory have proved fruitful, as elaborated in the following subsections.

2.4.2.2 Evidence on existence of procedural memory

A number of studies reinforce the existence of procedural memory through the research on the patients who are faced with brain deficiencies from accidents, pathology, or on the cases of animal models that are intentionally inflicted. Meanwhile, by distinguishing these two kinds of memory (declarative memory and procedural memory), the existence of procedural memory can be revealed.

Studies of amnesiacs have been the most common form of evidence used to distinguish declarative memory from procedural memory. Amnesiacs are known to lack the ability to add to their declarative memory stores (episodic or semantic).

A well-known case in history involves the patient known as HM, who had his anterior and medial portions of his temporal lobes removed to prevent epileptic seizures (Corkin, 1968). HM and similar patients have normal memory for events before their trauma while they cannot form new long-term memories. This suggests that the frontal and medial temporal lobe structures are related to adding information to declarative memory. This case has been accepted as support for the distinction of memory pathways (Gabrieli, 1998). Further evidence for the existence of declarative memory is shown by priming experiments in amnesiacs and normals who were asked general knowledge questions and then given a spelling test using homophones of words (i.e., heir/hair, reed/read) (Jacoby & Witherspoon, 1982). Both amnesiacs and normals were observed to spell the correct version seen in the questions presented (heir & reed) even though these were the less commonly used versions. Jacoby and Witherspoon (1982) reasoned that these observation of word priming utilizes semantic memory (i.e., recall meaning and application rules for words) in order to select the correct spellings. Therefore, declarative memory is present and being used.

Most of the evidence of a separate procedural long-term memory area in the brain is through studies involving patients with Korsakoff's psychosis or amnestic confabulatory syndrome. These people have damage to mammillary bodies (hippocampus, diencephalons), which are related to the other area of long-term memory, called declarative memory. First, Corkin (1968) studied this type of amnesic (HM) and found that he was able to learn a mirror tracing task, rotary pursuit, and bimanual tracking task. HM had to be told the instructions on how to perform each task all of the time because he had no recollection of doing the task before. Cermak, Lewis, Butters, and Goodglass (1973) examined the Korsakoff patients' learning performance on a declarative task (finger maze) vs. a procedural task (pursuit rotor) and found similar results when were able to learn a pursuit rotor task (procedural task) just as well as a normal control group, but were unable to learn a finger maze task (declarative task) as well as the control group. Cohen, Eichenbaum, Decedo and Corkin (1985) also found that Korsakoff patients were able to learn a different procedural task (Tower of Hanoi puzzle) just as well as a normal control group.

Separate learning patterns observed in Korsakoff patients were also reported by Cohen and Squire (1980). Their testing of mirror reading skills suggested that amnesiacs are able to acquire mental operations involving learning rules or procedures while operations involving specific, declarative, data-based information cannot be remembered (Squire, 1982). On the other hand, learning of pattern recognition was observed and attributed to the use of procedural LTM, thus, another indication of distinct pathways.

2.4.3 The definition of procedural memory for the present study

As noted above, procedural memory is a type of implicit memory subserved by frontal/basal ganglia circuits as well as portions of the parietal cortex, superior temporal cortex and the cerebellum (Ullman, 2001b, 2001c). It is the memory storage of skills and procedures. This type of memory has also been referred to as "tacit knowledge" or "implicit knowledge". Procedural memory is involved in tasks such as remembering how to play handball or how to ride a bike. This is memory, which is functionally defined as representing the learning and retention of motor skills and habits. Mishkin and Petrie (1984) referred to procedural memory as "a habit system", a memory system that includes retention of well-ingrained or "overpracticed" abilities such as the capacity to walk, swim, drive, eat, etc. Procedural memory is therefore of great importance in human motor performance.

Procedural memory has been mainly broken down into three separate groups: **conditioned reflexes**, **emotional associations**, and **skills and habits** (Rhoades & Bell, 2008). Each of these memories is associated to probable anatomical structures in the brain. Memories and learning of conditioned reflexes such as pulling your hand away from a hot fire are related to the cerebellum. On the other hand, emotional associations such as knowing when to be afraid or mad in a particular situation are related to the amygdala. Motor skills and habits require the cortex and the cerebellum.

Based on the findings of the studies on procedural memory, especially on Ullman's DP model, procedural memory in this dissertation refers to the skill-based, rule-based or proceduralized knowledge which is activated autonomously and unconsciously due to cognitive or motor skills and habits.

In addition, it is necessary to define declarative memory here because of its importance in Ullman's DP model. In this dissertation, declarative memory refers to knowledge that we have conscious access to, including personal and world knowledge.

In **Chapter Four**, an adapted version of the framework will be introduced for the identification of the effects of procedural memory in oral production.

2.5 Studies of the Role of Procedural Memory in Language Learning

The section reviews the major findings related to the role of procedural memory and language learning. In addition, in consideration of the relevance of procedural memory to rule-based, skill-based and related theories, this section also reviews some related studies at home and abroad.

2.5.1 Major findings of the studies of the relevance between procedural memory and language learning at home and abroad

This part reviews major findings of the studies of the relevance between procedural memory and language learning at home and abroad.

2.5.1.1 Major findings in China

Because of its importance in language process and production, the studies of procedural memory have attracted the research interest of more and more Chinese researchers. Chen (2002a, 2002b, 2002c) proposed that automaticity should be embraced into linguistic competence. Chen (2009) developed his previous views of linguistic competence by stating that the contents of memory and automaticity should be entailed in linguistic competence. The former includes grammatical rules, lexical knowledge, exemplar storage, four-channel mental representation of language and encyclopedia knowledge. Among these aspects, four-channel mental representation of language includes auditory representation, visual representation, memory of pronunciation procedures and memory of writing procedures. We can see this aspect is connected to procedural memory and input, storage, retrieval and output of information. The latter emphasizes the important role of automaticity in the complex mental procedural activities such as listening, speaking, reading and writing.

In addition, Shi and Chen (2006) surveyed the role of implicit memory including procedural memory in learning a foreign language. Zhou et al. (2008) explored the neural mechanism of procedural memory and its relevance to language learning.

It is worth noticing that Chen (2009) stated that procedural memory has its special characteristics. On one hand, procedural memory can be separately stored in the brain. That indicates that the knowledge acquired by the characteristic of procedural memory will not cover declarative knowledge. And the language learned by this type of procedural memory cannot be analyzed. For example, it is common that the two or three-year old children can say "How are you?" in English without understanding the English grammar of such expressions. They can remember and speak some English expressions or simple sentences because their parents or teachers have repeated the expressions or simple sentences for many times. In such case as parroting what other people say, the language they utter has not been analyzed. For another example, in the case of the native English speakers, they acquire language in the native language atmosphere and learn the use of a specific sentence pattern from the communication with their parents, teachers, friends and so on. Therefore, they can use it correctly in the face-to-face communication without knowing and analyzing its grammar.

On the other hand, procedural memory can **parasitize** in declarative memory and influence the automatic processing of its retrieval and application (Chen, 2009). In this case, the learners can first master declarative knowledge and then with the functioning of declarative knowledge and procedural memory, they can learn and master the knowledge they need. That means declarative and procedural memory systems interact in a number of ways. In English classes in China, the teachers often teach students English grammar knowledge first and ask the students to do some exercises concerning the knowledge taught. And then gradually the students can master the knowledge better.

These studies contribute to broadening the views of the researchers in the field of linguistics and pedagogy in China. They also work as the basis of the present study.

2.5.1.2 Major findings abroad

Comparatively speaking, the studies of the relationship between procedural memory and language learning was initiated earlier in western countries than those in China and the results of the such studies have proved fruitful, especially with the help of experimental instruments in neurology and cognitive neuroscience (Anderson, 1976, 1982, 1995; Tulving, 1983, 1985, 1987; Ullman, 2004).

The major up-to-date findings are as follows.

(1) *Declarative memory and procedural memory play different roles in L2 learning.*

As mentioned above, the case of the patient HM is of great significance to the distinction of declarative memory and procedural memory. Meanwhile, Anderson's ACT models, Ullman's DP model and other neural studies have proved the different roles these two types of memory play in L2 (Anderson, 1976, 1982, 1995; Tulving, 1983, 1985, 1987; Ullman, 2004). These studies have the implication that as one type of long-term memory, procedural memory is beneficial to the output of proceduralized issues such as grammar rules and motor skills. From this aspect, it is worthy to have a further investigation on procedural memory and its role in L2 leaning.

(2) *The declarative and procedural memory systems often interact together.*

Essentially, the two systems form a dynamically interacting network that yields both cooperative and competitive learning and processing, such that memory functions may be optimized. This characteristic will be expounded as follows.

First of all, the two systems can complement each other in acquiring the same or analogous knowledge, including knowledge of sequences. As was initially shown in the amnesic patient H.M., the declarative memory system need not be intact for the procedural memory system to learn (Corkin, 1984; Eichenbaum & Cohen, 2001; Squire & Knowlton, 2000). However, when both systems are functioning, they can be used cooperatively to learn a given task (Willingham, 1998). The declarative memory system may be expected to acquire knowledge initially, thanks to its rapid learning abilities, while the procedural system may gradually learn the same or analogous knowledge (Packard & McGaugh, 1996; Poldrack & Packard, 2003).

Second, animal and human studies suggest that these two systems also interact competitively (Ullman, 2004). This leads to a 'see-saw effect', such that a dysfunction of one system results in enhanced learning in the other or that learning in one system depresses the functionality of the other (McDonald & White, 1993; Packard, Hirsh, & White, 1989; Poldrack & Packard, 2003; Poldrack et al., 2001; Ullman, 2004). The see-saw effect may be explained by a number of factors, including estrogen, direct anatomical projections between the two systems and a role for acetylcholine, which may not only enhance declarative memory but might also play an inhibitory role in brain structures underlying procedural memory (Sanz, 2005; Sørensen & Witter, 1983; Ullman, 2004).

(3) *Motor skill learning associated with the procedural system is subject to early critical period effects.*

Evidence from humans and animals suggests that motor skill learning associated with the procedural system is subject to early critical period effects (Fredriksson, 2000; Schlaug, 2001; Walton, Lieberman, Llinas, Begin & Llinas, 1992). In contrast, there are obvious improvements in declarative memory during childhood, with a possible plateau in adolescence (Campbell & Spear, 1972; Kail & Hagen, 1977; Ornstein, 1978; Ullman, 2005). The changes in both procedural and declarative memory may be at least partly explained by the increasing levels of estrogen that occur during childhood/adolescence (in boys as well as girls, though estrogen levels are higher in girls) since estrogen may somehow inhibit the procedural memory system and enhance declarative memory (Phillips & Sherwin,1992; Ullman, 2004; Ullman, 2005). Additionally, the competitive interaction between the two memory systems (for example, learning in one system depresses functionality of the other), leads to the possibility that the improvements in declarative memory during childhood may be accompanied by an attenuation of procedural learning abilities (Poldrack & Packard, 2003; Ullman, 2004).

(4) *Age can be a factor influencing the use of memory types.*

Young adult L2 learners could tend to rely heavily on declarative memory, even for functions that depend upon the procedural system in L1 (Hartshorne & Ullman, 2006; Pinker, 1999; Prasada & Pinker, 1993). In particular, L2 learners could tend to memorize complex linguistic forms (e.g., walked) that can be computed compositionally by L1 speakers (e.g., walk + -ed). Associative properties of lexical memory may lead to productivity in L2.

(5) *Practice plays an important role in procedural learning.*

In accordance with multiple studies of the adult acquisition of non-linguistic skills by procedural memory (Mishkin, Malamut & Bachevalier, 1984; Schacter & Tulving, 1994; Squire & Knowlton, 2000), practice should lead to procedural learning and improved performance. Thus, with sufficient experience with L2, the language is expected to become L1-like in its grammatical dependence on the procedural system, with the potential for a high degree of proficiency. Whether or not a given individual acquires a given set of grammatical knowledge in the procedural system will depend on factors such as the type of grammatical knowledge, the nature of the L2 exposure, and characteristics of the learner, such as intrinsic procedural learning abilities.

(6) *Gender plays a role in L2 learning.*

Women could tend to show a faster learning rate than men during early stages of L2 learning (due to females' superior declarative memory abilities), men may show an advantage in later stages (due to a possible male advantage at procedural memory) (Eastabrooke et al., 2002; Ullman, 2004).

In addition, women may tend to show an advantage over men at verbal memory tasks which depend on declarative memory. However, men may tend to show superior performance at a variety of tasks, such as aimed throwing and mental rotation, which are expected to depend on the procedural system network (Squire & Knowlton, 2000; Wagner et al., 1998; Ullman et al., 2002; Ullman & Pierpont, 2005).

2.5.2 Other related theories and studies of procedural memory and language learning

As an important part in the multiple memory system and information processing system, procedural memory subserves the implicit learning and use of a symbol-manipulating grammar across subdomains that include syntax, morphology and possibly phonology (how sounds are combined) (Anderson, 1983a, 1983b, 1983c, 1983d; Mishkin, Malamut & Bachevalier, 1984; Schacter & Tulving, 1994; Squire & Knowlton, 2000; Ullman, 2004). Additionally, the system might be especially important in grammatical-structure building and abstract representations into complex structures. The learning of rules should depend on parts of the system that are involved in procedural learning.

In the following part, the dissertation will review some other important theories and studies related to procedural memory to a greater or lesser extent, such as automaticity, schema theory, formulaic language (e.g., chunking, idiomaticity), rule-based system & exemplar-based system, and implicit learning.

2.5.2.1 Automaticity

Automaticity mainly refers to the ability to perform an action automatically without focusing upon it (Bargh, 1989, 1992; Carr, 1992; Hasher & Zacks, 1979; Logan & Cowan, 1984; Mortimore, 2003; Neumann, 1984; Posner, 1978). It is usually the result of learning, repetition, and practice. Examples of automaticity are common activities such as walking, speaking, bicycle riding, assembly-line work, and driving a car.

Schneider and Fisk (1983) explained the mechanisms of skill acquisition in terms of contrasting automatic and controlled types of cognitive and memory processing: Automatic processing is a fast, parallel, fairly effortless process which is not under direct subject control and performs well-developed skilled behaviors while controlled processing is characterized as a slow, generally serial, effortful, capacity limited, subject controlled processing mode that must be used to deal with novel or inconsistent information. Tzelgov (1997, 1999) emphasized the distinction between intentional and autonomous automatic processing. Automatic processing is autonomous when it is not part of the task requirements, like in the case of "reading" the color word in the Stroop effect (MacLeod, 1991) while it is intentional when it is a component of a more general task performed intentionally, like in the case of processing of the individual words when a sentence is read for meaning. Taking the processing in the autonomous mode as a working definition of automaticity, he investigated the mechanisms of skill-based automatic processing and believed that a general memory-based mechanism could be enough to describe automatization and automatic processing (Logan, 1980; Tzelgov, Henik, & Berger, 1992).

From the above review, it is found that automaticity plays an important role in the effective acquisition of skill-related knowledge. Hence, it is possibly closely to language acquisition and learning.

The development of automaticity follows some stages. Figure 2-7 shows the continuum of automatization adapted from Whitaker (1983, p.199):

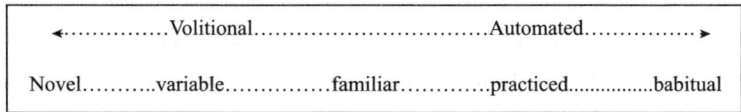

Figure 2-7　The Continuum of Automatization (adapted from Whitaker, 1983)

Whitaker (1983) held that the stages of behavior acquisition are best expressed as a continuum, not a dichotomy. Starting from the left end of this continuum, we gradually acquire the automaticity of a behavior with repeated practice. In learning the speaking of L2 language, people also must start from the novel (or novice) stage. Gradually, with sufficient practice and improvement, they acquire the speaking skills necessary to speak fluently and accurately.

Oral production involves linguistic units. Generally speaking, linguistic units refer to such units as **phoneme**, **syllable**, **word**, **phrases**, **clause**, **sentence**, and **discourse**. These units are connected with each other and form various types of hierarchical structures embedded into each other. Various types of experiments have shown that because of the horizontal and embedded relationships, lower level units make up their immediate higher-level units, forming various types of hierarchical structures, each of which is a cognitive model that can be activated by some implicit or explicit factors and gives rise to chains of reactions in different directions (Carroll, 2000; Fodor, 1983; Langacker, 1987, 1991). About this feature, some who are opposed to behaviorism have gone farther than behaviorists. For instance, Fodor's modularity hypothesis (Fodor, 1983) not only admits automatic responses, but also emphasizes the fast speech and the integrated nature of responses. In the study of grammar, some people have defined cognitive grammatical units as linguistic units or structures that the language user has mastered and can use at will without considering their implicit components and the relations between these components (Langacker, 1987, 1991). In the study of speech perception and comprehension, many experiments have indicated that linguistic units can function as a whole (Carroll, 2000).

Linguistic automaticity can be seen in such aspects as the use of formal units of language, the use of meaning and non-linguistic knowledge and so on.

Similar to Whitaker's a continuum of automatization, there are also three stages of the understanding of automaticity in language (Whitaker, 1983). The first stage is involved in mental operations, which refers to the formation of concepts, words and imagery. The second stage is involved in sensorimotor activities and the third stage refers to the use of a cognitive framework that incorporates both mental operations and sensorimotor activities, with which linguistic units are taken as cognitive units that users can use at will without considering the internal constituents (Langacker, 1987, 1991).

The automatic functioning of procedural knowledge can be seen through an analysis of the mental activities in language use. In speaking, the intention and selection of linguistic units must ultimately be transformed into speech sounds. This process includes programming, sending the programs to the motor centers, sending the commands to the speech organs, and the execution of the commands by the speech organs.

To execute the pronouncing commands, the speech organs must use the flow of air as motive force and carry out a series of highly coordinated movements, with a speed uttering as many as 150-200 words per minute (Taylor & Taylor, 1983, p.212). The models for movements are what people usually call habits. The motor habits of language are in essence the same as other habits of movements. They can be understood as the integration of many minor movements that can be carried out at one stroke without special attention.

Anderson (1995) perceived the development of skill acquisition as the development of problem-solving operators. He divided the processes into three stages: the cognitive stage, the associative stage, and the autonomous stage. In the cognitive stage, learners commit to memorize a set of facts relevant to the skill. Typically they rehearse these facts as they first perform the skill. The process is slow. The information they have learned amounts to a set of problem-solving operators for the skill. In the associative stage, the connections among the various elements required for successful performance are strengthened. Errors are detected and eliminated as well. Learners, by this time, have converted the verbal knowledge once memorized into procedural knowledge. In the autonomous stage, the procedure becomes more skilled, more automated, and more rapid. In becoming so, it requires fewer and fewer attentional resources. Learners also develop more complex skills in the direction of becoming more automated and requiring fewer processing resources. Anderson (1995, p.274) stated, "it is the procedural, not the declarative, knowledge that governs the skilled performance."

2.5.2.2 Schema theory

In the field of cognitive science, schema theory is considered an information processing theory and schemas have been referred to as 'the building blocks of cognition' (Rumelhart, 1980, 1997). Schemas are structures stored in our long-term memory and are used for interpreting and processing information (Landry, 2002). The schemas help organize our knowledge and assumptions about new information. If the new information does not fit our schema, it may be more difficult for us to remember. Meanwhile, what we remember or how we conceive of the new information may also be affected by our prior schema. There are two information resources: (1) bottom-up processing or data-driven processing which relies on the data received via the senses from the outside world; (2) top-down or conceptual-driven processing which is influenced by prior knowledge stored in memory. Schemata help us interpret the bottom-up flow of information from the outside world by operating in a top-down direction. Research on functions of the schema stressed the impact of prior knowledge on comprehension and memory (Driscoll, 2000).

So far, the relationship between schema theory and language learning has attracted much attention (Anderson & Pearson, 1984; Bartlett, 1932; Rumelhart & Norman, 1978). Bartlett (1932) studied the role of memory and language processing in a natural context and proposed that people have schemata that represent an individual's generic knowledge about the world. Modern versions of schema theory adopt many of Bartlett's ideas. The core of Piaget's views of cognitive development is about schema, suggesting that learning process is iterative, in which new information is shaped to fit with the learner's existing knowledge, and existing knowledge is itself modified to accommodate the new information (Piaget, 1985). The major concepts in this cognitive process include: assimilation, accommodation and equilibration. Rumelhart and Norman (1978) proposed three different processes (accretion, turning and reconstructing) to account for changes in existing schemata and the acquisition of new schemata due to learning.

In China, the application of schema theory to L2 learning of listening, speaking, reading and writing has been emphasized (Zi, 2004). As to listening, Chen (1988, 2002a, 2002b, 2002c), Liu (1996) and Ni (2004) suggested schema theory should be used to account for the node of mental activities involved in listening. Yang and He (2007) expounded the effects of the schemas in interpretation and emphasized that the schemas can enhance the speed of comprehension process, simplify the memory process and improve the memory speed. Moreover, the research on Cognitive Load Theory also stresses the role of the schemas in relieving the cognitive load (Wu & Wei, 2009).

Schema theory is a cognitive model, which is closely related to the studies of memory. According to schema theory, the knowledge stored in memory is organized as a set of schemata or mental representations, each of which incorporates all the knowledge of a given type of object or event that we have acquired from past experience. Thus, one may turn to the schemata in his/her mind when he/she is required to memorize the skills of how to ride a bike and how to play a musical instrument. Schemata can facilitate both encoding and retrieval of information. Moreover, the mental structures are active. The mental representations used during perception and comprehension evolve as a result of these processes and combine to form a whole which is greater than the sum of its parts. As the theory suggests, schemata grow and change when the new information is acquired, which will influence the accurateness of certain knowledge.

Schema theory is closely related to the current study due to the role of the schemas in information processing, especially in helping automatize the process of encoding and retrieval. In addition, from the angle of knowledge, schema theory has much in common with the theory of procedural memory. For example, both theories stress the impact of prior knowledge on learning new information. Moreover, both theories emphasize the importance of self-regulatory skills in learning. In this sense, it can be inferred that schema theory can be applied to explore the effects of procedural memory in oral production.

2.5.2.3 Formulaic language

Formula, formulaic language, formulaicity and formulaic sequences attract more and more attention in the research on memory and language production. Jespersen (1924) was the first to state that formulas are drawn from memory. Formulaic language is a cover term for ready-made constructions which can be used without having to be built up from scratch. The formulaic language units include fixed phrases and idiomatic chunks such as *on the other hand*, or *all in all*, or *hold your horses*, and longer phrases, clauses, and sentence-building frameworks of words. Several theories of cognition can be integrated with knowledge about formulaic language and formulaic sequences to produce models of language production, including controlled and automatic processing (McLaughlin, Rossmann, & McLeod, 1983), declarative and procedural knowledge (Anderson, 1983c; Levelt, 1989), etc. Formulaic language and formulaic sequences are related to 'how-to-do' (procedural) knowledge.

The psycholinguistic significance of formulaic language is that they are stored and retrieved whole, hence serving a function in speech production by easing the pressure of simultaneous planning and execution of long stretches of speech. Like other automatisms, prepatterned formulas drawn from memory as stock items save time for planning. There is evidence that the ability to produce fluent speech depends partly on a sufficiently large stock of formulas (Conklin & Schmitt, 2008; Pawley & Syder, 1983; Tannen, 1989; Weinter, 1995). Bolinger (1976) also considered formulaicity as a basic property of language which makes it unnecessary to exploit fully for every utterance the productivity of grammar and, at the same time, curtails it.

Take chunking for example. Chunking is a fundamental operation occurring in the human memory. Various studies are related to how people learn and process information (e.g., that have considered the notion of "chunking" of information, Miller, 1956; Simon, 1974). According to Simon (1974), chunks refer to long term memory units that are used for perception and meaning and chunking is the learning mechanisms leading to the acquisition of these chunks. Humans process information by an absolute limit (7 plus or minus 2) to the amount of information people can understand and remember). By using chunking we reduce the number of channels during the input of data (for instance acquisition of a new language, chess playing, memorizing a phone number) so we use less processing power and less bandwidth (Miller, 1956). The storage in small chunks in memory is also more reliable because if a chunk is destroyed or removed, other parts of the data will not be affected according to hierarchical chunking.

As an important component of formulaic language units, the role of formulaic sequences or chunks has been stressed for years. Formulaic sequences or chunks are one of the major causes for the fluent and accurate output of language of native-speakers (Biber et al., 1999; Ellis, 1991; Howarth, 1998; Pawley & Syder, 1983). Deng (2006) made an investigation into formulaic sequences in Chinese EFL learners' spoken English and found that Chinese EFL learners' use of formulaic sequences displays a complex picture of underuse, overuse and misuse of the target formulaic sequences and that with the increase of their English proficiency level, Chinese EFL learners make use of more and more formulaic sequences in their oral production. Wei (2004, 2007) and Wei and Wang (2005) investigated the features of the chunks in Chinese EFL learners' spoken English. Song (2002), Zhou (2007), Wei (2007) and Zhang (2008) have recently realized that teaching L2 by 'chunk' is an effective approach to the improvement of learners' ability to produce their language output. Zhen (2009) revealed chunks positively influence Chinese EFL learners' speaking in fluency, accuracy and appropriateness in communication. Hence, we can see the importance of chunking in oral production.

Take idiomaticity for another example. In some sense, idiomaticity and idioms are entailed in formulaicity and formulaic language, so they have the features of formulaicity and formulaic language. Idiomaticity is related to the storage and use of multi-word expressions preferred by native speakers. Bolinger (1961) stated that idiomaticity is a pervasive phenomenon than we ever imagined, and vastly harder to separate from the pure freedom of syntax (ibid: 3).

An idiom is an expression whose meaning is not predictable from the usual meanings of its constituent elements or from the general grammatical rules of a language and that is not a constituent of a larger expression of like characteristics. In China, Zhu and Zhang (2007) explored the processing models of idiom semantics and factors influencing idiom semantic processing. Zhang and Ji (2008) proposed an explanatory model of the semantic structure of idiomatic expressions. From these studies, it is found that idioms and idiomaticity are connected with the issues in language processing, such as mental lexicons, grammaticalization, familiarity, contexts. In this sense, it has close relevance to procedural memory.

2.5.2.4 The rule-based system and exemplar-based system

Through a survey of information processing models and models of language learning, Skehan (1998) developed his dual-coding model on the basis of the rule-based system and the exemplar-based system.

On the one hand, in a typical linguistic model processing system, rules play a very important role. For example, it enables maximum creativity and flexibility in what is said and there is no constraint on the production of new combinations of meanings (Skehan, 1998). For another example, the memory storage system can be as small as possible since the parsimony should be the criteria for evaluating the worth of different proposed grammatical models.

On the other hand, the exemplar-based system also matters in langue processing and learning. The system consists of memorized phrases. Using this system allows for quicker communication. As a result, learners cannot create new meanings using the exemplar-based system (Skehan, 1998).

Language users access both systems according to Robinson who found that rule-based knowledge and implicit memory-based knowledge interact in decision making (Robinson, 1995, 1997). Skehan (1998), drawing on work from Bates and MacWhinney (1989), Nelson (1991) and Carr and Curren (1994), argued that the two systems are blended in the following stages: lexicalization, syntactilization, and relexicalization. The learning stages of the learners are as follows: First, in the lexicalization stage, learners use "contextually coded exemplars" (Skehan, 1998, p.90). Then, in the syntactilization stage, learners gain the benefits of the rule-based system. Finally, in the relexicalization stage, learners create new exemplars using the rules from the syntactilization stage. Movement through the three stages ensures that learners will have access to both rule-based knowledge and memory-based knowledge.

On the basis of the relationship between procedural memory and the storage of rules and exemplars, the duel-coding model is considered very supportive in the current study.

2.5.2.5 Implicit learning

Implicit learning plays an important role in skill acquisition and other types of learning (Reber, 1989; Schmidt, 1994; Stanley et al., 1989, Willingham et al., 1989). It is involved in learning new motor skills such as bike riding, learning new languages, picking up new cognitive skills such as chess playing, and in developing intuitions about how other people will act. Anderson (1983b, 1983c, 1995) developed his Adaptive Control of Thought (ACT) model, in which he stated that during the development of automatic skills, conscious representations are gradually transformed into unconscious ones. Hence, implicit learning is related to such a procedure in which conscious representations are gradually transformed into unconscious ones. Hence, it is found that it is related to procedural memory.

Implicit learning has attracted much attention by the researchers and language educators in China (Guo, 2004; Shi, 2008; Yang, 1991). Shi and Chen (2006) surveyed the role of implicit learning in L2. In addition, as an important component in implicit learning, implicit attention has also been stressed. Shi (2008) investigated short-term memory of English (L2) collocations under implicit attention with an experiment taking short term memory of English collocations embedded in sentences. His experiment produced some evidence for the effects of implicit attention and learning.

Through these related studies, we can see more clearly the importance of the research on proceduralized phenomenon in language learning. However, there still exist some unsettled issues as stated in the following section.

2.6 Drawbacks with Previous Studies

The research on procedural memory has achieved a great deal in theoretical and experimental aspects, however, in consideration of L2 learning and L2 speaking, at least two major unsettled issues still exist.

2.6.1 Unexplored issues in procedural memory and L2 oral production

According to the literature review, procedural memory involves the learning of variety of motor (e.g., the knowledge of how to ride a bike) and cognitive skills (e.g., the acquisition of reading skills). Few reports in literature describe the empirical studies of the relevance between procedural memory and L2 oral production though the role of procedural memory has been stressed in speech through the evidence of patients who are suffering from disorders in speech. In addition, Ullman's DP model (Ullman, 2004) points out that procedural memory subserves the implicit learning and use of a symbol-manipulating grammar across subdomains that include syntax, morphology and possibly phonology (how sounds are combined), but less literature presents the studies of the complex grammatical structures in oral production. Also, the effects of procedural memory on L2 oral production need to be explored.

2.6.2 Unexplored issues in procedural memory and L2 oral proficiency

Theoretically, there are some defects of the view of linguistic competence, such as neglect of language skills, ignorance of the automatic property of knowledge and so on (Chen, 2002a, 2002b, 2002c). In consideration of the importance of procedural memory and its principles, the present researcher holds that linguistic competence should entail not only the procedural knowledge of skills, but also the automatic property of all factual knowledge in the mind.

2.6.3 Unsolved methodological issues

So far, the research on L2 speaking proficiency and the research on procedural memory have been affiliated to two broad fields. The former is closely related to linguistics while the latter is in the charge of neuroscience or cognitive science. However, with the development of disciplines, more and more issues in academia are involved with multi-disciplinary research methods. Regretfully, in the previous studies, we can hardly find the reports of the empirical studies, applying multi-disciplinary methods and exploring the relationship between procedural memory and L2 speaking proficiency. On one hand, most of the empirical studies mentioned above were carried out by neural scientists, psychologists and experts in other disciplines who focused on designing the studies and discussing the results of their studies from the perspective of their own fields. On the other hand, lack of scientific research methods has become a common problem for most linguists and language educators in China. Without the support from other disciplines, the interdisciplinary research can be very hard in obtaining valid data.

An interdisciplinary and multi-dimensional approach is necessary for the studies of L2 oral production based on the principles of procedural memory.

2.7 Summary

This chapter presents a detailed review of the studies on procedural memory and its relevance to language learning and speaking. From the review, it is concluded with three unexplored issues concerning the investigation of the relationship between procedural memory and L2 oral production. The further exploration in this area is thus called for.

Chapter Three
FINDINGS ON ORAL PRODUCTION

3.1 Introduction

Since the beginning of the 20th century, thanks to the development of theories and methodology in disciplines like modern linguistics, sociology, psychology, etc., research on oral production has made great progress in many aspects such as research on children's speaking (Piaget, 1945, 1955), the relations between thought and language (Vygotsky, 1961) and the acquisition of children's language (Chomsky, 1968). With the development of cognitive science in 1960s, some researchers began to be concerned with issues in cognitive science and their relevance to oral production. For example, some researchers emphasize the importance of the role of knowledge in language competence (Neisser, 1967). In their opinion, issues concerning knowledge influence one's language competence. As far as oral production is concerned, the mastery of knowledge, the application of knowledge, the speed of knowledge retrieval, etc. have great impact on one's oral production proficiency (Chen, 2002a, 2002b, 2002c).

This chapter reviews the literature of oral production, from physiological mechanisms to psychological processes, to find out evidence for exploring the relevance of oral production to procedural memory. Furthermore, some studies relevant to oral production are reviewed. Finally, this chapter reviews major up-to-date solutions to problems in oral production and points out some unsettled problems existing in L2 oral production.

3.2 Physiological Mechanisms of Speech Production

Speech organs controlled by the motor center are the executive system of speech. When one speaks, his brain imports compiled programs into the motor center. The actions of the speech organs are dependent on the orders (or the programs) which are sent out by the motor center.

The process of speech production has been divided into two major stages: planning and executing. These two stages cannot be completely separated because it is always the case that during the production of speech, one tends to think of how to go on with his/her speech while speaking (Chen, 2002c).

The production of speech has to fall back on the motor habits because the articulatory movements are very complex due to the fact that the continuous articulation has to depend on the programs sent out by the brain. The motor habits are the motor movement models formed by the repetitive movements of speech organs. The reason that people do not realize the difficulty of the production of speech lies in the effects of these models.

In the following part, the principles and manners of oral production will be introduced in order to illustrate the complexity of the processes of speech production.

3.2.1 Principles of oral production

From the technical, signal-oriented point of view, the production of speech is widely described as a two-level process (Koreman, 1996). In the first stage, the sound is initiated and in the second stage, it is filtered on the second level (Fant, 1960; Titze, 1994). This distinction between phases has its organ in the source-filter model of speech production (Fant, 1960).

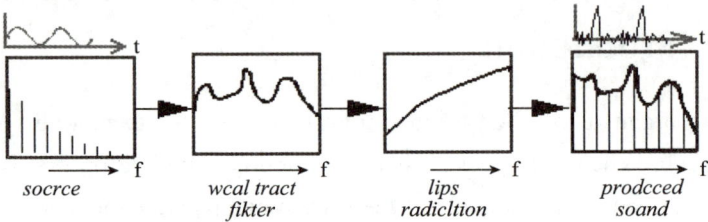

Figure 3-1　Speech Production

The basic assumption of the model is that the source signal produced at the glottal level is linearly filtered through the vocal tract. The resulting sound is emitted to the surrounding air through radiation loading (lips). The model assumes that source and filter are independent of each other. Although recent findings show some interaction between the vocal tract and a glottal source (Fant, 1986; Rothenberg, 1981), Fant's theory of speech production is still used as a framework for the description of the human voice, especially as far as the articulation of vowels is concerned.

From the linguistic phonetic point of view, the production of speech is regarded as a superposition of initiation, phonation, articulation and prosodic organization processes (Laver, 1994). An overview of the physiological constraints on speech production will be given later in this section. Figure 3-2 depicts the organs (including lungs, bronchial tubes, trachea or windpipe, larynx, vocal cords, pharynx, mouth cavity, nasal cavity, tongue and so on) involved in the production of speech.

Speech is produced by a cooperation of lungs, glottis (with vocal cords) and articulation tract (mouth and nose cavity). It involves four processes: initiation (the process when the air is expelled from the

Chapter Three
FINDINGS ON ORAL PRODUCTION

lungs), phonation (the process at the larynx), oro-nasal process (the process in the nasal or the oral cavity) and articulation (the process through most speech sounds can be produced) (Giegerich, 1992). Among these four processes, the articulation process is the most obvious one, taking place in the mouth and it is the process through which we can differentiate most speech sounds. In the mouth we can distinguish between the oral cavity, which acts as a resonator, and the articulators, which can be active or passive: upper and lower lips, upper and lower teeth, tongue (tip, blade, front, back) and roof of the mouth (alveolar ridge, palate and velum). So, speech sounds are distinguished from one another in terms of the place where and the manner how they are articulated.

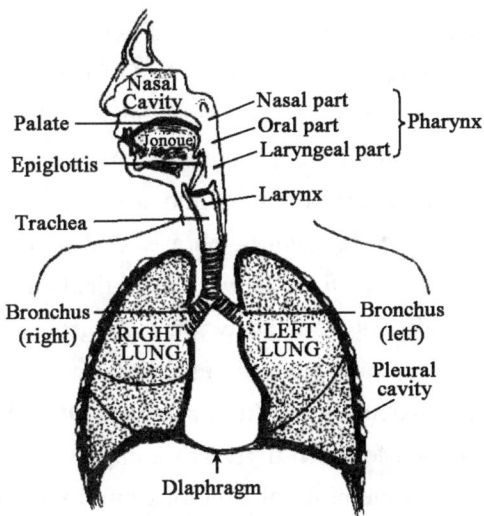

Figure 3-2   The Production of Speech Sounds -Lungs, Glottis, Vocal Tract (from Borden et al., 1994, p64)

In the process of articulation, the factors such as the strength of the air stream, the quality of vocal cords, the resonating effects of the pharynx, oral cavity and nasal cavity will influence the quality and degree of the sounds.

As briefly noted above, the articulation of any sound is dependent on a series of coordinated movements. However, why do not we feel the difficulty in the articulation of sounds? The major reasons lie in two aspects. On one hand, we were born with the conditions and abilities; on the other hand, we have developed the habits of how to produce sounds autonomously due to long-term practice, so we can control most motor movements without additional consciousness.

3.2.2 Manners of articulation

The manner of articulation literally means the way a sound is articulated. The factors such as geography, social status, education, age, gender and habits of utterances may result in the differences in the manners of articulation of different people (Jones, 1956; O'Connor, 1973).

Speech is a continuous process and the articulation of speech is a continuum. Generally, several levels of units of speech which are combined together to form the continuous pronunciation of speech, including sounds, syllables, words, phrases and sentences. Normally, there are no definite distinctions between the articulation of words while natural pauses are always needed between sense groups and sentences.

The articulatory programs, complied in working memory, are restricted by the capacity of working memory. Only one sequence of programs is compiled for each time. The compiling is implemented in a continuous way. In the brain, the motor center is responsible for the executing of the complied programs and sends out orders to speech organs for articulation in accordance with the programs at the fastest speed. The articulatory speed originates from the motor model which is dependent on the features of language. As noted above, speech is a continuous process.

From the perspective of language acquisition, the production of speech is that of linguistic units such as words, phrases, sentences, etc. rather than the production of a single sound. So the combination of linguistic units is a very common habit in articulation of speech.

In phonetics, manners of articulation include coarticulation (the phenomenon of producing more than one speech sound at a given time), parallel transmission, segment value spreading, progressive assimilation, regressive assimilation, allophone, ellipse and so on (Carroll, 2000; Gimson, 1980, pp. 286-296). To a native speaker, he/she has been accustomed to the phenomena and manners of articulation, so he/she does not find any difficulty in their production of speech.

The manners of articulation are activated by articulatory orders at any time or by chain reactions of the models. That is why clusters of sounds can be produced in an autonomous and continuous way, which helps people pay little attention to their pronunciation and every articulatory movement.

However, because of the complexity and variety of produced speech, not all the pronunciations can be produced autonomously.

First of all, the speech organs only react autonomously to familiar linguistic units rather than unfamiliar ones. Sometimes difficulties of speech production occur due to unfamiliar linguistic units. The best example to illustrate this principle is tongue twisters. What tongue twisters do is sabotage the articulatory program by mixing regular with irregular patterns in a way that confuses the articulatory organs (Schourup, 1973). That is why people find it difficult to say tongue twisters which contain the continuous pronunciations of sounds, such as "She sells sea shells.", "Six thick thistle sticks." and "Peter Piper picked a peck of pickled peppers." (Clark & Clark, 1977).

Second, because of physiological reasons, the articulatory speed is normally limited within 150-200 words per minute (Taylor & Taylor, 1983) , which cannot match with the speed of the planning of mental activities and the compiling of programs. If the order is sent out much faster, the mistakes in pronunciation will occur because speech organs need sufficient time to change their positions.

In brief, automaticity is the basic condition in oral production and it can occur in all the linguistic units. However, if a wrong autonomous reaction occurs due to some false stimulus, disagreement between what one thinks of and what he/she produces orally will come into being. In this case, speech errors will occur.

3.2.3 Disorders in speech production

The significance of the studies of disorders in speech production lies in the fact that such studies can reveal the functions of brain in language processing and production as well as in memory which is considered a factor influencing language processing and production.

The common examples of disorders in speech production are **dysphasia** and **aphasia**. **Dysphasia** is deemed for language abnormalities associated with malfunctioning in the area of the brain that process language. The forms of dysphasia involve articulation disorders, speech delays, disorders in the syntactic component of language, dyslexia and so on. Dysphasic children hear properly but without understanding the meanings of words or sentences. And when they speak, they have much trouble in making themselves understood. **Aphasia** is acquired due to the damage of the language-dominant brain hemisphere at a specific time in the life of an individual who had already fully mastered language. People with aphasia usually do not have any impairment of their cognitive faculties or of their ability to move the muscles used in articulating words. The two most common general forms of aphasia are **Broca's aphasia** and **Wernicke's aphasia** (Jay, 2003). **Broca's aphasia** (also known as motor aphasia or expressive aphasia) occurs as a result of lesions to Broca's area in the left frontal lobe. People with Broca's aphasia have trouble in articulating words, distinguishing sentence structures, etc. The combined result of all these problems in people with Broca's aphasia is to significantly impair their ability to engage in spontaneous oral communication. People with Broca's aphasia sometimes also suffer from partial paralysis of the right side of the body. This may have something to do with the fact that Broca's area is located close to other areas with motor functions in the posterior portion of the frontal lobe. **Wernicke's aphasia** occurs when lesions occur in the posterior portion of the superior temporal lobe in the dominant cerebral hemisphere, generally the left. These lesions reduce the understanding of spoken and written language, because this part of the brain plays a critical role in the relationship between the recognition of a word and its meaning. The patients with Wernicke's can read an instruction correctly, but cannot perform the action indicated by the meaning of the words. When Wernicke's aphasics speak, their language is littered with jargon, made-up terms, and other incomprehensible words. Their grammar is often intact while they misuse so many words that conversation with them is very difficult and somewhat reminiscent of Chomsky's famous sentence, "Colorless green ideas sleep furiously" (Chomsky, 1957).

3.3 Psychological Processes in Oral Production

As one of the basic skills of language as well as a psychological behavior, oral production is related to many issues in psychology. The psychological processes in speech production are very complex because they work almost simultaneously, forming a system, which cannot be separated from each other. However, for a better analysis on the psychological processing, most researchers tend to segment the whole system into several processes or stages (De Bot, 1992; Dell, 1986;

Fromkin, 1971, 1973; Levelt, 1989). Three representative models of psychological processing of oral production will be introduced in the following sections.

3.3.1 Dell's parallel model

An alternative to the serial models proposed by Fromkin (1971, 1973) and Garrett (1975) are parallel models which assume that multiple levels of processing take place simultaneously during the course of language production. As an interactive-activation-based theory, Dell's model differs from Fromkin and Garrett's serial models in two ways.

First, Dell (1986) assumed that there are four levels of nodes in permanent memory: semantic, syntactic, morphological, and phonological. Separate representations of the intended message occur at each level, much as in the serial model, but these representations work in parallel (Carroll, 2000).

Second, Dell's model differs from the Fromkin and Garrett's serial models in respect to the linguistic theory it instantiates (Liu & Liu, 2004). Dell noted the compatibility the activation-spreading theories developed in psychology and relational-network theories of language. In the relational-network theory, linguistic knowledge includes two major components: a realization network and a set of tactic patterns. The former realizes the language units like its concepts, words, phonemes and so forth, essentially as convergences of relation. In this theory, words are convergences of relations between concepts, phonemes, and tactic patterns.

According to the model, activation of a node at one level may trigger activation of nodes at other levels, and feedback may occur from morphological and phonological levels back to higher levels of processing (Carroll, 2000).

Dell's model can explain some phenomena in language such as

phonemic similarity effect and the lexical bias effect, so we can apply it to language learning. For example, to instruct students to speak more quickly can get rid of the lexical bias effect.

3.3.2 Levelt's model

Another influential model concerning psychological processes of speech production is Levelt's model (De Bot, 1992; Levelt, 1989). In some sense, the model expounds a linear view of speech production while it is different from the former two models in that it attempts to integrate independent, automatic modules into a complete system.

According to Levelt (1989), five modules involved in language production (conceptualizer, lexicon, formulator, monitor system and articulator) are put together. Basically, Levelt (1989) divides the processes of speech production into message generation, grammatical encoding, phonological encoding and articulation. These processes take place in three processing stages: conceptualization, formulation, and articulation.

As shown in Figure 3-3, during conceptualization, the prelinguistic thoughts of a speaker are generated and combined into propositional form. This step could be divided into macroplanning and microplanning. During the macroplanning process the speaker elaborates the communicative goals and retrieves the information needed to express such goals. During the microplanning process the speaker selects "the information whose expression may realize the communicative goals" (Levelt, 1989, p.5).

During formulation, the prelinguistic thoughts are translated into the appropriate linguistic units by searching through the mental lexicon and identifying the proper lemmas and lexical entries.

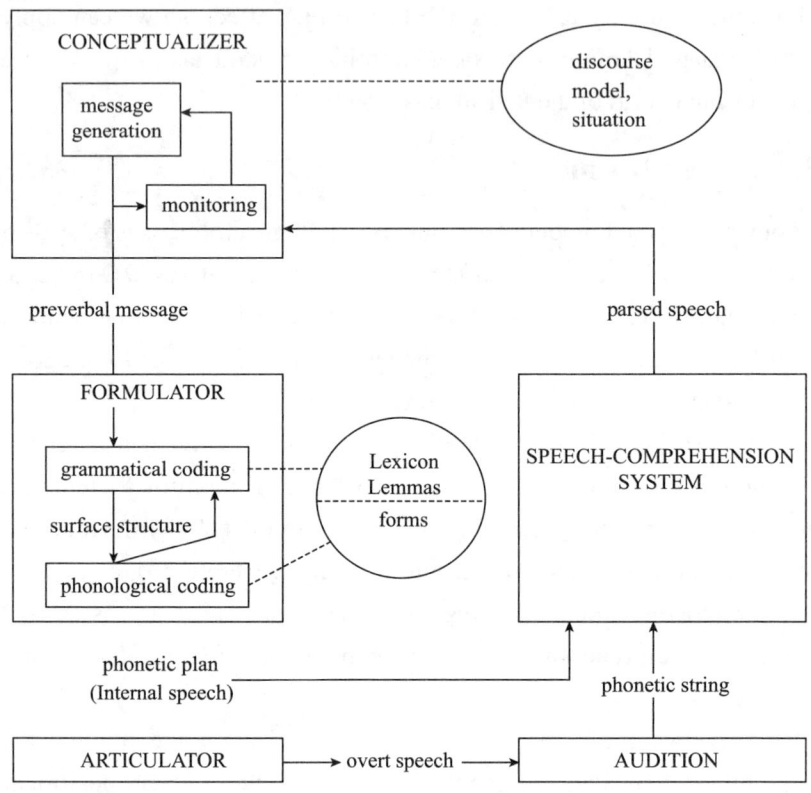

Figure 3-3　Levelt's Speech Production Model (Levelt, 1989)

During articulation, the motor plan for pronouncing the phonemes corresponding to the lexemes is created and executed. That is to say that, the "execution of the phonetic plan by the musculature of the respiratory, the laryngeal, and the supralaryngeal systems" (Levelt, 1989) is activated in order for the speaker to actually produce the utterance. In fact, conceptualization and formulation, the earlier stages of speech production, have typically been focused on the earlier stages of speech production as the possible beneficiaries of gesture.

Levelt's model (1989) was initially formed for speech production in L1, which places the lexicon at the centre of this process. A lexical item has two levels of representation: the lemma containing semantic and syntactic information; and the form containing morphological and phonological information.

There are at least three points taken from Levelt's model (Schuetze, 2002). First, the components in Levelt's model interact with each other in a dynamic process. Second, more than one language can be processed at the same time. Third, lexical items in different languages can be accessed simultaneously.

However, it is worth noticing that because real-life communication, with its discoursive interaction between multiple speakers, is much more complex, the core language regions identified in Levelt's model must "interact" in a much more non-linear than linear fashion.

3.3.3 De Bot's bilingual production model

The adaptation that De Bot made of Levelt's model is concerned with the whole speaker, and anything that influences his speech. In his model, De Bot concerned linguistic, psycholinguistic, and sociolinguistic factors to which the speaker is exposed. The model also followed Green (2000) in the assumption that the languages a bilingual speaks can be activated to varying degrees, being either selected, active, or dormant.

Influenced by Levelt's model, De Bot in his bilingual production model proposed that a part of the conceptualizer, the formulator and the lexicon are differentiated for the speaker's various languages. Because of individual competence factors, another language that is accessible to him may be activated simultaneously to the selected language, the one the speaker has chosen to speak in. The lemma and the form of an L1 item are potentially linked to the lemma and the form of an L2 item through the conceptual representation, thus forming a link between L1 and L2 (De Bot, 1992; De Bot, Cox, Ralston, Schaufeli, & Weltens,

1995; De Bot & Schreuder, 1993). The output of the formulators is sent to the articulator which makes use of a large set of non-language specific speech motor plans. The adapted version of Levelt's model appears to provide a good explanation of various aspects of language production, especially with respect to code switching and the storage and retrieval of lexical elements, and it may suggest a useful direction to take in future research on language processing in bilinguals.

Though De Bot's bilingual production model derived from Level's model, it should be considered that De Bot tried to keep the original model intact as much as possible and only to revert to adaptations only if empirical findings on language production cannot be explained with Levelt's model.

3.4 Studies Related to Non-linguistic Factors Influencing Oral Production

According to the findings of literature review, the factors influencing oral production can be categorized into two major types including internal and explicit ones.

The internal factors can at least be subcategorized into three aspects. The first is due to physiological disorders or language impairment by accidents (Gao, 1993; Wang et al., 1997). Stuttering and aphasia are among the major physiological disorders. The second is due to psychological problems such as anxiety, mood and so on. The third is concerned with individual differences such as motivation, interests, attitudes and so on (Zhou, 2003). Physiological disorders are disregarded in this dissertation.

The explicit factors include time pressure, nature of the task, planning, time for planning, learning atmosphere, teaching and learning materials, the quality of oral English teachers, etc. (Liu, 2004; Skehan,

1998; Skehan & Foster, 1997, 1999; Zhou, 2006). For example, Liu (2004) reviewed relevant studies and found that that planning exerts great influence on accuracy, fluency and complexity.

3.5 Studies Related to Indices of Oral Production Ability

So far, the importance of oral production ability has already been recognized in the evaluation of one's linguistic competence (Cai, 2002; Lennon, 1990; Riggenbach, 1991; Zhang, 2000; Zhang & Wu, 2001). However, the existing views on how to evaluate one's oral production ability are various from person to person. Skehan (1998) held in his task-based approach that fluency, accuracy and complexity are the major indices of evaluating an oral task. As far as fluency is concerned, speaking rate, articulatory rate, fillers, hesitations and so on are paid more attention to (Lennon, 1984, 1990; Riggenbach, 1991; Zhang, 2000). As to accuracy and complexity, many researchers stated that the more accurate and complex the grammar rules and words are applied in the oral production, the more proficient the speaker in oral production is (Halleck, 1995; Zhang, 2000). Some researchers such as Young and Milanovic (1992) were concerned with the processes of conversations and evaluated oral production from the perspective of the styles in conversations, which are dependent on interactional contingency, goal orientation and dominance.

In China, the syllabuses issued by Ministry of Education always play an important role in assessing English competency (Cai, 2002). Meanwhile, the changes in the different versions of syllabuses reflect the development of research focuses on students' English competency. Take College English Curriculum Requirements (CECR) (*For*

Trial implementation, 2004) for example. There are three levels of requirements for speaking: basic requirements, intermediate requirements and higher requirements. Accuracy, fluency and communicative abilities are the major components paid attention to though, to some extent, there are differences in different levels. In the Self-Assessment/Peer Assessment Forms of Students' English Competence (from Form I to Form III), it is easily found that more emphasis is laid on communicative abilities such as the application of communicative strategies.

Lou et al. (2006) reviewed the past related studies of speaking assessment from the following aspects: the contents of speaking assessment, the tasks of speaking assessment and the influential factors during assessment. When reviewing the first aspect, they mention that accuracy, fluency and complexity are the main indices of oral production discussed by researchers at home and abroad. Fluency is a very important index applied in assessing one's speaking ability, especially when communicative language teaching becomes more and more popular. Speaking rate, hesitation, pauses, silence and so on are the influential factors affecting fluency of speaking proficiency (Zhang, 2000; Zhang & Wu, 2001). Meanwhile, the accuracy of pronunciation and application of words, sentence patterns as well as complexity of vocabulary, sentence patterns and so on are also considered the major indices of oral production proficiency (Yang, 1999).

3.6 Problems with the Previous Studies

3.6.1 Difficulty in assessing one's oral production due to incomplete understanding of linguistic competence

The theories of linguistic competence play an important role in the assessment of one's abilities in listening, speaking, reading and writing.

The term of linguistic competence can be traced back to the dichotomous views by many scholars, such as langue/parole (F. D. Saussure); competence/performance (N. Chomsky); linguistic potential/ linguistic behavior (M. A. K. Halliday), communicative competence (D. Hymes) (Hu & Jiang, 2003). For their purpose of description, the first three scholars are of the view that a line must be drawn between inner ability and outward performance and their task is to study the internalized knowledge. Because of these influential views, it has been widely held that the ability to use language is **"competence"**, which mainly consists of linguistic knowledge while in the type of view by Hymes, the linguistic competence is for communication and it involves not only the ability to use the formal rules of language, but many types of interpersonal, sociocultural, and situational factors (Hymes, 1972, p.277). This view has changed the narrow perspective of linguistic competence and exerted great influence in linguistics and language teaching.

Nowadays, Hymes' views of linguistic competence are very popular in China, researchers lay more stress on communicative strategies when they assess students speaking competency. In fact, as noted above, oral production is a very complex issue which involves physiological, linguistic, psychological and cognitive aspects. We'd better assess the oral production in a more scientific and overall perspective.

According to Chen (2002a, 2002b, 2002c, 2009), the popularly accepted views on linguistic competency are imperfect though the connotations of views have been enriched many times with the development of relevant theories, linguistic competence should include the following aspects: (1) the formal and semantic systems of language, including abilities in terms of phonetic features, phonemes, syllables, words, phrases, sentences, discourses, semantic rules, and prosodic features. (2) the ability to use language in social interactions, or the pragmatic competence emphasized by scholars in sociolinguistics. (3) the procedural knowledge of skills as well as, but also the automatic property of all factual knowledge in the mind. Chen (2009) deemed that the first two points have been widely accepted while the third is relatively new and should be emphasized. In his understanding, the new concept of linguistic competence should include not only grammatical rules, lexical knowledge, exemplar storage, four-channel mental representation of language and encyclopedia knowledge but also automaticity in the complex mental procedural activities such as listening, speaking, reading and writing.

In view of the cognitive aspect of language processing and production (Skehan, 1998), the present study supports Chen Kaishun's proposal of new concept of linguistic competence. In the researcher's opinion, procedural memory and automaticity should be entailed in the indices of oral proficiency in the assessment of one's oral production.

3.6.2 Imbalance in research on oral production

(1) In current China, few researches are concerned with the ways for the English learners with high speaking proficiency to grasp words, patterns and strategies and so on though there is no doubt that communicative abilities are very important in oral production (Hymes, 1972). In other words, how those students with high speaking proficiency memorize words, grammar rules or communicative strategies has not been explored satisfactorily so far in China.

(2) When assessing oral production, most examiners are used to scoring according to their overall impressions on the examinees' performance. Such scoring method is called holistic/global scoring method, which is commonly applied in oral examinations at all levels, even in the national examinations. Undoubtedly, it is a time-saving way of scoring in formal large-scale examinations while it is not good to the English learners

because they do not know where their problems are in their oral production. As a result, they are at a loss about how to improve their oral production even after they have known their levels in the oral examinations.

(3) To most of the tertiary English learners in China, they have a good mastery of the basic knowledge of grammar and vocabulary and also are better at developing topics than those younger students in high schools. However, what troubles these students most is the problems in oral production of pronunciation, words, collocations, sentence patterns and so on which negatively influence their proficiency of oral production (See **Appendix 6** and also **Section 6.4**).

Influenced by knowledge of psychology and cognitive and neural science, more and more researchers have realized the importance of the role of combining linguistic units in oral production and rules in oral production. Recently, such research has been initiated on units of oral production such as pronunciations, words, sentences and so on (Yang & Chen, 2005). However, it is far from being satisfactory, though.

3.7 Summary

This chapter presents a detailed review of the related studies of oral production. From the review, it can be concluded that oral production is closely related to cognitive processing. However, more work needs to be done in this area due to drawbacks of the previous studies of oral production.

Chapter Four
A CONCEPTUAL FRAMEWORK FOR THE PRESENT STUDY

4.1 Introduction

In the chapter, based on the review of literature of the relevance between procedural memory and oral production, an information- processing theoretical framework is provided for the research design of empirical studies and for the explanation of the results obtained. In addition, this chapter expounds the issues such as the new approach to linguistic competence, the identification of functioning of procedural memory, and the procedural memory-based indices of oral production for the current study.

4.2 The Focus of the Present Study

As mentioned in **Chapter Three**, the research on oral production is complex since oral production is related to both psychological and linguistic issues and therefore, the present study has to narrow its focuses. Besides the reasons mentioned in **Section 1.2 "Need for the Study"** and the unsettled problems in **Section 2.6** and **Section 3.6**, the final decision of the focus on the object clause structure in indirect speech in oral production from the perspective of procedural memory is based on the reasons summarized as follows.

First, in oral production, the use of the object clause structure in indirect speech is very common in real communication of daily life as well as in classroom teaching and learning while the research literature on such structure is limited. From this point, the research on the use of such structure in oral production is of great significance and deserves much attention.

Second, the object clause structure in indirect speech is grammatically difficult for English learners in China. As mentioned in **Section 1.2.3**, many shifts are involved in the sentence structure, such as the shifts of the inflection of verbs, nouns for person, tense, voice, personal pronouns, word order and adverbials of time. It is a good breakthrough to explore oral production of such difficult structure among different subjects with oral proficiency at different levels. Furthermore, because of the difficulty of the tasks concerning the object clause structure in indirect speech, cognitive complexity of the speakers can be investigated by speakers' response time, accuracy, etc. In this sense, the effects of procedural memory may be explored.

Third, based on the nature of the grammar structure, the current study attempts to explore the effects of procedural memory in L2 oral production under the guidance of the theories including Ullman's DP model. According to Ullman's DP model, procedural memory is related to grammatical rules (Pinker & Ullman, 2002; Ullman, 2004). In the current study, the object clause structure in indirect speech is a typical grammatical phenomenon.

Fourth, the use of the object clause structure in indirect speech is related to syntagmatic relations. Lyons (2002, p.96) stressed the importance of linear and simultaneous syntagmatic relations in the stream of speech or writing and defined the rules of combining smaller units of any level of a language into bigger ones and compatibility of the former. According to Zhang's study of word association patterns in Chinese EFL learners' mental lexicon (Zhang, 2009), syntagmatic relations and paradigmatic relations influence learners' L2 proficiency in lexicon. In this sense, the use of the object clause structure in indirect speech is related to syntagmatic relations as it is involved with the shifts of subjects, verbs, adverbials and so on. In the oral training of the present study, the application of changing the words in the same word category may be beneficial to the flexible use of sentence patterns.

Fifth, the present study focuses on the type of procedural memory parasitizing in declarative memory and influencing the automatic processing of its retrieval and application. As mentioned in **Section 2.5**, there are two special types of procedural memory (Chen, 2009). The first is concerning the procedural memory stored in the brain, separate from declarative memory. The type of procedural memory can help with the production of comparatively simple and often-used linguistic units such as chunks, idiomatic expressions and collocations. However, it is hard to deal with more complex and longer sentences because these linguistic units have not been proceduralized. The second is about the procedural memory parasitizing in declarative memory. With the functioning of the two memory systems, the production of language units like chunks or idiomatic expressions learned in this type of procedural memory can be analyzed and hence leads to the easier processing in the working memory which helps increase the storage of knowledge information. The present study focuses on the second type of procedural memory because of the Chinese subjects who have grasped a certain grammatical knowledge of the object clause structure in indirect speech.

4.3 A General Information-Processing Framework

Besides its neural mechanisms, language processing is involved in the framework of information processing because it is closely related to the encoding, storage and retrieval of information. It is the information processing framework that the current study is based on.

According to the introduction in **Section 2.2**, the information processing system, multiple memory system and procedural memory are closely related to each other. In accordance with the influential information processing model of Atkinson and Shriffin (1968), information is thought to be processed in a serial and discontinuous manner as it moves from one stage to the next. Because of the components involved in this system, the information processing system is considered closely related to linguistic competence.

In the information processing system, the multiple memory system is the important place where the information is stored and analyzed as introduced in **Section 2.2.2**. An agreement has been reached among the researchers of memory and language that memory and the multiple memory system has a very close relevance to human abilities (Chen, 2009). As we know, the capacity of memory and duration of information storage play a decisive role in knowledge learning, therefore so far the research on memory has been carried out widely. In the multiple memory system, the long-term memory has been paid much attention to mainly because of its larger capacity and longer duration of information storage, compared with the short-term memory. According to Chen Kaishun's proposal of linguistic competence from the cognitive perspective, the proficiency of oral production is influenced by the concept of linguistic competence (Chen, 2002a, 2002b, 2002c). In the new approach to linguistic competence, besides other contents of information, the long-term memory entails the lexical storage, the storage of grammatical rules, the storage of linguistic exemplar and four-channel storage of language (Chen, 2009). Hence, there is no doubt as to the close relation between the long-term memory and linguistic competence.

As an essential component of long-term memory, procedural memory is the memory storage of skills and procedures, representing the learning and retention of motor skills and habits as introduced in **Section 2.4**. The newly-developed concept of linguistic competence entails procedural memory as part of contents on the basis that procedural memory is connected with the storage of proceduralized, rule-based and skill-based knowledge. Meanwhile, procedural memory influences automaticity in the language processing such as the retrieval and output of the stored information. The newly-developed concept of linguistic competence and the identification of procedural memory will be expounded in **Section 4.5**.

Meanwhile, the role of declarative memory cannot be ignored. Chen (2009) held that there are two types of procedural memory. One is stored in the brain, separated from declarative memory. The other type of procedural memory can parasitize in declarative memory and influence the automatic processing of its retrieval and application (Chen, 2009). The linguistic units produced with this type of procedural memory have been analyzed. With the functions of both memory systems, the effects of learning can be optimized (Poldrack & Packard, 2003).

For a better understanding of the general information-processing framework, Figure 4-1 was drawn to demonstrate the general complex relationships between the information processing system, the multiple memory system and linguistic competence.

Chapter Four
A CONCEPTUAL FRAMEWORK FOR THE PRESENT STUDY

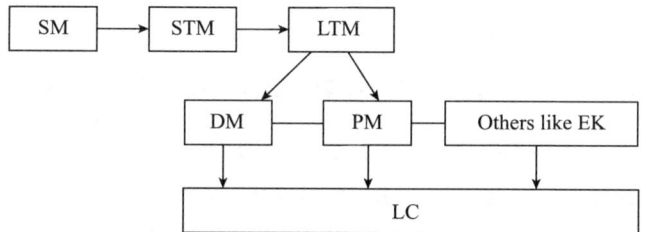

Figure 4-1 A General Information Processing Framework

(Note: SM: sensory memory; STM: short-term memory; LTM: long-term memory; DM: declarative memory; PM: procedural memory; EK: encyclopedia knowledge; LC: linguistic competence)

From Figure 4-1, we can see that the information processing system entails the multiple memory system. In the multiple memory system, some of the information in sensory memory (SM) is transferred to short-term memory (STM). However, compared with short-term memory, long-term memory (LTM) can store much larger quantities of information for potentially unlimited duration (sometimes a whole life span) (Solso et al., 2005). The long-term memory in this information processing system consists of declarative memory and procedural memory. Besides the other factors like encyclopedia knowledge, linguistic competence is supposed to be influenced by declarative memory and procedural memory because it involves not only declarative knowledge but also procedural knowledge as shown in Figure 2-4 "Models of Long-term Memory". Meanwhile, the combination of the two memory systems can improve the effects of memory and learning.

The following sections will deal with some terms in the framework in great detail.

4.4 A New Approach to Linguistic Competence

As mentioned in **Section 1.3.1**, the views on linguistic competence have changed with the disciplinary development in different eras. The dichotomous views by many scholars, such as langue/parole (F. D. Saussure); competence/performance (N. Chomsky); linguistic potential/linguistic behavior (M. A. K. Halliday), communicative competence (D. Hymes) still have great impact in the field of linguistics while influenced by the information processing theory, the concept of linguistics competence needs to be enriched from the perspective of cognitive science.

According to Chen (2009), the new concept of linguistic competence should include not only grammatical rules, lexical knowledge, exemplar storage, four-channel mental representation of language and encyclopedia knowledge but also automaticity in the complex mental procedural activities such as listening, speaking, reading and writing.

Because of the cognitive aspect of language processing and production (Skehan, 1998), the present study supports Chen's proposal of the new concept of linguistic competence. In the current researcher's opinion, procedural memory and automaticity should be entailed into the indices of one's linguistic competence.

Figure 4-2 shows the newly-developed linguistic competence which combines the existing ideas of linguistic competence and Chen's opinion (Chen, 2009).

Generally speaking, linguistic competence entails the skills of listening, speaking, reading and writing. Compared with other linguistic skills, oral production is very complex because of the characteristics in its physiological mechanisms and influencing factors as mentioned in

Chapter Four
A CONCEPTUAL FRAMEWORK FOR THE PRESENT STUDY

Chapter Three. As part of the new approach to linguistic competence, the proficiency of oral production is supposed to be influenced by declarative memory and procedural memory because it involves not only declarative knowledge but also procedural knowledge as shown in Figure 2-4 "Models of Long-term Memory".

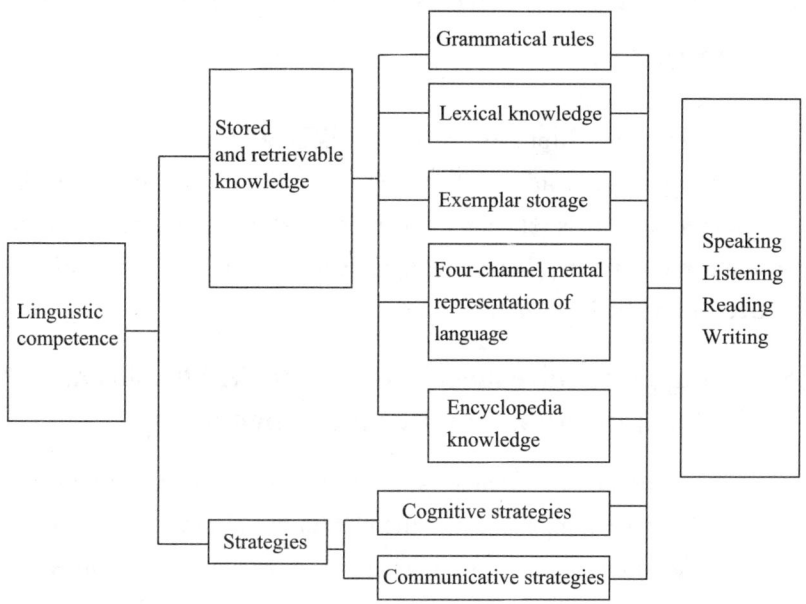

Figure 4-2 Linguistic Competence

From Figure 4-2, we can see that speaking or oral production is influenced by the new concept of linguistic competence. It is worth noticing that we do not find automaticity in this figure because automaticity parasitizes all the information involved in language processing. Though automaticity is invisible in Figure 4-2, its effects cannot be ignored. In addition, the strategies such as cognitive strategies and communicative strategies are involved in the assessment of proficiency of listening, speaking, reading or writing. Nevertheless, because the current study focuses only on procedural memory, the investigation of the strategies is ignored.

The relation between procedural memory and oral production in the current study will be expounded in the following sections.

4.5 Identification of Functioning of Procedural Memory

On the basis of the literature review, this section will first sort out schema theory, Anderson's ACT models and Ullman's DP model as the major cognitive models relevant to the identification of the application of procedural memory and then provide an adapted version for identifying the effects of procedural memory in oral production.

4.5.1 Major cognitive models relevant to the identification of the application of procedural memory

As we know, cognitive science is concerned with understanding the processes that the brain, especially the human brain, uses to accomplish complex tasks including perceiving, learning, remembering, thinking, predicting, inference, problem solving, decision making, planning, and moving around the environment. The major goal of cognitive models is to scientifically explain one or more of these basic cognitive processes, or explain how these processes interact. Cognitive models appear in all fields of cognition at a rapidly increasing rate, ranging from perception to memory to problem solving and decision-making.

Cognitive models have been applied in a wide variety of areas. For example, clinical psychologists use cognitive models to assess individual differences in cognitive processing between normal individuals and clinical patients (e.g., schizophrenics). In cognitive neuroscience, cognitive models are applied to the understanding of the psychological function of different brain regions.

It is well known that memory plays an important role in cognitive processes. There are a variety of cognitive theories and models of memory introduced in the previous chapters. From the perspective of the information processing, the current study sorts out schema theory introduced in **Section 2.5.2.2,** Anderson's ACT models introduced in **Section 2.4.1.2,** and Ullman's DP model introduced in **Section 2.4.1.3,** as the supportive models to the information-processing framework of the current study.

The major reasons for selection of these three models lie in the following aspects.

1. As important theories of learning, these three cognitive models emphasize the unity as far as the output of knowledge is concerned. In the three models, prior knowledge influences the output of new knowledge. For example, schema theory views organized knowledge as an elaborate network of abstract mental structures representing one's understanding of the world. Shallert (1982) indicated that abstract concepts are best understood after a foundation of concrete, relevant information has been established. The general knowledge provides a framework into which the newly-formed structure can be fitted. Anderson's ACT models and Ullman's DP model also emphasize the importance of prior knowledge such as declarative knowledge.

As to procedural memory, it also relies on declarative knowledge to learn new information. In other words, in all these models and the theories of procedural memory, stored knowledge parasitizes in the learning processes and helps with the skill-based knowledge.

2. All the three models emphasize the importance of the rate of retrieval of knowledge. For example, schema theory is connected to automaticity and fluency, accuracy and complexity in language

production. This theory emphasizes the complexity of processing and learning knowledge and offers ways to deal with the complex processing, i.e. by establishing schemata to ease the pressure of retrieving knowledge and hence enhance the rate of retrieval of knowledge. Anderson's ACT models and Ullman's DP model also stress the role of the rate of retrieval of knowledge. In this sense, these three models are closely related to procedural memory.

3. All the three models emphasize the concept of proceduralization. Both Anderson's ACT models and Ullman's DP model deal with declarative and procedural memory though their focuses are different. The former is explanatory, paying attention to the approaches of processing information and the latter stresses the functions of these two types of memory in language learning and processing. Schema theory does not directly put forward the concept of proceduralization. However, the quality of the output of knowledge on the basis of this theory has close relevance to the degree of proceduralization.

Based on the illustrations above, the three models are connected to oral production in the information processing framework, which is also connected to complex cognitive activities and motor skills.

4.5.2 An adapted version for identifying the effects of procedural memory in oral production

In this dissertation, the adapted version of the framework for the identification of the effects of procedural memory consists of the following aspects.

Firstly, in accordance with the opinions of researchers in the field of memory research, such as Ryle, Anderson and Ullman, procedural memory is equivalent to procedural knowledge. In this sense, this dissertation will adopt this view and hence the effects of procedural memory have been transferred to the effects of procedural knowledge which is about how to do things. Now the issue of identification of the effects of procedural memory in oral production is simplified as adding up the effects of procedural knowledge, which could be realized by identifying the use of units of oral production and communicative strategies. The units include phonemes, syllables, morphemes, words, phrases, sentences and texts. More important, the use of formulaic language like chunks, collocations and idioms is a significant index of identifying the effects of procedural memory in oral production.

Secondly, the identification of the effects of procedural memory can be reflected by the errors in oral production, such as the errors in pronunciation, disfluency in communication, wrong usage of phrases and collocations and incorrect use of pauses. In the field of psycholinguistics, speech errors help with the research on linguistic mental processes (Jiang, 2001). Speech errors have been utilized and contributed to the present study in the investigation of the use of linguistic units.

Thirdly, procedural memory is a kind of nondeclarative (implicit) memories (Gazzaniga et al., 2002, p.213-215) which has been widely explored in psychology and cognitive neuroscience with the help of modern technology. In neural science, fMRI, ERP studies and other experimental studies have been taken to distinguish the similarities and differences among the subjects through electric brain potentials evoked by pictures, sounds, words and so on (Friederici et al., 2000; Gao et al., 2006; Hao & Li, 2002; Li & Li, 2006; Ullman, 2001a, 2001b, 2001c; Zhang & Chen, 1995). Nevertheless, since the present study focuses on oral production, which is not feasible to investigate by fMRI and ERP experiments because of lack of the effective technical support and restrictions of the current research on oral production. Instead, some cognitive behavioral experiments were designed and conducted to explore the subjects' oral proficiency and the effects of procedural memory.

4.5.3 Systematic effects of procedural memory on L2 oral production

As revealed in the previous sections, existing studies on L2 oral production have been fragmentary rather than systematic. A more systematic and comprehensive investigation of the effects of procedural memory on L2 oral production is therefore called for.

Concerning the various aspects of procedural memory and the complex features of oral production, the current study attempts to offer a conceptual framework for better descriptions (See Figure 4-3).

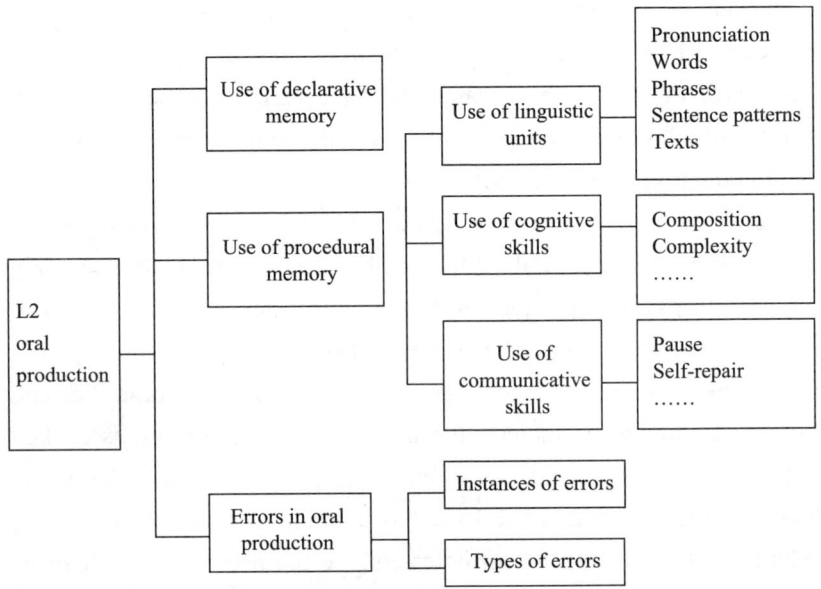

Figure 4-3　Systematic Effects of Procedural Memory on L2 Oral Production

Though the use of declarative memory is part of L2 oral production, this conceptual framework first emphasizes the importance of use of procedural knowledge which affects L2 oral production. Procedural knowledge is said to be concerning about how to perform a cognitive skill and is inaccessible to conscious processes (Anderson, 1983b, 1983c, 1983d; Turban & Aronson, 1988). The researchers prefer to use the term "procedural knowledge" rather than "procedural memory", because procedural memory is more abstract and implicit, which cannot be revealed without advanced technology and equipment in the fields of psychology or cognitive science.

Based on the review of literature concerning procedural memory and oral production, in this dissertation, procedural knowledge involves the use of linguistic units, the use of cognitive skills and use of communicative skills which can be measured by the empirical studies.

However, as far as the oral production of the object clause in indirect speech is concerned, the current study simplifies procedural memory and procedural knowledge in a more specific way. In order to explore the effects of procedural memory on L2 oral production, the current study only investigates fluency, accuracy, and complexity in use of linguistic units of the object clause in indirect speech, ignoring part of cognitive skills and the communicative skills under the controlled condition in a language lab.

Second, this conceptual framework emphasizes the role of errors in oral production. A speech error is a speech pattern that differs from some standard pattern. Within the field of psycholinguistics, speech errors are categorized in language production. For example, speech errors occur in use of pronunciation, vocabulary and grammar. The types of speech errors mainly include blends, additions, deletions, exchange errors, perseveration, anticipation, shift, substitution, etc. (Eysenck & Keane, 2005). Over the years, speech error data have come to be regarded as a kind of "window" into linguistic mental processes, providing the investigators with empirical evidence for testing hypotheses about language and language behavior (Jiang, 2001). In this dissertation, the speech error data will be applied to assess the subjects' oral proficiency.

4.6 Oral Proficiency in the Newly-developed Concept of Linguistic Competence

From the perspective of cognitive science and psychology, linguistic competence should entail not only grammatical rules, lexical knowledge, exemplar storage, four-channel mental representation of language and encyclopedia knowledge but also automaticity in the complex mental procedural activities such as listening, speaking, reading and writing (Chen, 2009).

Besides procedural memory introduced in **Chapter Two**, automaticity will be added into the indices of oral proficiency based on the newly-developed concept of linguistic competence in the following section.

4.6.1 Oral proficiency in general

Influenced by the theorists such as Saussure, Chomsky, Halliday, Hymes, the concepts of linguistic competence entail the indices covering from linguistic units to communicative strategies. Each concept of linguistic competence is featured and limited by the era when the theorists were in and also by the development of multiple disciplines. It is certain that the indices of oral proficiency are influenced by the accepted concepts of linguistic competence. It has been acknowledged that the way of establishing the indices of oral proficiency has gradually become mature. As shown in **Appendix 2**, the indices include fluency, accuracy, appropriateness and so on in the performance of the speakers. However, some drawbacks still exist in these indices. For example, in **Appendix 2**, the cognitive processing is not paid special attention to since these indices emphasize more on the functions of language and the communicative strategies in communication. This current study will perfect these indices by adding the procedural memory-based items to the indices of oral proficiency.

4.6.2 Procedural memory-based indices of oral proficiency for the present study

Based on the literature review in this dissertation, especially on Skehan's opinion (1998) of cognitive abilities and Chen's proposal (2002a, 2002b, 2002c, 2009) of linguistic competence, the present study adds the item "**automaticity**" into the index "fluency" of oral proficiency. The reason for the change is that fluency is always revealed by the time. The following indices in Table 4-1 are established in consideration of the principles of procedural memory.

Table 4-1 Indices of Oral Proficiency

Indices	Items involved		
Fluency	Time	Speech time	Syllables
			Pauses
			Chunks
Accuracy	Macro assessment	Sentence patterns	
	Micro assessment	Pronunciation	
		Use of linguistic units	
Complexity	Complexity in language structure	Syntactic variety and lexical variety	
		Syntactical complex	
	Cognitive complexity	Familiarity, task difficulty, information organization, etc.	

As mentioned in **Chapter Three**, oral production is very complex because it is connected with many elements such as declarative knowledge, procedural knowledge, communicative strategies and the organization of discourses. That means procedural memory is merely one of the elements influencing oral production. Among all these elements, this dissertation only focuses on the elements related to procedural memory, especially under the equivalent condition of the mastery of declarative knowledge.

Fluency, accuracy and complexity are the major indices of assessing L2 oral production proficiency (Yang, 1999; Zhang, 2000; Zhang & Wu, 2001; Zhou, 2002). From the perspective of memory, fluency is the external manifestation of automaticity and proceduralization. Accuracy and complexity are more influenced by declarative knowledge, but with intensive automaticity and proceduralization, they can be bettered in oral production. These indices work together and influence the proficiency of one's oral production. Through the assessment of these indices, we can explore proceduralization. The assessment of these three indices will be introduced, combining the literature of previous studies and the theme of the current study.

4.6.2.1 Fluency

Skehan (1996) defined fluency as the rate of production and learner's capacity to produce language without undue pausing or hesitation. Schmidt (1990) termed fluency as an 'automatic procedural skill'. So far, some accepted measures have been applied in the research on fluency. For example, speech rate has been used in almost all the previous studies concerning language production. It is considered as the best single index of fluency since it can capture the overall workings of language production (Fillmore, 1979; Towell, Hawkins, & Bazergui, 1996). In addition, research has shown that speech rate is the measure found to be consistently statistically significant on native speakers' judgments of fluency of L2 production (Lennon, 1990).

The assessment of fluency includes indices such as speech rate (SR), articulation rate (AR), phonation time ratio (PTR), mean length of runs (MLR) and average length of pause (ALP) (Zhang & Wu, 2001; Zhou, 2002).

(1) Speech Rate (SR): syllables per minute, total number of syllables uttered by total length (in seconds) of speech sample multiplied by 60.

(2) Articulation Rate (AR): total syllables produced in speech sample divided by total time required to produce those syllables multiplied by 60.

(3) Phonation time ratio (PTR): total time spent speaking divided by total time to produce speech sample, ST/TR.

(4) Mean Length of Run (MLR): total number of syllables / phonemes in speech sample divided by total number of run of speech.

(5) Average Length of Pause (ALP): The time of pausing divided by the number of pauses (Note: Pause is the measure central to the analysis of oral fluency). In this study, a pause is defined as "a break of 0.3 seconds or longer, either within a sentence or between sentences" (Zhang, 2002). All filled and unfilled pauses of 0.3 seconds and above are marked.

In this study, considering the fact that the subject of the current study is related to procedural memory, the researcher paid more attention to the temporal analysis of the indices when assessing fluency. In addition, similar to Yuan and Guo's study (2010) concerning the relevance of chunks and fluency, the present study selected SR, PTR, MLR and ALP as indices of fluency, ignoring AR (Articulation Rate). Besides SR, PTR, MLR and ALP, TRT (Total Response Time) was employed as another index to assess fluency in oral production of the object clause structure in indirect speech between the high-proficiency and low-proficiency L2 speakers as shown in Table 4-2. It is worth mentioning that because the length of the tested sentences is controlled and limited, the tested sentences are separated from each other, the researcher makes some adjustments of part of the calculation of the indices, which is slightly different from those analysis of a speech or a discourse (Zhou, 2002; Zhou & Zhang, 2006). In the analysis of Mean Length of Run (MLR) in a speech or a discourse, the "run" only refers to the one between two pauses, each of which is as long as 0.3 seconds or longer. Nevertheless, in the current study, the researcher attempts to investigate all the runs before and after the pauses.

Table 4-2　Fluency Indices and Their Calculation

Indices	Calculation
TRT (Total Response Time)	total response time
SR (Speech Rate)	total number of syllables ÷ total amount of speaking time (including the pause time) × 60
MLR (Mean Length of Run)	total number of syllables ÷ (total number of pauses+1)
PTR (Phonation Time Ratio)	the time spent speaking ÷ total amount of speaking time (including the pause time)
ALP (Average Length of Pause)	total time of pausing ÷ total number of pauses

In Table 4-2, the total response time refers to the total amount of speaking time including pause time and the time spent by other non-voice speech. The calculation of the total response time helps to get a global impression of frequency.

Wei (2007) reported the length of chunks is a determinant factor influencing fluency. As to fluency of the pronounced chunks, this study applies the opinion of Zhen (2009) who revealed that frequency of chunks has a positive correlation with fluency and accuracy. The present study attempts to investigate the influence of chunks in oral production of the object clause structure in indirect speech.

So far, the definitions of chunks have had different versions. Yuan and Guo (2010) defined the chunk as: (1) the lexical bundle which contains two or more than two words; (2) the idiomatic expression which is established by usage or has a fixed structure; or semi-structured sentence builders such as "I think that⋯" and "People say that⋯"; (3) fixed expressions, or collocations which are temporarily generated without being limited by grammatical rules, such as "solve the problem" and "means of transportation"; (4) no pause(s) within a chunk. (Note: Here pauses including those lasting less than 0.3 seconds). Wei (2007) categorized the chunks into three types: full clauses (independent clauses and dependent clauses), clause constituents (multiple clause constituents and single clause constituents) and incomplete phrases. He also finds that 3-word chunks are most frequently used in COLSEC (College Learners' Spoken English Corpus). Based on the literature and the feature of the current study, the current study applied Yuan and Guo's definition of chunks and investigated chunks from chunk frequency. Zhen (2009) deemed that frequency of chunks has a positive correlation with fluency. That means if SR is faster, then the time spent in the pronunciation of chunks is also less. Zhen (2009) calculated the frequency of chunks by the formula: total number of chunks ÷ the number of tokens in a speech. Tokens refer to the words in the speech (Yang, 2002). Taking consideration of the types of tasks in the current study, the present researcher calculates the frequency of chunks by the operational formula: total number of chunks ÷ the number of tested sentences as shown in Table 4-3. In addition, the recognition response time for the speakers to retrieve chunks will be explored in the parts where necessary. The response time is applied to explore the speakers' familiarity with the chunks. Meanwhile, it can reveal how the subjects deal with the cognitive complexity in a subjective way.

Table 4-3   The Calculation of Chunk Frequency

Items	Calculation
Chunk frequency (CF)	Total number of chunks ÷ the number of sentences

With the help of Adobe Audition 3.0 software, the researcher will manually calculate the values.

4.6.2.2 Accuracy

Skehan (1996) held that accuracy refers to how well the language is produced in relation to the rules of the target language. Mehnert (1998) assessed accuracy by the ratio of error-free T-units (REFT). This is calculated by the formula "total error-free T-units ÷ total T-units". Hunt (1970) defined a T-unit as a main clause plus all subordinate clauses and non-clausal structures attached or embedded in it. The current study explores the linguistic structures within a sentence, rather than in a text with many sentences or clauses, so the approach of REFT applied by Mehnert of oral language will not be used in the current study.

As a measurement of oral proficiency in the current study, accuracy is assessed by the two types: macro assessment and micro assessment as shown in Table 4-4.

Table 4-4   Accuracy Indices and Their Calculation

	Indices	Calculation
Macro assessment	The number of sentences which are correct in sentence builders and sentence patterns (NC)	Assessed by knowledge of standard English

Chapter Four
A CONCEPTUAL FRAMEWORK FOR THE PRESENT STUDY

continued

	Indices	Calculation
Micro assessment	Ratio of errors of pronunciation (REP)	The number of total inaccurately pronounced words ÷ the number of the tested sentences
	Ratio of errors of use of linguistic units (REULU)	The number of total inaccurately used linguistic units ÷ the number of the tested sentences

(1) The macro assessment is to judge the correctness of sentence builders and sentence patterns. The sentence builder and the sentence patterns in the current study involve the specific clause: the object clause structure in indirect speech, and relevant grammatical issues. In the experiments designed in the present study, they can be revealed by such tasks in which the subjects are required to judge whether the sentence builders of the tested sentences belong to the object clause structure in indirect speech or they are required to make sentences which apply correct sentence builders and sentence patterns in accordance with the object clause structure in indirect speech. The present study will calculate the number of sentences which are correct in sentence builders and sentence patterns (NC).

(2) The micro assessment is measured by the following indices: ratio of errors in pronunciation and ratio of errors in use of linguistic units (REULU), feeding back on the ratio of inaccurately pronounced words per tested sentence or the ratio of inaccurately used linguistic units.

In the current study, the assessment of pronunciation involves the pronunciation of syllables and stress, which is made word by word. The formula is shown as Table 4-4. The use of linguistic units includes the changes of the following items in each sentence concerning five aspects in the object clause structure in indirect speech: the subject (change of person); predicate verb(s) (tense, voice and word order), the objects (change or person), adverbials of time and place, conjunction.

As to the definition and judgment of "error", Corder (1967) distinguished the terms of "error" and "mistake". He claimed that the former is the error of competence, systematic, produced by the lack of internal knowledge on language rules, while the latter is the error of performance, unsystematic, caused by some explicit factors like fatigue, anxiety and excitement. Zhang (1999a, 1999b) deemed that based on standard English and the observation of the researchers, the errors are those which break grammatical rules or those which are incorrectly used by the speakers. On the basis of the literature, the judgment of errors will be made by the researcher according to the commonly accepted grammatical rules and usage of words, phrases, etc.

4.6.2.3 Complexity

Complexity is concerned about how elaborate the language is. According to Foster and Skehan (1996), complexity reflects how learners can use the forms "closer to the cutting edge of interlanguage development" and is more associated with learners' willingness to take risks to use the language they are not familiar with. In the current study, it includes the complexity in language structure and cognitive complexity.

4.6.2.3.1 **Complexity in language structure**

Syntactic complexity, syntactic variety and lexical variety are the measures that have been widely employed to measure how the complex language was used for production (Crookes, 1989).

In the current study, syntactic variety and lexical variety (SVLV) are applied as one of the indices of complexity and judged by the researcher.

In the task of translation or something similar to this, another index is needed for comparing syntactical complexity. Previous research has applied a couple of approaches to assess syntactic complexity.

For example, Arnold et al. (2000) and Hawkins (1990) used length—the number of words, syllables, intonation units, etc.— as a proxy for syntactic complexity. For another example, Johnson (1966), Ferreira (1991), Hawkins (1994) and Rickford et al. (1995) counted nodes to determine syntactic complexity of phrases and sentences. The current study will assess syntactic complexity (SC for short) by counting the number of words included in a sentence.

In addition, the current study attempts to assess the complexity in language structure by judging the degree of difficulties (DD) in pronunciation, words, phrases and sentence patterns. Taking the translation of "展览中心" into English for example. Suppose that Subject A's answer is "exhibition hall" and Subject B's answer is "museum" or "show center", the former is considered more complex in the difficulties in pronunciation and word choice. The judgment of this aspect will be made by the researcher.

4.6.2.3.2 Cognitive complexity

As a driving force for irreversible developments, learning is a permanent process that changes our long-term knowledge base in an irreversible and invisible way. In our life time, with the increase of learning, the structure of our long-term memory changes to more complexity and higher abstraction.

Pervin (1984) deemed that the analysis of cognitive complexity is an aspect of a person's cognitive functioning which at one end is defined by the use of many constructs with many relationships to one another (complexity) and at the other end by the use of few constructs with limited relationships to one another (simplicity). Therefore, cognitive complexity involves a person component (unobservable cognition and observable behavior) and a task structure component (Oxford, 2006). Skehan (1996) suggested three general categories in his task framework: code complexity, cognitive complexity, and communicative stress.

Cognitive complexity is subdivided by Skehan into cognitive familiarity and cognitive processing. The former refers to the ability of the learner to access "packaged" solutions to tasks, such as familiarity of topic, discourse genre and task whereas the latter means the need to work out solutions "on line", such as information organization, amount of "computation", clarity and sufficiency of information given (Skehan, 1996, 1998; Skehan & Foster, 1999, 2001).

Observing the behavior of people solving a specific problem or task is our basis for estimating "cognitive complexity". The cognitive structures of users are not directly observable, so we need a method and a theory to use the observable behavior as one parameter to estimate cognitive complexity. Rauterberg (1992, 1993) stated that the estimate of the cognitive complexity is based on the measurement of the behavioral complexity, the measurement of the system complexity and the measurement of the task complexity.

The focus of the current research is the objective clause structure in indirect speech. In terms of the task difficulty, the structure is difficult because it is involved with a series of changes in subjects, predicates, objects, adverbials, etc. when changed from direct speech to indirect speech. Therefore, it is not hard to understand that a difficult task should be cognitively complex.

It is worth noticing that not every cognitively complex task is viewed as difficult. Oxford (2006) stated the student's familiarity with the kind of cognitive operations required is considerably important when he / she actually perceives a given, cognitively complex task to be difficult.

In cognitive neural science, complexity can be measured by such equipments as ERP and fMRI which can scan the changes in the brain when the subjects are taking different types of tasks (Chang, 2009). However, the theme of the present study is about oral production, which is not suitable to conduct the experiments with ERP, fMRI, etc.

Inspired by the report of O'Keefe et al. and Applecate et al.'s concerning the reliability and comparability of alternative forms of Role Category Questionnaire (RCQ) in the measurement of cognitive complexity (O'Keefe et al.,1982; Applecate et al.,1991), the present researcher attempts to assess cognitive complexity by designing some difficult tasks followed by retrospective interviews and follow-up questionnaire to indirectly investigate the cognitive processing.

According to Krashen's Affective Filter Hypothesis (Krashen, 1982, 1988), learners with high motivation, self-confidence and low-proficiency anxiety can more easily access to SLA. Besides, according to Ellis's statement of SLA (Ellis, 1999) and Krashen's Monitor Hypothesis (Krashen, 1982), hesitation and self-repair have a close relevance to SLA (Wang, 2009). In the current study, the questions in the retrospective interviews and follow-up questionnaire are about psychological issues such as anxiety, pauses, hesitation, self-repair, etc.

Meanwhile, in order to explore the ability to process more difficult tasks (such as the tasks related to the object clause structure in indirect speech), the current study attempts to supplement by testing and comparing the recognition response time (that is the time for the speaker to plan and organize his/her utterance before speaking) of the speakers with different levels of speaking. By this way, subjects' familiarity with the object clause structure in indirect speech will also be investigated.

4.7 Summary

Chapter Four establishes an information processing conceptual framework for the present study on the basis of the review of literature on the relevance between procedural memory and oral production. Under the guidance of the newly-developed concept of linguistic competence, the indices of oral proficiency are also displayed.

Chapter Five
RESEARCH DESIGN

5.1 Introduction

This chapter presents the research design for the present study. In this part, a series of studies including a cross-sectional study and three other case studies were involved to explore the research questions mentioned in **Section 5.3**.

To begin with, the research principles are made clear for a better understanding of the research design. Then, four research questions are presented focusing on the theme of the present study: L2 oral production and the effects of the principles of procedural memory on the L2 oral production of the object clause structure in indirect speech.

A pilot study was designed to determine the optimality of the designed cognitive behavioral experiments and interviews before the main experiments. With two cognitive behavioral experiments, **Section 5.5** investigates the differences in the effects of procedural memory between high-proficiency and low-proficiency L2 speakers among Chinese tertiary English learners when they utter the object clause structure of indirect speech.

Section 5.6, **Section 5.7** and **Section 5.8** provide further insight into the effects of procedural memory on oral production of the object clause structure of indirect speech by investigating individual similarities and differences among the following groups of subjects: (1) the high-proficiency English speakers among Chinese tertiary English learners and the native English speakers; (2) a subject with lower English speaking proficiency; (3) the 16 high-proficiency subjects in Cognitive Behavioral Experiment One in **Section 5.5**.

The subjects, instruments and tools, procedures for data collection and data analysis are also introduced in this chapter.

5.2 Research Principles

This section explains the major principles that the research design was based on.

5.2.1 The type of procedural memory explored in the present study

As mentioned in **Section 4.2**, the present study focuses on the type of procedural memory which can be analyzed because it **parasitizes** in declarative memory and influences the automatic processing of its retrieval and application (Chen, 2009). The subjects participating in the experiments were required to master enough grammatical knowledge about the object clause structure of indirect speech. Under such equivalent condition, the study can explore the effects of the principles of procedural memory on L2 oral proficiency because their way of learning English is by analyzing the grammar of linguistic units, rather than parroting what other people say.

Meanwhile, the present study selected chunk frequency as an index to explore the effects of procedural memory because of the following reasons. First, formulaic language and formulaic sequences have been thought of to be related to "how-to-do" (procedural) knowledge (Anderson, 1983c; Bolinger, 1976; Conklin & Schmitt, 2008; Levelt, 1989; McLaughlin, Rossmann & McLeod, 1983; Pawley & Syder, 1983;

Tannen, 1989). Second, chunking has been considered a fundamental operation occurring in the human memory (Miller, 1956; Simon, 1974). Chunks refer to long-term memory units that are used for perception and meaning and chunking is the learning mechanisms leading to the acquisition of these chunks (Simon, 1974). By using chunking the number of channels during the input of data can be reduced, so less processing power and less bandwidth will be used (Miller, 1956). Third, formulaic sequences or chunks are one of the major causes for the fluent and accurate output of language of native-speakers and L2 speakers (Biber et al., 1999; Deng, 2006; Ellis, 1991; Howarth, 1998; Pawley & Syder, 1983; Wei, 2004, 2007; Wei & Wang, 2005; Zhen, 2009).

There are two types of chunks as well. The first type cannot be analyzed because such chunks are learned by parroting what other persons utter. The second type can be analyzed because such chunks are learned when the learners have mastered the grammatical knowledge of chunks and other linguistic phenomena. In the present study, the second type of chunks was explored, which accords with the focus of the present study: exploring the type of procedural memory which is parasitic with declarative memory and can be analyzed.

5.2.2 The design of the experiments

The present research abode by some principles as follows to design the experiments.

5.2.2.1 The principles for the implementation of the experiments

To ensure the validity of the collected data, the design of the number, gender and groups of subjects and procedures of the experiments was based on the principles of experimental psychology (Gui, 1991; Murphy & Davidshofer, 2005; Zhang & Shu, 2004; Zhu, 2000) as well as of the feedbacks from the subjects in the pilot study.

5.2.2.2 The types of the tasks

The design of the task types such as *Listen and Repeat/Listen, Judge and Speak* and *Question and Answers* in the cognitive behavioral experiments was influenced by the Input Hypothesis of Krashen and the Output Hypothesis of Swain in L2 acquisition (Krashen, 1982; Swain, 1985, 1995). These two hypotheses emphasize the role of input and output in L2. As mentioned in **Chapter Four**, oral production is closely related to the input and output process in the information processing framework. On the basis of these reasons, the present researcher designed the tasks which were applicable to investigate the two aspects in oral production. Meanwhile, the major difference between the tasks *Listen and Repeat* and *Listen Judge and Speak* lie in the difficulty of the tasks. The former is more difficult than the latter because of the requirements of tasks, which will be further explained in **Section 5.5.2.1** and **Section 5.5.2.3**.

5.2.2.3 The selection of the materials and the speed rate of recorded sound files

In the oral test made to screen the subjects, the forms and the level of difficulty of the materials as well as the speed rate of recorded sound files were referred to the items in CET-SET (short for College English Test-Spoken English Test).

5.2.2.4 The selection of sentences used in the cognitive behavioral experiments

Based on the research purposes of the present study, the selection of sentences used in the cognitive behavioral experiments was mainly referred to the feedbacks from the pilot study. As mentioned above, the present study was aimed to explore L2 oral proficiency and the role of procedural memory in L2 oral production. In accordance with the research purposes, the number of words in the most selected sentences was mostly limited in 9 to 15 so that the subjects could concentrate on the requirements of the tasks in the experiments.

5.2.2.5 The calculation of the numerical values

The calculation of the numerical values of fluency, accuracy and complexity was referred to the criteria mentioned in **Section 4.6.2**. Aimed with different requirements of research purposes, the dissertation will give a more detailed and specific description of the ways to analyze data in the necessary parts.

Since the subjects were asked to utter their answers immediately after they heard the recorded sentences or dialogues in the cognitive behavioral experiments, the response time and the pause time before the sentences were not calculated. That is to say, in the cognitive behavioral experiments, the present study only concerns the response time and the pause time before the words or multi-word expressions (including chunks) which are included within a tested sentence.

5.2.3 The ignorance of the communicative aspects of oral production

The present study ignored part of the communicative aspects of oral production when exploring the research questions concerning fluency, accuracy and complexity in the object clause structure in indirect speech. The reasons are as follows. First, the current research focuses only on the sentence patterns and other linguistic units of the object clauses structure in indirect speech, so it did not deal with the communicative strategies. Second, all the experiments were conducted under the controlled condition in the language lab or a particular room, so it was different from the face-to-face communication and not involved with the communicative strategies.

Chapter Five
RESEARCH DESIGN 103

5.3 Research Questions

As mentioned in **Chapter One** "**Introduction**", the present study explores oral production of Chinese tertiary non-English majors by taking the object clause structure of indirect speech as the research focus. Based on the conceptual framework and indices of oral proficiency in **Chapter Four**, the following research questions are raised with respect to the investigation of the effects of procedural memory on L2 oral production of L2 speakers of non-English majors in China under the equivalent condition of the mastery of declarative knowledge.

Question 1: Concerning the oral production of the object clause structure in indirect speech, what are the distinctive features of high-proficiency and low-proficiency L2 speakers in the application of procedural memory?

1.1 Concerning the oral production of the object clause structure in indirect speech, what are the major differences between the high-proficiency and low-proficiency L2 speakers as to fluency, accuracy and complexity?

1.2 What are the major differences between the high-proficiency and low-proficiency L2 speakers in the mental processing?

1.3 What are the major effects related to procedural memory on the high-proficiency L2 speakers in the oral production of such complex grammatical structure as the object clause structure in indirect speech?

Question 2: Concerning the oral production of the object clause structure in indirect speech, what are the distinctive features of native English speakers and non-native English speakers with high oral proficiency in the application of procedural memory?

2.1 Concerning the oral production of the object clause structure in indirect speech, what are the major similarities and differences between the native English speakers and the non-native English speakers with high oral proficiency as to fluency, accuracy and complexity?

2.2 What are the major effects related to procedural memory on oral production of native-English speakers and non-native English speakers?

Question 3: What are the effects of procedural memory on the improvement of oral production of the object clause structure in indirect speech?

3.1 What progress does the low-proficiency L2 subject make with the oral training approaches in light of the principles of procedural memory?

3.2 If the oral training approaches in light of the principles of procedural memory have effects on oral production, what aspects of oral production (for example, pronunciation, use of linguistic use, etc.) will benefit most in the case of the oral production of the object clause structure in indirect speech?

Question 4: What are the major implicit and explicit factors influencing the application of procedural memory in oral production of the object clause structure in indirect speech and in oral production in general?

The four research questions mentioned above are logically related to each other. By investigating the subjects' performance of the oral production of the object clause structure in indirect speech and the effects of procedural memory on such oral production in the first and second sets of research questions, the present study trains a subject orally in the light of the principles of procedural memory to test the effects of procedural memory on the improvement of oral production of the object clause structure in indirect speech (**Question 3**). Finally, the present study explores the factors influencing the application of procedural memory in oral production of the object clause structure in indirect speech and in oral production in general with the purpose of putting forward suggestions on improving the teaching and learning of

L2 oral proficiency (**Question 4**).

The research questions will be addressed in the following sections.

5.4 The Pilot Study

In order to determine if the research design of the cognitive behavioral experiments in the quantitative part was optimal, a pilot study was carried out a week before the main experiments. Generally speaking, the pilot study shared the same research questions with the main cognitive behavioral experiments, except for the fact that it emphasized more on the determination of the selection of sentences and the operability of each experiment.

Four subjects from School of Computer Science and School of Engineering of Southeast University participated in the pilot study. They were 2 males and 2 females with their average age being 21. The researcher chose these subjects because she taught them college English one year ago and knew well about their comprehensive English proficiency and the level of oral English. Their scores of CET 4 ranged from 532 to 608. Among them, two males were considered high-proficiency oral English speakers and two females were considered low-proficiency. When the researcher introduced her study to these students, they showed great interest in it and agreed to participate in their spare time.

With the help of the research assistant, the pilot study was carried out in the multimedia language lab of Learning Center of School of Foreign Languages, Southeast University. Except for the limited number of the subjects, the pilot study displayed the main procedures of all the cognitive behavioral experiments designed by the researcher.

The retrospective interview was made when the two cognitive behavioral experiments finished. The questions involved were mainly about the feedbacks of these subjects on the selection of sentences and difficulties in doing the designed tasks.

The major feedbacks from the subjects included the following aspects.

(1) The length of sentences. Two female subjects and one male subject thought two of selected sentences were somewhat long, which influenced the effects of their recognition and production of sentences.

(2) The degree of difficulty of the first task. Two female subjects thought the first task-*Listen, Judge and Speak*-was somewhat difficult. They could easily repeat the sentences they heard, but it was hard for them to judge whether these sentences were wrong or not and then uttered the revised sentences within a very short time. However, the other male subjects had no difficulty in doing this task.

(3) Need for clarifying the purpose of the experiments. In the pilot study, the subjects were not told the purpose of the experiments before the pilot study. What they were told was to do according to the direction of each experiment. After the experiments, two subjects held that they could have behaved better if they had been informed of the purpose of the experiments.

Hence, the researcher revised the design of the two cognitive behavioral experiments according to the principles of the methodology of the study and the feedbacks of the subjects in the pilot study, which will be introduced in **Section 5.5**, **Section 5.6** and **Section 5.7**.

5.5 A Cross-sectional Study between High-proficiency and Low-proficiency L2 Speakers

This section will introduce the research purposes as well as the research questions, the subjects, data collection and data analysis of two cognitive behavioral experiments, retrospective interviews and follow-up questionnaires in the cross-sectional study between the high-proficiency and low-proficiency English speakers from China.

5.5.1 Research purposes

In this section, the cross-sectional study between the high-proficiency and low-proficiency English speakers was conducted in order to address the first set of research questions concerning the distinctive features of high-proficiency and low-proficiency L2 speakers in the application of procedural memory in the oral production of the object clause structure in indirect speech.

The subjects' proficiency of oral production was distinguished in the oral test. However, the oral test applied in the selection of the subjects did not involve the specific sentence pattern: the object clause structure in indirect speech since the researcher meant to select the subjects whose oral proficiency could be leveled according to the indices reflecting the subjects' overall oral performance. To further explore the differences of the subjects in the application of procedural memory in the oral production of the object clause structure in indirect speech was supposed to help with the exploration of effects of procedural memory and other issues concerning oral teaching and learning and hence lay a foundation for the later experiments in the present study. The screening of the high-proficiency and low-proficiency subjects in the two cognitive behavioral experiments will be introduced in **Section 5.5.2.2.1**.

In this cross-sectional study, two cognitive behavioral experiments, retrospective interviews and follow-up questionnaires were conducted to obtain the research purposes.

5.5.2 Cognitive Behavioral Experiment One: Listen, Judge and Speak & Listen and Repeat

5.5.2.1 Research questions

This experiment was designed to address the first research question made in **Section 5.3** in two task types: *Listen, Judge and Speak* and

Listen and Repeat.

The reason for designing two types of the tasks was mainly due to the feedback from the pilot study. The subjects in the pilot study thought *"Listen, Judge and Speak"* very hard to complete. As introduced in **Chapter Four**, the difficulty of the tasks lies in the increase of the complexity of oral production from the perspectives of language structure and cognitive processing. Considering this reason, the researcher designed the two types of tasks with different difficulties in an attempt to explore whether the different difficulties in the tasks would affect the performance of the subjects, which will serve as a finding affiliated to the major findings.

5.5.2.2 Subjects

5.5.2.2.1 Selection of the subjects

Ninety five non-English majors from School of Computer Science, School of Economics and Management, School of Engineering, School of Liberal Arts, Medical College, Department of Mathematics of Southeast University participated in the selection of the subjects. All the subjects were tertiary non-English majors including junior students, senior students and the first-year graduate students, ranging in age from 22-25. Among them, 48 were male and 47 were female. Their scores of CET 4 ranged from 538 to 610.

Step One: A diagnostic study was carried out on oral production of the subjects in order to select two groups of subjects: the high-proficiency group and the low-proficiency group.

First, the subjects were asked to participate in an oral test in the multimedia language lab of Learning Center of School of Foreign Languages, Southeast University. Limited by the capacity of the language lab and the governable time of the subjects, the subjects were divided into three groups to take the oral test in three different chosen times. The subjects in each group shared the same oral test. Before the oral test, the researcher emphasized the same procedures and requirements of the test to ensure that every subject could be clear about these issues. The researcher played the role of the examiner and all these subjects were the examinees.

Similar to CET-SET, the oral test consisted of three parts (See **Appendix 1**). **The first part** was a greeting between the examiner (the researcher) and the examinees (participants) and self-introductions of the subjects themselves. The subjects were asked to introduce themselves as much as possible. **The second part** was "Questions and Answers", lasting about three minutes. In this part, the subjects were asked three questions about living in Nanjing. The questions involved were "yes or no" questions or "wh" questions which needed the subjects to express their opinions on the theme. **The third part** is an oral presentation which was a discussion on the topic entitled "The Advantages and Disadvantages of the Internet". The subjects were required to make an oral presentation with the five words/phrases listed in the given box. They had one minute to prepare and two minutes to talk about the topic. The researcher might interrupt them when the time was up.

It was worth mentioning that thanks to the powerful function of CMT-XP Language Learning System developed by Nanjing Lima Technology Corporation Limited and installed in the computers of the language lab, the researcher was able to collect the recorded sound files one at a time without much effort.

Step Two: After the sound data was collected, two experienced raters who participated in CET-SET scoring for times helped with grading the subjects' performance and screening the subjects. The scoring standards of the oral test were made by referring to the indices of oral production in the **Section 4.6.2**, the syllabus of CET-SET (See

Appendix 2) and research principles in **Section 5.2**. According to the scoring standards listed in Table 5-1, the raters listened to all the recorded sound files of the subjects and scored their performance in the oral test.

Table 5-1　Scoring Standards of the Oral Test

Indices	Items involved		
Fluency	Time	Speaking time	Syllables
			Pauses
			Chunks
Accuracy	Macro assessment	Sentence patterns	
	Micro assessment	Pronunciation	
		Use of linguistic units	
Complexity	Complexity in language structure	Syntactic variety and lexical variety	
		Syntactical complex	
	Cognitive complexity	Familiarity, information organization, etc.	
Appropriateness	The application of communicative strategies		

It is worth mentioning that appropriateness was applied as an index to assess the subjects' oral proficiency in the oral test because the subjects needed to show their communicative abilities in some items such as greetings and dialogues between the subjects and the examiner. In addition, in the section of selection of the subjects, the scoring approach was holistic, which is thought with high validity (Yang, 1999). The final score of each item was averaged by the two raters' scores. Based on the results of scoring, 36 subjects were ranked as the ones with the higher proficiency of oral production and 48 with the lower proficiency of oral production. The rest were not included in the following selection because of their moderate proficiency of oral production.

Step Three: The researcher selected 84 subjects including 36 with a higher proficiency of oral production and 48 with a lower proficiency of oral production and asked them to do a grammar test concerning the knowledge of indirect speech. The test consisted of 15 multiple choices (See Appendix 3). The results revealed that 75 subjects got fully scored in the grammar test, among whom 35 were the ones with higher proficiency of oral production and 40 with the lower proficiency of oral production. The time spent in the grammar test ranged from 12 to 26 minutes (*Note:* "Time" is not a norm for the judgment of the mastery of declarative knowledge of indirect speech.).

From the 75 subjects who got full scores in the grammar test, 8 males and 8 females with the higher proficiency of oral production and 8 males and 8 females with the lower proficiency were selected at random by the researcher.

5.5.2.2.2 Grouping of the subjects

Then these 32 subjects were divided into two groups: Group A and Group B. In each group, there were 16 subjects including 8 (4 males and 4 females) with the higher proficiency of oral production and 8 (4 males and 4 females) with the lower proficiency of oral production.

Both of the cognitive behavioral experiments were conducted among these two groups of subjects.

5.5.2.3 Instruments and tools

In this part, a 2 × 2 cognitive behavioral experiment was designed. The first "2" refers to the number of groups (Group A and Group B). The second "2" refers to the number of task types (*Listen and Repeat* and *Listen, Judge and Speak*).

The reasons for designing such experiment are as follows:

First: Generally speaking, oral performance includes the face-to-face communication and the performance in language lab or examinations. In order to display and imitate the face-to-face communication, the test of the subjects' oral production of indirect speech was designed by asking them to listen and repeat.

Second: The time span of each sentence recorded in the sound file and the length of selected sentences were revised due to the feedbacks from the pilot study as well as the literature of the researches on sensory stores and working memory. According to the literature of the researches on listening, sensory stores consist of auditory memory and phonetic memory, which can last 1-4 seconds (Carroll, 2000; Crowder & Morton, 1969; Spearling, 1960). In addition, working memory is restricted by storage time and memory capacity (Hormann, 1979; Moore, 1977). Besides the factors of memory, the feedbacks from the pilot study were also taken into account. In the main experiment, the number of words in each sentence was controlled within 8-12, which could be read within 4 seconds. The sound file of the 20 sentences was recorded ahead of time with the help of a skilled oral English teacher. The speed of speaking is about 150 words per minute (*Note*: According to the new "*College English Syllabus*", the speed of speaking in the Section of Listening in CET 4 is 130 to 150 words per minute and in CET 6, 140 to 160 words per minute). Between two sentences, there was a pause lasting 15 seconds during which the subjects could finish the task and have a rest for the preparation of the next sentence.

Third: The feedbacks of the pilot study showed that it might be difficult for some subjects to utter the revised sentences and make a judgment of whether the sentences were right or not within a short time. Therefore, in the real experiment, two task types with different difficulties, *Listen and Repeat* and *Listen, Judge and Speak*, were designed. By this way, the present study intended to obtain data indicating the differences or similarities in the subjects' performance

Chapter Five
RESEARCH DESIGN

when the subjects were assigned two task types with different difficulties. Meanwhile, this study attempted to explore the differences or similarities in the subjects' performance when they have different cognitive complexity caused by the task types with different difficulties in oral production.

The experiment was conducted in the multi-media language lab. The testing system of Nanjing Lima Corporation Limited played a very important role in collecting the data of sound files.

It was the researcher who operated the computer system and controlled the whole procedure of the experiment. When entering into the testing system, the researcher pressed the button "Start" and the system began to record the sounds uttered by the subjects through the microphones in the headphones they wore.

Picture 5-1 shows what the screen of the computer was like during the process of the experiment.

Picture 5-1:

Picture 5-2 shows what the screen of the computer was like when the experiment was over.

Picture 5-2:

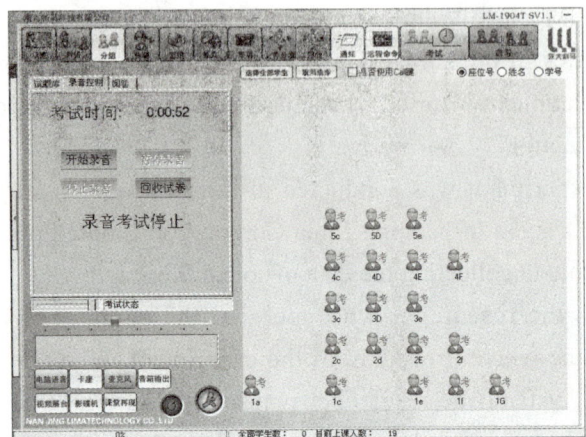

When analyzing recorded sound files, the researcher applied Adobe Audition 3.0 software, a powerful and professional audio editing and mixing instrument, which could help with displaying and navigating the sound waves and the time that the subjects took when uttering sentences as showed in Picture 5-3.

Picture 5-3:

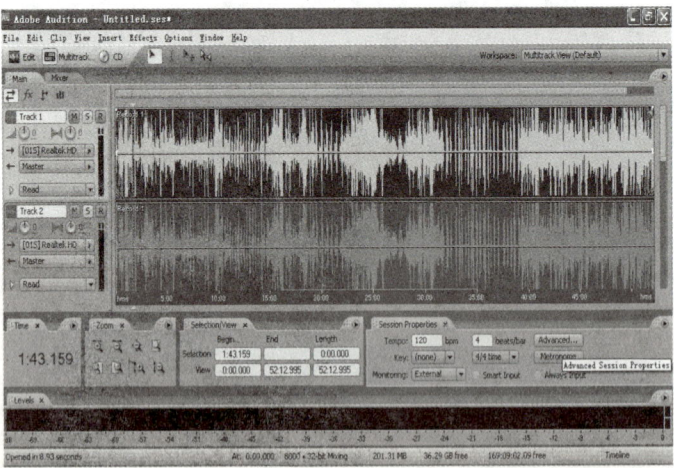

5.5.2.4 Procedures of data collection

Actually, in order to simplify the procedures of data collection and analysis, the subjects were asked in Group A to do the two cognitive behavioral experiments one by one first. After the subjects in Group A finished their tasks, the subjects in Group B were asked to do according to the same procedures. However, the researcher addressed the procedures of data collection and data analysis experiment by experiment to make the report of the two experiments clearer.

It was worth mentioning that before the experiments, the subjects were informed that they were going to be tested about indirect speech according to the direction of each experiment. However, they did not know which aspect of indirect speech would be examined.

5.5.2.4.1 The procedures of Group A

The following are the major procedures of the implementation of the experiment with Group A.

Step One: A training session of the cognitive behavioral experiment

The training session was given to the 16 subjects in Group A to familiarize themselves with the whole process of the quantitative part of the pilot study in early January of 2010 with the researcher and the research assistant of the language lab of Learning Center of School of Foreign Languages of Southeast University.

The 16 subjects were asked to familiarize themselves with the computer system in the language lab and enter into the testing section in the system of Lima Corporation which was developed to facilitate the language learning, especially in speaking and listening. Before the experiment began, these subjects were required to say any sentences they thought of and recorded what they had said to check whether the testing system worked.

Step Two: The task of Group A: Listen, Judge and Speak

The subjects in Group A were asked to listen to 20 sentences recorded in a sound file and judge whether these sentences had some mistakes or not. If there were some mistakes in the sentence, the subjects were asked to utter the revised sentence immediately and if there were no mistakes, the subjects were needed to repeat the sentence immediately.

After the equipment had been checked and the preparation of the subjects had been done, the experiment was announced to begin by the researcher. The sound file was played, from which the subjects could hear the recorded 20 sentences. The subjects had no difficulties following the requirements and doing the task.

Step Three: Data collection

After the subjects had finished the task, the received sound files were copied and stored by the researcher from the computer in the main console desk.

Step Four: An episode for disturbing the thinking of the subjects

The subjects were required to have a rest and do a math calculation. The calculation was as follows:

"What is it when you add 58 to 89?"

The subjects were active with the calculation. Then the researcher checked the answer with them.

The calculation was applied to help the subjects forget the previous task so that they could pay much attention to the following task.

5.5.2.4.2　The procedures of Group B

The subjects in Group B followed the same four steps as those in Group A except for the task in the second step **"Listen and Repeat"** which required the subjects to repeat the sentences they heard one by one.

After the subjects had finished the task, the researcher asked the subjects to have a rest and do another math calculation to avoid the disturbance of the previous task so that they could pay great attention to the following task.

5.5.2.5 Procedures for data analysis

In this section, the procedures and methods of data analysis are displayed and explained.

All the received sound files of the subjects in the computer of the main console desk in the front of the language lab were stored and transcribed word by word by the researcher.

The results of this experiment were obtained through manual calculation, the Audition 3.0 software or Microsoft Excel. It is worth noticing that though in the experiment the number of total tested sentences was 20, 8 sentences (including Sentence 2, Sentence 6, Sentence 8, Sentence 11, Sentence 13, Sentence 15, Sentence 17 and Sentence 18) were not included in calculation because they were not about indirect speech. The reason for asking the subjects to listen to 20 sentences was that the researcher did not intend to give away the purpose of this experiment to the subjects.

5.5.2.5.1 The analysis of fluency

As to the analysis of fluency of the oral production of the subjects, the researcher fed back to Adobe Audition 3.0 software, whose function will be introduced in **Section 5.5.3**.

According to research principles in **Section 5.2** and Table 5-1, in order to obtain data concerning fluency, four indices are taken into account. They are Total Response Time (TRT), Speech Rate (SR), Mean Length of Run (MLR) and Average Length of Pause (ALP). Besides, Chunk Frequency (CF) was collected and analyzed for exploring the effects of chunks on fluency of oral production.

Take one sound file of Subject X for example.

First, the researcher turned on the Adobe Audition 3.0 software installed in her computer and imported the sound file. Then she double clicked the left key of the mouse and then the imported sound file appeared on the screen.

Picture 5-4:

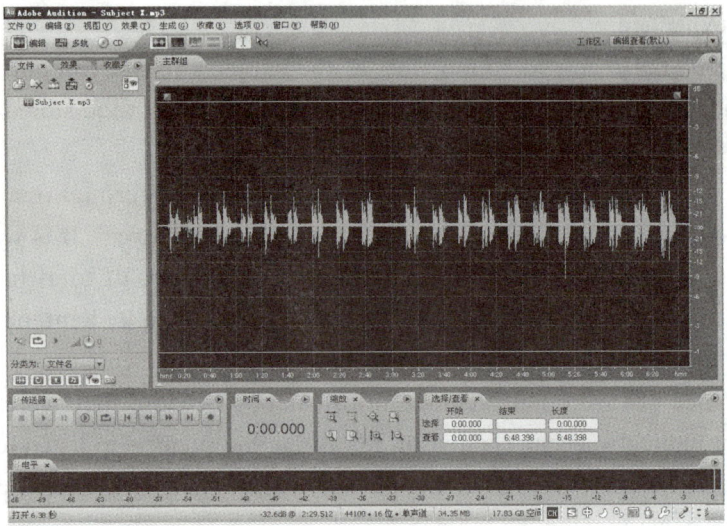

From Picture 5-4, we can see the 20 groups of sound waves. Each group of the sound waves includes the sound wave of the reader followed by the sound wave of the subject.

Because the software could present the time and the sound wave, the researcher could collect the numerical values of the time that subject spent in uttering each sentence and the time that the subject spent in pausing and hesitating.

In the case of Subject X, the data in the production of 12 sentences were taken down respectively. Take Sentence One for example. The record of the production was taken down as follows.

-1-She said that (0.782 /3)[0.317] -2-Jacky would be busy(1.538 / 7) [0.231] -3-with his study(1.247 / 4).

There are 13 syllables in the uttered sentence. The number between two short lines refers to the sequential order of run of speech such as "-1-" and "-2-". In the brackets, we can see two numbers. The first number (for example 0.582) refers to the time of the run of speech 'I said' and the second number (for example 2) is the number of the syllables in the run of speech. The number in the square brackets (for example 0.309) is the pausing time. In this example, the times of pauses are twice (*Note:* A pause is defined as "a break of 0.3 seconds or longer, either within a sentence or between sentences" (Zhang, 2002). The way of recognizing chunks in the current study can be referred to **Section 4.6.2.1.**

Table 5-2   The Performance of Subject X in Producing Sentence 1

Items	Numerical Value
TRT	4.115 seconds
SR	189.6 syllables per minute
PTR	0.867
MLR	13 syllables per run of speech
ALP	0.317 seconds
NCF	3

Note: TRT: total response time; SR: speech rate; PTR: phonation time ratio; MLR: length of run; ALP: average length of pause; NCF: The number of chunks in one sentence. The calculation can be referred to Table 4-2 and Table 4-3.

Then the researcher collected numerical values of the same items of the other 11 sentences concerning the object clause structure and calculated the mean value of each item as indicated in Table 5-3.

Table 5-3   The Performance of Subject X in Producing 12 Sentences

Subjects	MTRT	MPTR	MSR	MMLR	MALP	MNCF
Subject X	4.299	180	0.832	12.31	0.527	2.1

Note: MTRT: the mean value of total response time; MPTR: the mean value of phonation time ratio; MSR: the mean speech rates; MMLR; MALP: the mean value of average length of pause; MNCF: the mean number of chunks.

According to the approach of the calculation displayed in Table 4-2, the researcher calculated the numerical value of each item and then filled in the table of the performance of each subject in this experiment as indicated in Table 5-5.

The data of the mean values of the indices of all the 32 subjects of both Group A and Group B were collected. Based on the purpose of this experiment, the data in the following aspects were analyzed with univariate analysis: (1)the performance of all the subjects in Group A and Group B in fluency; (2) the interactive effect between two different tasks of Group A and Group B; (3)the performance of the 8 high-proficiency subjects and 8 low-proficiency subjects in Group A and the performance of the 8 high-proficiency subjects and 8 low-proficiency subjects in Group B in fluency (*Note*: The third aspect is analyzed if there exists no interactive effect between the subjects and groups). In addition, chunk frequency (CF) was collected and analyzed for exploring the effects of chunks on fluency of oral production.

All the mean values of the indices were analyzed by univariate analysis with SPSS for comparison. The results of univariate analysis will be reported in Table 6-1, **Chapter Six**.

5.5.2.5.2　The analysis of accuracy

The sound files received were played through Adobe Audition 3.0 program and listened to carefully one by one.

The analysis of accuracy of the tasks of Group A and Group B was made respectively as follows.

A. The analysis of accuracy for Group A

As to the analysis of accuracy, this index included the following aspects according to the calculation in **Section 4.6.2.2**.

(1) Macro assessment involving the judgment of correctness of sentence builders and sentence patterns.

The subjects were required to make a judgment in the task "*Listen,*

Judge and Speak". Since the judgment was processing in an invisible way, the assessment of whether the subjects' judgment was correct or not was made by the researcher by checking the scripts of the recorded files and comparing with the keys (See **Appendix 4**). In Table 5-5, there are four situations listed in the *Note*. In S1 and S2, the subject was considered familiar with the sentence pattern of the object clause structure in indirect speech in oral production. The researcher took down the number of the sentences which were correctly judged in Table 5-5.

(2) Micro assessment involving pronunciation and the use of linguistic units

The assessment of pronunciation involves syllables and stress. In the current study, the ratio of errors in pronunciation (REP) was assessed by the formula: The number of total inaccurately pronounced words ÷ the number of the tested sentences.

The correctness of pronunciation was judged by two ways: (1) by the judgment of the researcher if the pronunciation was not so hard to recognize; (2) with the help of Adobe Audition 3.0 software under the condition that the pronunciation should be very hard to recognize or the researcher should intend to compare the pronunciation of two subjects as shown in Picture 5-3.

As indicated in **Section 4.6.2.3**, the use of linguistic units includes the changes of the following five items in each sentence concerning the object clause structure in indirect speech: the subject; predicate verb(s) (tense, voice and word order), objects, conjunction, adverbials of time and adverbials of place. This index is assessed by the ratio of errors of the use of linguistic units (REULU) with the formula: The number of total inaccurately used linguistic units ÷ the number of the tested sentences.

Take Sentence X for example. The results of accuracy of the use of linguistic units of Sentence X are presented in Table 5-4.

Table 5-4 Accuracy of the Use of Linguistic Units of Sentence X

Sentence	Subject	Predicate verb(s)	Objects	Conjunction	Adverbials
SX	√	√	√	×	√

Note: Tense, voice and word order are involved to assess accuracy of predicate verb(s).

The errors made in use of the object clause structure, such as the use of word order, the change of the subject and tense in indirect speech were judged by the researcher who transcribed what the subjects uttered in some forms after carefully listening to all the 12 selected sentences by each subject.

Take Sentence 1 and Sentence 3 (See **Appendix 4**) uttered by Subject X for example:

Sentence 1: She said why Jacky would be busy with his study.

The utterance of Subject X:

She said why… Jacky would be busy with his study.

Sentence 3: His mother asked him what had he done the day before.

The utterance of Subject X:

His mother ask…ed him what had he…uhm…he had …done… the day before.

After listening to the recorded file and making the judgment, the researcher filled in Table 5-5 about the performance of each subject in this experiment as indicated.

Table 5-5 The Performance of Subject X in Cognitive Behavioral Experiment One

Sentence	Correctness of judgment		Situations	TRT (Seconds)	
	The key	The answers of Subject X		The reader	Subject X
No. 1	×	×	S2-1	3.591	4.115
No. 3	×	×	S2-1	3.613	4.084
No. 4	×	×	S2-1	3.352	4.010

continued

Sentence	Correctness of judgment		Situations	TRT (Seconds)	
	The key	The answers of Subject X		The reader	Subject X
No. 5	×	×	S2-2	3.532	3.951
No. 7	×	√	S4	3.651	3.727
No. 9	√	×	S3	3.472	4.130
No. 10	×	×	S2-2	4.549	4.609
No. 12	×	√	S3	3.352	3.651
No. 14	√	√	S1	4.425	4.443
No. 16	×	×	S2-1	3.698	3.952
No. 19	√	√	S1	4.939	5.806
No. 20	×	√	S4	5.126	5.108
Average				3.942	4.299

Note: In the column "**Situations**".

S1 refers to the situation in which the original sentence was correct and the subject repeated the original sentence.

S2 refers to the situation in which the original sentence was wrong and then the subject repeated the revised sentence. (S2-1: The revised sentence was correct. S2-2: The revised sentence was wrong.)

S3 refers to the situation in which the original sentence was correct but the subject thought the sentence he/she heard was wrong and repeated the revised sentence.

S4 refers to the situation in which the original sentence was wrong but the subject thought the sentence he/she heard was correct and repeated the original sentence.

The data for accuracy of Group A in Cognitive Behavioral Experiment One were collected. With SPSS, the researcher applied univariate analysis to analyze these data. The results of the data analysis will be reported in Table 6-4, **Chapter Six**.

B. The analysis of accuracy for Group B

As to the analysis of accuracy, the index in the task '*Listen and Repeat*' includes the ratio of errors of pronunciation and the ratio of errors of the use of linguistic units.

The procedure of the analysis of pronunciation is the same as that of Group A. After being collected, the data were analyzed by univariate analysis with SPSS. The results of the data analysis will be reported in **Section 6.2.2**.

5.5.2.5.3 The analysis of complexity for Group A and Group B
Because the type of task "*Listen, Judge and Speak*" is much more difficult than the task "*Listen and Repeat*", cognitive complexity was explored by retrospective interviews and follow-up questionnaires. Detailed descriptions of this aspect will be introduced in **Section 5.5.4** and **Section 5.5.5**. The results of retrospective interviews and follow-up questionnaires will be reported in **Section 6.2.3** and **Section 6.4**.

5.5.3 Cognitive Behavioral Experiment Two: Questions and Answers

5.5.3.1 Research questions

This experiment was designed to address the first research questions in **Section 5.3** with the task "*Questions and Answers*". The researcher intended to investigate the subjects' ability to interpret Chinese sentences concerning indirect speech to English from the perspective of fluency, accuracy and complexity.

The type of the experiment and the materials used in the experiment will be introduced in **Section 5.5.3.3**.

5.5.3.2 Subjects

The subjects involved were the same 32 ones in the first cognitive behavioral experiment. As introduced in **Section 5.5.2.2**, among the 32 subjects, there were 16 high-proficiency subjects and 16 low-proficiency subjects. When the data were calculated, the 32 subjects were divided into two groups according of their oral proficiency. Group One consisted of 16 subjects with higher proficiency of production, among whom there were 8 males and 8 females. Group Two consisted of the 16 subjects with lower proficiency of production, among whom there were 8 males and 8 females (*Note*: The way of grouping in the second cognitive behavioral experiment was different from the one in **Section 5.5.2.2.2**).

The process of selection of the subjects was displayed in **Section 5.5.2.2**, which will not be mentioned in this section again.

5.5.3.3 Instruments

In the pilot study, the subjects were asked to interpret the Chinese sentences recorded in the sound file they heard. The problem found in the pilot study was that because these sentences were read in Chinese, it was very hard for the subjects to pay attention to the grammatical aspects the researcher intended to explore. As a result, the testing result of the pilot study was unsatisfactory. The subjects failed in changing tense and the adverbial parts related to time.

In order to help the subjects focus on indirect speech, taking consideration of the feedbacks from the pilot study, the experiment followed by was designed in another way: **Questions and Answers**.

Take the first dialogue for example.

Dialogue 1:
M: 小明和小芳还没有来呢。
W: 他们今天上午不可能到达国际展览中心了。
Q: What did the woman say to the man?

The dialogue was made between a man and a woman in Chinese language as indicated above. Then a question was asked like "What did the woman say to the man?". By this way, the subjects were led to a situation in which (1) they were required to answer the question in English; (2) meanwhile, they interpreted what the woman said into English in a complete way; (3) furthermore, indirect speech could be focused. By doing so, the task proved to be of much validity.

5.5.3.4 Procedures of data collection

The major procedures of data collection were referred to **Section 5.5.2.4**, which were similar to that of Cognitive Behavioral Experiment One. There were three steps: Step One: A training session; Step Two: The task; Step Three: Data collection. After the researcher collected the data, she made the retrospective interviews with the subjects.

5.5.3.5 Procedures of data analysis

In this section, the procedures and methods of data analysis are demonstrated and described.

In this experiment, all the 32 subjects took the same task *"Questions and Answers"* and they were divided into two groups: Group One (including 16 high-proficiency subjects) and Group Two (including 16 low-proficiency subjects) for comparison. All the received sound files of the subjects in the computer of the main console desk in the front of the language lab were stored and transcribed word by word by the researcher.

5.5.3.5.1 The analysis of fluency

The procedures are not reported here because they were similar to that in **Section 5.5.2.5.1**.

According to **Section 4.6.2.1** and Table 5-1, in order to obtain data concerning fluency, five indices (TRT, SR, MLR, PTR, ALP) are taken into account.

In the case of Subject X, the data in the production of 4 answers were taken down respectively. Take Answer One for example, the record of the production was taken down as follows.

Answer One: *-1- She said that (0.592/3)[0.429] -2- they couldn't get to (1.235 /5)[0.451]-3- the International Exhibition Center (5.896/12) [0.102]-4-that morning (0.757/3).*

The way of encoding oral production can be referred to **Section 5.5.2.5.1**.

Table 5-6   The Performance of Subject X in Producing Answer 1

Indices	Numerical Value
TRT	9.462 seconds
SR	145.8 syllables per minute
MLR	7.67 syllables per run of speech
PTR	0.896
ALP	0.44 seconds
NCF	3

Note: TRT: total response time; SR: speech rate; MLR: mean length of run; PTR: phonation time ratio; ALP: average length of pause; NCF: the number of chunks in the answer. the calculation can be referred to Table 4-2.

In this case, TRT is 9.462. The number of the total syllables is 23. The times of pauses are 2. The total pausing time is 0.88. According to the approach of the calculation shown in Table 4-2, the numerical value of each item was calculated and then filled in Table 5-6 concerning the performance of each subject in this experiment as indicated.

Then the numerical values of the same items of the other 11 sentences concerning the object clause structure were collected and calculated the mean value of each item. Univariate analysis was made to compare the performance in fluency between high-proficiency and low-proficiency subjects. The results of the Independent Samples *t*-Test will be exhibited in Table 6-3, **Chapter Six**.

5.5.3.5.2   The analysis of accuracy

The procedures were similar to that in **Section 5.5.2.5.2**, which is not reported here. As to the analysis of accuracy, the indices included the following aspects.

(1) Macro assessment involving the judgment of familiarity with the sentence builders and sentence patterns of the object clause structure in the answers (i.e., NC, the number of sentences which are correct in sentence builders and sentence patterns.)

The assessment of this aspect was made by the researcher who compared with the keys (See **Appendix 5**). However, the keys were applied just for reference. In other words, the answers of the subjects were acceptable if they accorded with the questions in the dialogues.

(2) Micro assessment involving pronunciation and the use of linguistic units

The assessment of pronunciation is made through the ratio of inaccurately pronounced words (*Note*: This is REP, ratio of errors in pronunciation) and the ratio of inaccurate use of linguistic units (*Note:* This is REULU, ratio of errors in use of linguistic units). The analysis of pronunciation and the use of linguistic units can be referred to **Section 5.5.2.5.2** and the items applied to assess the use of linguistic units can be referred to Table 5-6.

The errors made in use of the object clause structure in indirect speech such as word order, the change of the subject and tense were judged by the researcher who carefully listened to all the six answers by each subject and transcribed what the subjects uttered in some forms.

The researcher manually calculated the number of the inaccurately pronounced words and the number of the inaccurately used linguistic units and then calculated the ratio of accuracy. Then she collected the data of the performance of all the subjects in accuracy. With the collected data, Independent Samples *t*-Test was carried out between the groups of subjects and the results will be reported in Table 6-6.

5.5.3.5.3　The analysis of complexity

The researcher attempted to explore complexity in the subjects' answers, taking consideration of the answers of the subjects might be different from the reference keys.

As mentioned in **Section 4.6.2.3**, observing the behavior of people solving a specific problem or task is our basis for estimating cognitive complexity. The cognitive structures of users are not directly observable, so we need a method and a theory to use the observable behavior as one parameter to estimate cognitive complexity. Rauterberg (1992, 1993) stated that the estimate of the cognitive complexity is based on the measurement of the behavioral complexity, the measurement of the system complexity and the measurement of the task complexity.

The judgment was made by the researcher according to **Section 4.6.2.3**. The indices include: (1) the complexity in language structure SVLV (syntactic variety and lexical variety); (2) SC (syntactic complexity); (3) DD (the degree of difficulties in pronunciation, words, phrases and sentence patterns).

After listening to the recorded file and making the judgment, the researcher filled in the table of the performance of complexity of each subject in this experiment. Take Subject X for example.

Table 5-7 **The Performance of Complexity of Subject X in CBE II**

Dialogues	SVLV	SC	DD
No. 1	3	4	3
No. 2	3	4	2
No. 3	4	4	3
No. 4	4	4	2
No. 5	3	3	2
No. 6	4	3	2

Note: SVLV: syntactic variety and lexical variety; SC: syntactic complexity; DD: the degree of difficulties in pronunciation and use of linguistic units; CBE II: cognitive Behavioral Experiment Two.

In Table 5-7, the degrees of each item were divided into four ranks. The number "1" stands for the lowest degree. The number "2" stands for the low degree. The number "3" stands for the high degree. The number "4" stands for the highest degree. According to the judgment of the researcher, she ranked the performance of each subject. After calculation of all the subjects' performance, she compared the data.

The data of complexity of all the subjects will be analyzed with SPSS and the results of Independent Samples t-Test will be reported in Table 6-7 in **Chapter Six**.

In addition, the analysis of cognitive complexity was referred to retrospective interviews and follow-up questionnaires in **Section 5.5.4** and **Section 5.5.5**.

5.5.4　Retrospective interviews

5.5.4.1　Research purposes

Retrospective interviews were employed immediately after the subjects finished the three cognitive behavioral experiments. According to the different contents involved, the interview schedules were made up of retrospective and opinion interviews. Data from this channel can reveal some hidden truth about the subjects and their major thinking processes and cognitive complexity when they orally produced the object clause structure of indirect speech and the factors which facilitate or constrain the oral production of the object clause structure of indirect speech, thus supplementing the information obtained from the experimental part.

5.5.4.2　Subjects

The 32 subjects who participated in the two cognitive behavioral experiments were involved in the retrospective interviews. Among the 32 subjects, there were 16 high-proficiency ones (8 males and 8 females) and 16 with low-proficiency ones (8 males and 8 females).

5.5.4.3 Instruments

The instruments included two types of interviews: the retrospective interview and the opinion interview. The retrospective interview was made to ask the subjects some questions concerning their behaviors and cognitive processing in the process of the two cognitive behavioral experiments. The questions were raised by the researcher to different subjects according to their different performances in the process of three cognitive behavioral experiments.

Examples of questions about the thinking process were listed as follows.

1. Why did you utter the second sentence so quickly/so slowly?

2. Why did you revise the fifth sentence which was originally correct?

3. Why did you hesitate before uttering the object clause?

4. Did you feel stressed when you were doing the experiments?

5. I found you did a very good job when asked to revise the wrong sentences after the experiments, but in oral production, your performance was unsatisfactory. What are the major causes?

The opinion interview was given immediately after the retrospective interview, which was aimed to explore the subjects' opinions about and attitudes towards oral production of indirect speech and oral English practice. This type of interview was semi-structured. Some of the questions were prepared by the researcher beforehand. All the questions were asked in Chinese.

Examples of the questions asked by the researcher were listed as follows.

1. Which is most difficult in the production of indirect speech, the selection of subjects, word order, collocations, the change of adverbial structure?

2. Did Chinese language affect your performance?

3. Do you often do such types of oral English practice?

5.5.4.4　Procedures for data collection

The retrospective and opinion interviews were employed immediately after the subjects finished the three cognitive behavioral experiments.

　　The subjects were given the interviews one by one. With the digital recorder, the whole process of each interview was recorded for transcribing. The researcher might be able to get a clearer picture of relevant issues after synthesizing and analyzing all the interview data.

5.5.4.5　Procedures for data analysis

The interviews were carefully examined in order to supplement the analyses of the mechanism in the cognitive behavioral experiments. The recorded interviews were transcribed and the scripts were read very closely by the researcher in an attempt to analyze the implicit and explicit factors influencing oral production of the object clause structure of indirect speech.

　　The researcher generally went through three steps in the interview-based analysis.

　　First, find general patterns. The researcher tried to read through the transcribed interviews for the purpose of identifying the broad patterns.

　　Second, make categories. The researcher tried to find and organize specific components into each category.

　　Third, establish taxonomies. By establishing taxonomies, the researcher tried to make clear the logic relationships between procedural memory and oral production between all the components within each category. For instance, there appeared many factors influencing oral production and the relationship among the factors were revealed though the establishment of a taxonomy.

　　The results of the retrospective interview will be reported in **Section 6.4**.

5.5.5 Follow-up questionnaire

5.5.5.1 Research questions

The follow-up questionnaire was designed to investigate the following questions.
1. What are the subjects' attitudes towards oral English?
2. What are the most difficult problems of their oral production?
3. What are the major approaches applied to improve their oral English?

5.5.5.2 Subjects

The subjects were the same 32 ones who had participated in the two cognitive behavioral experiments in the cross-sectional study. They were non-English majors from different schools or departments of Southeast University including School of Computer Science, School of Economics and Management, School of Engineering, School of Liberal Arts, Medical College, Research Center of Learning Science and Department of Mathematics.

5.5.5.3 Instruments

The questionnaire consisted of three parts. The first part was concerned with personal details of the subjects, including their sex, age, majors, histories of English learning, time spent in oral English practice, etc. The second part collected information about the subjects' opinions of performance in the cognitive behavioral experiments concerning the object clause structure in indirect speech. The third part was involved with the subjects' attitudes towards oral English and their opinions of the improvement of oral English. The items involved with personal opinions in the questionnaire were semi-structured or open questions. In the second and third part, the subjects were needed to respond to the questions on a 4-or-5-point scale.

For example, What do you think of the factors influencing the improvement of your oral English? (***Note***: Rank the opinions according to your identity. For example, you may fill in the letter standing for the opinion that you are most agreeable in the first box. The least agreeable one should be filled in the last box.)

Most Agreeable	Very Agreeable	Agreeable	A Little Agreeable	Least Agreeable

A) Psychological problems such as shyness, fear for making mistake, incorrect approaches of learning oral English, lack of initiative, lack of ways to deal with cultural shocks.

B) Unfavorable atmosphere for practicing oral English.

C) Lack of qualified oral English teacher.

D) Less emphasis on oral English.

5.5.5.4 Procedures for data collection

The subjects were asked to fill in the questionnaire after they had finished the three cognitive behavioral experiments and retrospective interviews. Chinese was used to generate questionnaire information in avoidance of any language failure in expression (See **Appendix 6**). The samples and the major results presented in this section were translated by the researcher. All the data were edited, sorted and filed into the computer by the researcher after she had collected all data of the questionnaire.

5.5.5.5 Procedures for data analysis

In order to conduct the descriptive statistical analysis, Statistical Package for Social Science 15.0 (SPSS 15.0) was applied in this part. It was found that no subjects missed any part of the sessions in the questionnaire and therefore all of them were included in data analysis.

Because the first part was about the subjects' personal information, attitudes and opinions it was referred to when needed in the section "**Results and Discussion**". The dissertation paid more attention to the second part in which the object clause structure in indirect speech in oral production was focused.

The results of the retrospective interview will be reported in **Section 6.4**.

5.6 A Comparative Case Study between Native English Speakers and Non-native English Speakers

This section will introduce the research purposes as well as the research questions, the subjects, data collection and data analysis of the comparative study between native English speakers and non-native English speakers with high oral proficiency and retrospective interviews.

5.6.1 Research purposes and questions

This case study was conducted to address the second research question in **Section 5.3**. The research question was about the distinctive features of native English speakers and non-native English speakers with high oral proficiency in the application of procedural memory when uttering the object clause structure in indirect speech. In addition, the researcher attempted to explore the question "What effects of procedural memory are on oral production of native-English speakers and non-native English speakers in general?"

5.6.2 Subjects

Four subjects participated in the case study.

Nick was an overseas student in Southeast University. Born in

Edmonton, Alberta, Canada, he was 24 years old. Before he came to China, he majored in International Business and got his bachelor degree of Commerce from University of Alberta. His mother was English and his father was Taiwanese. He came to Nanjing in 2008 to learn Chinese.

Kate was also an overseas student. Born in Boston, Massachusetts, the United States, she was 22 years old. Before she came to China, she majored in Art and Design and got her bachelor degree of Fine Arts from University of Troy Michigan. Her parents are both American. In August, 2009, she came to Nanjing to learn Chinese and at the same time, she also teaches oral English in a university.

The selection of the subjects, Nick and Kate, is representative and typical. Nick and Kate are among the middle class in social status. So far they have been educated in different majors. They are not trained specially in English language though taught some grammar in this form or that in primary school and middle school. They can represent those educated native speakers of middle class. Though in this dissertation the number of the subjects from English speaking countries is limited, the performance of them can more or less reflect the oral production of people of the middle class in English-speaking countries. In this sense, the sample of the subjects can be considered representative and significant.

The Chinese subjects were Li and Gang who were from Southeast University. Several days before they participated in this case study, they took part in the two cognitive behavioral experiments mentioned in **Section 5.5**. They were selected from the high-proficiency subjects. Compared with the low-proficiency ones, the data of the high-proficiency subjects could be more significant in comparing the distinctive features of native English speakers and non-native English speakers in the application of procedural memory when uttering the object clause structure in indirect speech. Their personal information was indicated in Table 5-8.

It is worth mentioning that though all the four subjects participated in their tasks, the results of their performance will be reported where necessary. For example, when compared with the performance of Jun, the subject in the longitudinal case study in **Section 5.7**, the performance of Nick and Kate was not included because of their nationalities.

Table 5-8 Basic Profiles of the Subjects

Name	Gender	Age	Nationality	Major	Score in Band 4	Time of Learning English (years)
Li	Female	23	Chinese	Economics	590	12
Gang	Male	24	Chinese	Mathematics	558	15
Nick	Male	24	Canadian	Chinese		
Kate	Female	22	American	Chinese		

5.6.3 Instruments and tools

The instruments included a behavioral experiment with the E-prime 1.0 software, followed by a retrospective interview. The behavioral experiment was designed to explore the similarities and differences between the native speakers and the non-native speakers with higher proficiency of oral English of the response time (RT) in recognition and oral production. The retrospective interview was designed to supplement the behavioral experiment and obtain their opinions in their performance of the cognitive behavioral experiment.

It was worth mentioning that because the E-prime 1.0 software was not available for the storage of sound, the researcher recorded what the subject uttered with a digital voice recorder in order to obtain the sound data concerning the performance of each subject in fluency, accuracy and complexity during the process of the experiment.

5.6.3.1　The behavioral experiment with the E-prime program

The most important component of fluency is response time (Zhang, 1999a, 1999b). In this study, the behavioral experiment with E-prime program was designed to test the subjects' response time in recognition and output.

The type of the task was the change of sentences patterns from direct speech into indirect speech. The researcher chose 20 sentences, which had irregular length and were required to change into three sentence patterns according to the requirements at the end of each sentence. These three sentence patterns involved were as follows: (1) from passive voice to active voice; (2) from active voice to passive voice; (3) from direct speech to indirect speech (See **Appendix 7**). The sentences the researcher chose were programmed in the E-prime file before the pilot study. In order to show how to operate the E-prime program, another two sentences were programmed before the other 20 sentences in the E-prime program for practice. The 20 sentences were programmed to appear at random in order to avoid the case in which the subjects could easily get what the researcher intended to test by guess.

When programming the E-prime file, the researcher designed a procedure. That is, after opening the E-prime file, the subjects would see a greeting sentence on the screen which was black.

Welcome to the Experiment
And if you feel OK,
Please start the experiment by pressing the Spacebar.

Then the subject pressed the Spacebar if he felt OK. Then he may see a "+" in the middle of the screen which was set there to guide the eye balls of the subject to focus on this area. A duration of 2000

Chapter Five
RESEARCH DESIGN 139

milliseconds was set between the appearance of the "+" and the first sentence for demonstration. When the sentence appeared automatically, the subject was asked to read the sentence and the requirement at the end of the sentence as quickly as possible. The sentence was displayed as follows:

> **His cat was found by the girl.** ⟶ **Active Voice**

When he finished reading the sentence and got the requirement of it, he pressed the Spacebar immediately. It was programmed that the E-prime program began to calculate the reaction time at the click of the Spacebar. During his utterance, the screen turned black without any words on it. When the subject uttered the last word of his answer, he was asked to press the Spacebar as quickly as possible. That means he had finished his utterance. The reaction time was the duration between these two clicks of the Spacebar. At the same time, the second click of the Spacebar also means another sentence would appear. The subject would see another "+" in the middle of the screen. Then the same procedure was repeated until the subject uttered the last word and pressed the Spacebar. The practice was over and then he would see the direction in the middle of the screen:

> **Have a rest**
> **And if you feel OK,**
> **Please start the experiment by pressing the Spacebar.**

The subject would start the experiment when he felt OK. The 20 sentences chosen by the research would appear at random and after he finished ten sentences, the direction would remind him to have a rest in case the subject would be tired.

> **Have a rest**
> **And**
> **If you feel OK,**
> **Please restart the experiment by pressing the Spacebar.**

When the subject finished the task of the other ten sentences, the sentence "It's over and thanks for your participation." would appear in the center of the screen. The researcher was responsible for saving the E-prime file.

When analyzing recorded sound files, the researcher applied Adobe Audition 3.0.

Both E-prime 1.0 software and Adobe Audition 3.0 software can show time value minimized to milliseconds, which was one of the very important reasons for the researcher to choose these two types of software to analyze sound files. They had obvious advantages over other kinds of software in displaying time value.

5.6.3.2 Retrospective interviews

The retrospective interviews were made after each subject finished the experiment with E-prime program. The questions were controlled, which were about what they reacted in the experiment of the change of sentence patterns. Meanwhile, with these questions, the researcher could get some information about cognitive complexity as mentioned in **Section 4.6.2.3**. The questions are as follows.

"Why did you pause for a long time before you uttered the answer to Sentence X?"

"What did you think when you paused?"

"Did you find any new words in the sentences?"

"Did you recognize what was the research designed to explore?"

"What do you think of the length of selected sentences?"

"Did you recognize you had made a mistake in the utterance of Sentence Y?"

5.6.4　Procedures for data collection

Because of the inconsistence of the four subjects' time, the experiment was carried out in 4 different times. The major procedures were the same, so we take one subject's procedure for example.

Step One: A training session of the operation of E-prime 1.0 program

The training session started before the cognitive behavioral experiment. The researcher demonstrated the operation of E-prime 1.0 program and then asked the subject to familiarize himself or herself with it.

The training session lasted for about 10 minutes and it was over until the subject had no difficulties in operating the program.

Step Two: The experiment: "The change of the sentence patterns"

The subject was asked to do the task with the E-prime program by himself/herself. When the subject was doing the task, the researcher kept a suitable distance from him/her in the lab. In order to collect the sound data to analyze fluency, accuracy and complex, a voice recorder was applied to record the whole procedure of the experiment.

The procedure of the operation was introduced in **Section 5.6.3** and the selected sentences were listed in **Appendix 7**.

Step Three: A retrospective interview

The retrospective interview was made after the subject finished the experiment with the E-prime program. The main questions of the retrospective interview can be referred to the relevant introduction in **Section 5.6.3.2**.

5.6.5　Procedures for data analysis

This section will introduce the analysis of the E-prime experiment and the retrospective interview respectively.

5.6.5.1 The analysis of the E-prime experiment

The analysis involves three aspects of the subjects' performance in their oral production of the object clause structure in indirect speech: fluency, accuracy and complexity.

5.6.5.1.1 The analysis of fluency

Similarly, according to **Section 4.6.2.1** and Table 4-2, four indices are taken into account. They are Speech Rate (SR), Mean Length of Run (MLR), Phonation Time Ratio (PTR), and Average Length of Pause (ALP). The data of these four indices were collected by the digital recorder and analyzed with Audition 3.0 software. The analysis procedure is not introduced here since it is the same as that in **Section 5.5.2.5.1**.

It is worth mentioning that another temporal index was also analyzed in the E-prime experiment: the response time (RT). In this behavioral cognitive experiment the response time had two types: recognition response time (RRT) and output response time (ORT). Feeding back on the E-prime program, the researcher could collect each subject's raw data and then she put the numerical data of each subject into Microsoft Excel in order to make the data easier for grouping. In addition, she applied an SPSS file for descriptive analysis to see the tendency of the two types of response time.

The results for fluency will be reported in **Section 7.2**.

5.6.5.1.2 The analysis of accuracy

In this experiment, there were 12 sentences related to the change of sentence patterns from direct speech into indirect speech. The analysis of accuracy included the macro assessment and micro assessment. The macro assessment dealt with the use of sentence builders and sentence patterns and the micro assessment stresses the accuracy of pronunciation and use of linguistic units. The analysis procedures and the items to be involved can be referred to **Section 5.5.2.5.2** and Table 5-3.

The results and discussion for accuracy will be reported in **Section 7.2**.

5.6.5.1.3 The analysis of complexity

According to **Section 4.6.2.3**, the indices of assessing complexity include complexity in language structure and cognitive complexity. However, in this case study the type of the task was not concerned with complexity in language structure, so the researcher explored the cognitive complexity by comparing the recognition time spent by the subjects. The recognition response time is the time for the subjects for planning the organization. From the length of the recognition time, we may find the speed and the difficulty of the processing. The recognition time was collected from the E-prime program and edited with Microsoft Excel for comparison. Meanwhile, the researcher also got to know the cognitive processing by the retrospective interviews in which she asked some questions about the cognitive processing of the object clause structure in indirect speech.

The results and discussion for complexity will be reported in **Section 7.2** and **Section 7.4**.

5.6.5.2 The analysis of the interview

Similarly as presented in **Section 5.5.4**, the interviews were carefully examined in order to supplement the cognitive behavioral experiment. The recorded interviews were transcribed and the scripts were read very closely by the researcher in an attempt to explore the implicit and explicit factors influencing the change of sentence patterns concerning indirect speech in oral production.

The researcher generally went through three major steps in the interview-based analysis as mentioned in **Section 5.5.4.5**. The results and discussion will be reported in **Section 7.4**.

5.7 A Longitudinal Case Study of a Low-proficiency Subject

In order to explore the effects of the principles of procedural memory, a case study was designed and carried out, in which Jun, a low-proficiency subject, was trained to improve his oral production by the oral training approaches in light of the principles of procedural memory.

5.7.1 Research purposes and questions

This case study dealt with Question 3 and Question 4 in **Section 5.3**. It explored the effects of procedural memory on the improvement of oral production of the object clause structure in indirect speech as well as the major implicit and explicit factors influencing the application of procedural memory both in oral production of the object clause structure in indirect speech and in oral production in general.

5.7.2 The subject

The subject, Jun, came from the city of Guangzhou, Guangdong Province and now is a first-year graduate student in Medical College of Southeast University. His score in CET 4 was 538. He was considered a low-proficiency subject of English speaking in the researcher's class.

He liked learning English and spent much time in English learning when he was a middle school student. The score of English in the university entrance examination was 128 (*Note*: The full score was 150). In the first two years of college, he spent 6-10 hours each week in English learning under the pressure of passing CET 4. At the end of the second academic year, he passed CET 4 with the score 528. Later on, because of his tight schedule, he wasn't able to spend much time learning English. As to oral English, he thought it very important. However, he did not spare efforts to the practice of oral English since in China oral English is least stressed compared to English writing and reading.

After the researcher explained the aim and the procedures of the study, Jun was willing to be the subject and cherished the chance of being trained. He expected to take the chance to improve his oral English.

5.7.3 Instruments and tools

In order to explore fluency, accuracy and complexity, two kinds of tasks were involved.

The first was the task *"The Change of the Sentence Patterns"* with the E-prime 1.0 software, as introduced in **Section 5.6**. The second task was *"Questions and Answers"* as introduced in **Section 5.5.3**.

In order to investigate the changes of the subject in fluency, accuracy and complexity, the two tasks involved three times of oral test respectively according to the designed training plans presented in **Appendix 8**. The tested sentences were the same as those listed in **Appendix 5** and **Appendix 7**.

Each time, the oral test was followed by a retrospective interview, aimed at getting to know how the psychological processes were when the subject was doing the experiments. The questions were controlled or semi-controlled, which were about what Jun reacted in the experiment of the change of sentence patterns. Nevertheless, taking consideration of the performance of Jun, each time the questions were somewhat different from other times. The major questions are as follows:

"Why did you pause for a long time before you uttered the answer to Sentence X?"

"What did you think when you paused?"

"Did you find any new words in the sentences?"
"Did you recognize what was the research designed to explore?"
"What do you think of the length of selected sentences?"
"Did you recognize you had made a mistake in the utterance of Sentence Y?"

Similarly, as mentioned in **Section 5.4**, a digital voice recorder was applied to collect sound files. During the analysis of the recorded sound files, the powerful and professional Adobe Audition 3.0 software was applied to help with displaying and navigating the sound waves as well as the time that the subjects took when uttering sentences.

5.7.4 Procedures for data collection

The case study began in early October, 2009 and lasted for three months. It involved five tests, four training plans as well as six interviews before or after the tests. The series of tests and training plans are reported in **Appendix 8**. The procedures of data collection of each time can be referred to the relevant parts in **Section 5.5.3** and **Section 5.6**.

Before the first test began, the researcher made an interview with Jun, in which she asked him some questions about his personal information, education, interests and so on. The interview was made in Chinese for a better understanding and recorded for data collection.

Jun was not selected from the 16 low-proficiency subjects as introduced in **Section 5.4**. To know his mastery of the knowledge of indirect speech, Jun was asked to do a grammar test in which 15 multiple choices were included about different cases of indirect speech (See **Appendix 3**). Jun spent 20 minutes doing the test and after that, the researcher checked his answers and found all the answers were correct. Jun told the researcher though he had got full scores in the test, he was not sure about some choices such as Choice 1, Choice 7 and Choice 10 because he had not reviewed the grammatical knowledge of indirect speech for a very long time. The researcher asked Jun to point out the most difficult sentences in the 15 multiple choices and explained the detailed grammatical points to him until he understood completely.

5.7.5 Procedures for data analysis

This section will introduce the analysis of fluency, accuracy and complexity respectively. The data from a series of oral tests will be analyzed and compared in order to find out the changes of the subject in the performance of fluency, accuracy and complexity in oral production of the subject clause structure in indirect speech.

5.7.5.1 The analysis of fluency

The analysis of fluency involved the data collected from three different oral tests concerning Task One: *The Change of the Sentence Patterns*, and the other three times of oral tests concerning Task Two: *Questions and Answers*.

In Task One, besides the four indices including Speech Rate (SR), Mean Length of Run (MLR), Phonation Time Ratio (PTR) and Average Length of Pause (ALP), another temporal index, the response time (RT), was also applied to assess the fluency of the subjects. As introduced in **Section 5.6.5.1.1**, RT included two types: recognition response time, or RRT and output response time, or ORT.

As to the analysis of fluency in the task *"Questions and Answers"*, the four indices were SR, MLR, PTR and ALP. The procedure of analysis can be referred to **Section 5.5.3**.

Similarly as done in **Section 5.6**, with the E-prime program, the researcher collected each subject's raw data and then edited the numerical data of each subject into Excel in order to make the data easier for grouping. Meanwhile, the univariate analysis with the help of the SPSS file was applied for descriptive analysis to explore the tendency of the two types of response time: ORT and RRT. The results will be reported in **Section 8.2**.

5.7.5.2 The analysis of accuracy

As to the analysis of accuracy, the indices included NC (the number of sentences which are correct in sentence builders and sentence patterns), REP (ratio of errors in pronunciation) and REULU (ratio of errors in use of linguistic units). The analysis of accuracy involved the data collected from three different oral tests concerning Task One: *The Change of the Sentence Patterns* and the other three times of oral tests concerning Task Two: *Questions and Answers*.

The procedure can be referred to **Section 5.5.3** and **Section 5.6**. The results will be reported in **Section 8.3**.

5.7.5.3 The analysis of complexity

The assessment of complexity included complexity in language structure and cognitive complexity.

In Task One: *The Change of the Sentence Patterns*, the researcher assessed the cognitive complexity by comparing the recognition response time (RRT) which indicated the time for the subjects to plan and organize the utterances in order to test the familiarity of the subjects with the object clause structure in indirect speech.

In Task Two: *Questions and Answers*, the researcher assessed complexity by comparing (1) complexity in language structure including SVLV (syntactic variety and lexical variety), SC (syntactic complexity) and DD (the degree of difficulties in pronunciation, words, phrases and sentence patterns); and (2) cognitive complexity. It was explored by the relevant questions in the three retrospective interviews after each oral test concerning Task Two.

The procedure of the analysis can be referred to **Section 5.5.3**. The cognitive complexity was involved in the retrospective interviews.

The results and discussion will be reported in **Section 8.4**.

5.7.5.4 The analysis of the interviews

This case study included five interviews which were made to explore the research questions concerning the effects of the principles of procedural memory on oral production of object clause structure in indirect speech as well as the implicit and explicit factors influencing the change of sentence patterns concerning indirect speech in oral production.

The researcher transcribed each of the recorded interviews and read the scripts very closely. She generally went through three major steps in the interview-based analysis as mentioned in **Section 5.5.4.5**.

The results and discussion will be reported in **Section 8.5**.

5.8 A Cross–comparative Case Study between and within Subjects

Because of the importance of the indices such as fluency, accuracy and complexity in oral production, the present study designed and carried out the cross-comparative study to further explore the effects of the training of Jun's oral English and also supplement the behavioral experiments in **Section 5.5**, **Section 5.6** and **Section 5.7** by comparing the performance of Jun in two tasks: *"The Change of the Sentence Patterns"* and *"Questions and Answers"*.

5.8.1 Research questions

The research questions focused on the changes of Jun in the performance of fluency, accuracy and complexity in the object clause structure in indirect speech during the process of the oral training in order to explore the effects of procedural memory in oral training. These questions are as follows:

1. What are the significant changes that Jun made in fluency, accuracy and complexity in the object clause structure in indirect speech during the process of the oral training?

2. Compared with the Chinese high-proficiency speakers, what are the characteristics of the progress that Jun made in fluency, accuracy and complexity in the object clause structure in indirect speech during the process of the oral training?

3. What aspects in the object clause structure in indirect speech do the principles of procedural memory influence most?

5.8.2　Subjects

In Task One, the subjects included Jun and Gang and Li, who participated in the same task "*The Change of the Sentence Patterns*" in **Section 5.6**.

In Task Two, the subjects consisted of Jun and the high-proficiency subjects in Cognitive Behavioral Experiment Two "*Questions and Answers*" in **Section 5.5**.

5.8.3　Instruments and tools

The instruments included the following two items: (1) The E-prime experiment concerning Task One: *The Change of the Sentence Patterns* in **Section 5.6**; (2) The cognitive Behavioral Experiment concerning Task Two: "*Questions and Answers*" in **Section 5.5** and **Section 5.7**. The researcher directly made good use of the existing data collected from the experiments done in these previous sections, rather than redoing the experiments.

5.8.4　Procedures for data collection

The data had already been collected in the process of data collection of the previous tasks, so what the researcher did was to enter the data into SPSS software and retrieve the data relevant to the research purposes.

After that, she was able to make a series of comparisons between Jun and different groups of subjects.

5.8.5 Procedures for data analysis

This analysis of this part was mainly through comparison according to different research purposes and research questions. SPSS 15.0 and Microsoft Office Excel 2003 were fed back to analyze the data. The results and discussion will be reported in **Section 8.6**.

5.9 Summary

The chapter presents the research design for the present study. To address the research questions, four major studies were conducted. The research procedures of collecting and analyzing the data were described in detail. The results and discussion of the data collected will be presented in **Chapter Six, Chapter Seven** and **Chapter Eight**.

Chapter Six
RESULTS AND DISCUSSION (1): DIFFERENCES BETWEEN HIGH-PROFICIENCY AND LOW-PROFICIENCY L2 SPEAKERS

6.1 Introduction

Chapter Six addresses the first research question by reporting and discussing the major results of the two cognitive behavioral experiments, retrospective interviews and follow-up questionnaires in **Section 5.5**. The research question is presented as follows.

Question 1: Concerning the oral production of the object clause structure in indirect speech, what are the distinctive features of high-proficiency and low-proficiency L2 speakers in the application of procedural memory?

1.1 Concerning the oral production of the object clause structure in indirect speech, what are the major differences between the high-proficiency and low-proficiency L2 speakers as to fluency, accuracy and complexity?

1.2 What are the major differences between the high-proficiency and low-proficiency L2 speakers in the mental processing?

1.3 What are the major effects related to procedural memory on the high-proficiency L2 speakers in the oral production of the object clause structure in indirect speech?

Meanwhile, this chapter also explores the fourth research question concerning the major factors influencing the application of procedural memory in oral production of the object clause structure in indirect speech and in oral production in general.

The data were obtained from the two cognitive behavioral experiments of the study in **Section 5.5**. **Section 6.2** will present the results and discussion for the differences of oral production between high-proficiency and low-proficiency L2 speakers in fluency, accuracy and complexity. **Section 6.3** will report and discuss about the effects of chunks in oral production and **Section 6.4** will present the implicit and explicit factors influencing the proficiency of oral production.

6.2 Differences of Oral Production between High-proficiency and Low-proficiency L2 Speakers

Section 5.5 introduces the cross-sectional study conducted between high-proficiency and low-proficiency English speakers in order to address the first set of research questions mentioned above.

This section (**Section 6.2**) reports the major results for fluency, accuracy and complexity in Cognitive Behavioral Experiment One and Cognitive Behavioral Experiment Two respectively and then has some discussions about the results.

6.2.1 Major results and discussion for fluency

This section explores the performance of the subjects concerning fluency by combining the major results in Cognitive Behavioral Experiment One with those in Cognitive Behavioral Experiment Two.

As to the assessment of fluency of the subjects' oral production in the two cognitive behavioral experiments in **Section 5.5**, the independent variable was the indices of time spent by the subjects in producing each sentence and the dependent variable was fluency.

As introduced in **Section 5.5**, in Cognitive Behavioral Experiment One, the subjects in Group A and Group B took the tasks of *"Listen, Judge and Speak"* and *"Listen and Repeat"* respectively. The indices of fluency selected in the present study included Total Response Time (TRT), Speech Rate (SR), Mean Length of Run (MLR) and Average Length of Pause (ALP). The data of the mean values of the indices of fluency were collected and calculated for analysis of Group A and Group B.

Table 6-1 presents the results of univariate analysis of the indices of fluency in both Group A and Group B (*Note:* The time unit is the second.).

Table 6-1 Univariate Analysis of the Indices of Fluency for CBE I

	Between Levels				Between Groups			
	F	p	Mean H	Mean L	F	p	Mean GA	Mean GB
MTRT	88.237	0.000	4.192	4.965	10.327	0.003	4.711	4.446
MSR	82.561	0.000	179.560	149.190	53.166	0.000	152.190	176.560
MPTR	86.640	0.000	0.884	0.760	83.514	0.000	0.762	0.883
MMLR	214.984	0.000	12.019	8.883	15.319	0.000	10.003	10.853
MALP	200.195	0.000	0.480	0.680	34.747	0.000	0.622	0.539

Note: MTRT: the mean value of total response time; MSR: the mean speech rate; MPTR: the mean value of phonation time ratio; MSR: the mean speech rates; MMLR: the mean value of mean length of run; MALP: the mean value of average length of pause; MNCF: the mean number of chunks; Mean H: mean value of high-proficiency subject; Mean L: mean value of low-proficiency subject; Mean GA: mean value of Group A; Mean GB: mean value of Group B; CBE I: Cognitive Behavioral Experiment One.

As shown in Table 6-1, when compared between levels, the high-proficiency subjects performed much better than the low-proficiency subjects in MTRT, MSR, MPTR, MMLR and MALP ($p=0.000$). When compared between the two groups ("*Listen, Judge and Speak*" and "*Listen and Repeat*"), there was a significant difference between Group A and Group B ($p<0.05$). It indicates that the subjects in Group A did not perform better than those in Group B in MTRT, MSR, MPTR, MMLR and MALP. In order words, the subjects in Group A spent longer time than those in Group B in MTRT, MSR, MPTR, MMLR and MALP. This may be explained due to the following reasons on the basis of literature review and the information processing framework.

(1) The difficulty of different tasks. As introduced in **Section 5.5.2.4.1** and **Section 5.5.2.5**, the subjects in Group A were asked to listen to 20 sentences recorded in a sound file and judge whether these sentences had some mistakes or not. After the judgment, the subjects were required to utter the revised sentence immediately if they found mistakes in the sentence or to repeat the original sentence immediately if they found no mistakes in the sentence. Different from the subjects in Group A, the subjects in Group B were only required to repeat the sentences they heard one by one. Obviously, compared with the task of Group B "*Listen and Repeat*", the task of Group A "*Listen, Judge and Speak*" was much more difficult. The more difficult task would lead to more cognitive complexity (See **Section 4.6.3**). According to Oxford (2006), cognitive complexity involves a person component (unobservable cognition and observable behavior) and a task structure component. Though the sentences in both two tasks were not difficult in vocabulary, the task in Group A needed more unobservable mental operations of the subjects. For example, the judgment of the sentences would take more unobservable cognition of the subjects, which was verified by the retrospective interviews after the task.

(2) Automaticity. In oral production, automaticity influences fluency of one's oral proficiency as automatic processes are effortless, unconscious, and involuntary (Hasher & Zacks, 1979; Posner, 1978). From the perspective of memory, automatic processing is a fast, parallel, fairly effortless process which is not limited by short-term memory capacity (Schneider & Fisk, 1983). According to Anderson (1995), Langacker (1987, 1991) and Whitaker (1983), automaticity in language involves several stages. Each stage is decisive in the continuum of automatization. Since oral production involves many processes as what Levelt's Speech Production Model (Levelt, 1989) presents, each process in oral production will require due attention to complete and thus influence automaticity. In this sense, more complex tasks require more attention and cost more time for the subjects in Group A to retrieve relevant knowledge about the object clause structure in indirect speech from memory and to plan and organize the mental representation. In addition, such tasks were connected to the use of grammar and were related to skill-related knowledge and memory (i.e. procedural memory). When the subjects in Group A were not familiar with the oral task, automaticity could be reduced because, as Tzelgov (1999) held, automatic processing becomes intentional when it is a component of a more general task performed intentionally. The subjects in Group B undertook an easier task and automaticity in their oral production was not much influenced as automatic processing worked during the task (Schneider & Fisk, 1983; Tzelgov, 1999).

In order to further explore the interaction effects between two levels and two groups, univariate analysis was made as indicated in Table 6-2 (*Note*: The time unit is the second.).

Table 6-2   Univariate Analysis of the Interaction Effects of the Indices of Fluency in CBE I

	F	p	Mean			
			Mean Group A		Mean Group B	
			Mean H	Mean L	Mean H	Mean L
MTRT	3.292	0.080	4.399	3.984	5.023	4.908
MSR	1.812	0.189	165.130	139.250	194.000	159.130
MPTR	2.035	0.165	0.814	0.709	0.954	0.812
MMLR	0.355	0.556	11.659	8.347	12.379	9.326
MALP	20.742	0.000	0.568	0.676	0.393	0.635

Note: MTRT: the mean value of total response time; MSR: the mean speech rate; MPTR: the mean value of phonation time ratio; MSR: the mean speech rates; MMLR: the mean value of mean length of run; MALP: the mean value of average length of pause; MNCF: the mean number of chunks; Mean H: mean value of high-proficiency subject; Mean L: mean value of low-proficiency subject; CBE I: Cognitive Behavioral Experiment One.

In addition, Table 6-2 also indicates that the low-proficiency subjects in Group B took shorter average length of pause time (ALP) than the low-proficiency subjects in Group A (***Note***: Mean L of Group A: 0.676; Mean L of Group B: 0.635). As supposed, the low-proficiency subjects in Group B should have taken longer pause time. The possible reason for the phenomenon may lie in the following two aspects. First, compared with Group A, the task of Group B was easier and required less attention and therefore the subjects in Group B spent less time for pauses. Second, it may be because of the limited number of the subjects and the tested sentences. If the number of the subjects and the tested sentences is increased, there would be possibly no interaction effects in MALP, which would possibly accord with the general tendency of the performance in MTRT, MSR, MPTR and MMLR as shown in Table 6-1.

As to the assessment of fluency in Cognitive Behavioral Experiment Two, the indices included Total Response Time (TRT),

Speech Rate (SR), Phonation Time Ratio (PTR), Mean Length of Run (MLR) and Average Length of Pause (ALP). Based on the data and the purpose of this experiment, the researcher analyzed the data of Group One (high-proficiency subjects) and Group Two (low-proficiency subjects) with Independent Samples *t*-Test. Table 6-3 shows the results of the analysis with Independent Samples *t*-Test of fluency in Cognitive Behavioral Experiment Two (*Note*: The time unit is the second.).

Table 6-3   Independent Samples t-Test of Fluency in CBE II

Items	Mean H	Std D	Mean L	Std D	t	df	Sig. (2-tailed)
MTRT	6.080	0.11784	7.445	0.49429	-10.749	16.70	0.000
MSR	170.250	9.57427	134.188	9.09372	10.924	30	0.000
MPTR	0.803	0.01534	0.596	0.06709	12.053	16.565	0.000
MMLR	10.940	.13302	7.840	.37896	30.874	18.641	0.000
MALP	1.184	.22056	1.507	.06585	-5.608	17.653	0.000

Note: MTRT: the mean value of total response time; MSR: the mean speech rate; MPTR: the mean value of phonation time ratio; MSR: the mean speech rates; MMLR: the mean value of mean length of run; MALP: the mean value of average length of pause; MNCF: the mean number of chunks; Mean H: mean value of high-proficiency subject; Mean L: mean value of low-proficiency subject; CBE II: Cognitive Behavioral Experiment Two.

Table 6-3 indicates that Cognitive Behavioral Experiment Two is almost consistent with Cognitive Behavioral Experiment One in the findings of fluency of the high-proficiency and low-proficiency subjects. That is, the high-proficiency subjects in Group One performed better than the low-proficiency subjects Group Two in MTRT, MSR, MPTR, MMLR and MALP ($p=0.000$).

In summary, from the analysis of fluency in Cognitive Behavioral Experiment One and Cognitive Behavioral Experiment Two, it is found that the high-proficiency subjects performed better in fluency than the low-proficiency subjects no matter whether the comparison was made between the levels within a task group or between two task groups.

Besides, in order to explore the effects of procedural memory on oral production, the researcher will analyze the correlation between chunks and accuracy in **Section 6.3**.

6.2.2 Results and discussion for accuracy

This section explores the performance of the subjects concerning accuracy in **Section 5.5** by combining the major results in Cognitive Behavioral Experiment One with those in Cognitive Behavioral Experiment Two.

According to **Section 4.6.2**, accuracy is assessed by different indices in different tasks. As introduced in **Section 5.5**, the indices in the task "*Listen, Judge and Speak*" were different from those of the task "*Listen and Repeat*" in the fact that the former task involved the macro assessment in which the correctness of sentence builders and sentence patterns was required to judge.

Table 6-4 presents univariate analysis of the collected data concerning the indices of accuracy of the subjects in both Group A and Group B.

Table 6-4   Univariate Analysis of the Indices of Accuracy for CBE I

	Between levels				Between Groups			
	F	p	Mean H	Mean L	F	p	Mean GA	
MREP	80.911	0.000	0.457	0.744	120.867	0.000	0.776	0.426
MREULU	135.920	0.000	0.402	0.667	910.817	0.000	0.877	0.193
NC	26.843	0.000	7.150	5.125				

Note: MREP: the mean ratio of errors in pronunciation; MREULU: the mean of errors in use of linguistic units; NC: the number of sentences which are correct in sentence builders and sentence patterns; Mean H: mean value of high-proficiency subject; Mean L: mean value of low-proficiency subject; Mean GA: mean value of Group A; Mean GB: mean value of Group B; CBE I: Cognitive Behavioral Experiment One.

As shown in Table 6-4, when compared between levels, the high-proficiency subjects performed much better than the low-proficiency subjects in NC, MREP and MREULU ($p=0.000$). Take NC for example. In detailed analysis, it can be found that compared with the low-proficiency subjects, the high-proficiency subjects in Group A did better in correctness of judgment of sentence builders and sentence patterns (Mean H:7.150; Mean L:5.125). Meanwhile, the ratio of errors in pronunciation (MREP) and in use of linguistic units (MREULU) of the high-proficiency subjects is lower than that of the low-proficiency subjects no matter whether the comparison was made in Group A or in Group B. This phenomenon shows that the high-proficiency subjects were better in accuracy than the low-proficiency ones. This may be because the high-proficiency subjects stressed not only fluency but also accuracy when they dealt with procedural knowledge and procedural learning. According to Chen (2002a, 2002b; 2009), who develops a new approach to linguistic competence, the elements of memory and automaticity should be entailed in a sound theory of linguistic competence. The contents of memory include grammatical rules, lexical knowledge, exemplar storage, four-channel mental representation of language and encyclopedia knowledge. Among these aspects, four-channel mental representation of language includes auditory representation, visual representation, memory of pronunciation procedures and memory of writing procedures. In this experiment, the finding that the high-proficiency subjects were better at accuracy may be due to the following reasons. First, they may be better at memorizing grammatical rules, lexical knowledge, exemplar storage, four-channel mental representation of language and encyclopedia knowledge. Second, they may be better at memorizing pronunciation procedures. The correct pronunciation procedures are beneficial to the accuracy of their oral production. Besides these two abilities, they may be more familiar with the retrieval and the use of procedural knowledge as well as the stored grammatical rules and pronunciations. The familiarity with the combination of linguistic units such as syllables, phrases and sentence patterns is very important in such tasks in Cognitive Behavioral Experiment One and Cognitive Behavioral Experiment Two.

From the mean values it can be found that when compared between the two groups (*"Listen, Judge and Speak"* and *"Listen and Repeat"*), the subjects in Group A did not perform better than those in Group B in MREP (Mean GA:0.776; Mean GB:0.426) and MREULU (Mean GA:0.877; Mean GB:0.193). The possible reason for the phenomenon may lie in the fact that the task of Group A was much more difficult than that of Group B, which may have influenced the performance of the subjects in Group A as discussed in **Section 6.2.1**.

From the data in Table 6-4, we can find out the general tendency that the high-proficiency subjects performed better than the low-proficiency subjects in the tasks *"Listen, Judge and Speak"* and *"Listen and Repeat"*.

Though the selected sentences were not exactly the same in *"Listen, Judge and Speak"* and *"Listen and Repeat"*, the sentence length and the difficulty of words in the corresponding sentences were similar, so the researcher made a comparison with univariate analysis between the subjects in both groups to explore the differences between the two tasks and between high-proficiency and low-proficiency subjects (See Table 6-5).

Table 6-5 shows that there were no interaction effects in MREP ($p=0.628$). It indicates that in both of the two groups, the average ratio of errors of pronunciation (MREP) of the high-proficiency subjects is lower than that of the low-proficiency subjects. However, as to the average ratio of errors in use of linguistic units (MREULU), there existed significant interaction effects ($p=0.000$). It indicates that the different

Table 6-5 Univariate Analysis of the Interaction Effects of the Indices of Accuracy

	F	p	Mean			
			Mean Group A		Mean Group B	
			Mean H	Mean L	Mean H	Mean L
MREP	0.240	0.628	0.625	0.928	0.290	0.561
MREULU	23.264	0.000	0.690	1.064	0.115	0.270

Note: MREP: the mean ratio of errors in pronunciation; MREULU: the mean of errors in use of linguistic units; NC: the number of sentences which are correct in sentence builders and sentence patterns; Mean H: mean value of high-proficiency subject; Mean L: mean value of low-proficiency subject; CBE I: Cognitive Behavioral Experiment One.

tasks may lead to different performances of the subjects. Compared with Group A whose task was "*Listen, Judge and Speak*", the ratio of errors in use of linguistic units (REULU) of Group B decreased greatly in the cases of both high-proficiency and low-proficiency subjects (Mean H: 0.690 in Group A; 0.115 in Group B; Mean L: 1.064 in Group A; 0.270 in Group B). This may be due to the difficulty of the tasks. The task of Group A was "*Listen, Judge and Speak*", involving the more complex processing of judgment which might influence the performance in use of linguistic units. It may be the case that to some of the high-proficiency subjects, their oral production may be more fluent than low-proficiency subjects, but in order to speak as fluently as the native English speakers do, they may ignore the accuracy of the use of linguistic units. According to the information processing framework of the present study, this may be because their working memory could not load much information in a short time. Ignoring the accuracy of the use of linguistic units would help them save much time in retrieving information about grammatical rules and pronunciation processes. The finding was verified in the retrospective interview made after the experiment. It indicates that in China, though some high-proficiency learners seem to be fluent in oral production, accuracy of the use of linguistic units is unsatisfactory. To solve the problem calls for more practice of the use of linguistic units in oral production. Meanwhile, accuracy in oral production needs to be paid due attention to.

Table 6-6 shows the results of analysis of accuracy with Independent Samples t-Test in Cognitive Behavioral Experiment Two (CBE II).

Table 6-6   Independent Samples t-Test of Accuracy in CBE II

Items	Mean H	Std D	Mean L	Std D	t	df	Sig.(2-tailed)
NC	3.688	0.60208	2.000	0.51640	8.510	30	0.000
MREP	1.178	0.24667	1.698	0.04056	-7.045	30	0.000
MREULU	0.689	0.25706	2.083	0.18289	-17.679	30	0.000

Note: NC: the number of sentences which are correct in sentence builders and sentence patterns; MREP: the mean ratio of errors in pronunciation; MREULU: the mean ratio of errors in use of linguistic units; Mean H: mean value of high-proficiency subject; Mean L: mean value of low-proficiency subject; CBE II: Cognitive Behavioral Experiment Two.

The task "*Questions and Answers*" was cognitively complex because of the requirements of the task. The dialogues were made in Chinese while the subjects were required to answer the questions in English. Meanwhile, the answers were related to object clause structure in indirect speech.

As shown in Table 6-6, we can also find out the general tendency that the high-proficiency subjects in Group One performed better than the low-proficiency subjects Group Two in NC, MREP and MREULU (p=0.000). It indicates that when undertaking the same difficult task, the high-proficiency subjects performed better than the low-proficiency subjects possibly because of the high-proficiency subjects who were more familiar with such difficult structures (Oxford, 2006). The finding was also verified in the retrospective interview made after the experiment. From the retrospective interview, it was found that the high-proficiency subjects were more frequently exposed to the object clause structure in indirect speech from novels, movies, videos and other approaches. This finding is consistent with schema theory. According to schema theory, the exposure to the object clause structure in indirect speech from novels, movies, videos and other approaches helped with the formation of a set of schemata or mental representations. These schemata or mental representations incorporate all the knowledge of a given type of object or event that the high-proficiency subjects acquired from past experience. Because of the functioning of schemata, the prior knowledge influenced the subjects' comprehension and memory (Driscoll, 2000).

Besides, in order to explore the effects of procedural memory on oral production, the researcher will analyze the correlation between chunks and accuracy in **Section 6.4**.

6.2.3 Results and discussion for complexity

This section investigates the performance of the subjects concerning complexity in **Section 5.5** by combining the major results in Cognitive Behavioral Experiment One with those in Cognitive Behavioral Experiment Two.

Considering the fact that the subjects with different levels of oral production may have various answers with different complexity in the task "Questions and Answers", the researcher explored complexity only in Cognitive Behavioral Experiment Two.

According to **Section 4.6.2.3**, the indices of assessing the complexity in the current study include complexity in language structure and cognitive complexity. The indices are SVLV (syntactic variety and lexical variety), SC (syntactic complexity) and DD (the degree of difficulties in pronunciation and use of linguistic units such as words, phrases and sentence patterns).The researcher reports the data of the performance of the subjects in complexity. The results of Independent Samples t-Test are presented in Table 6-7.

Table 6-7 Independent Samples t-Test of Complexity in CBE II

Items	Mean H	Std D	Mean L	Std D	t	df	Sig.(2-tailed)
MSVLV	2.698	0.24553	2.157	0.21445	6.636	30	0.000
MSC	2.719	0.25692	2.209	0.14132	6.966	23.316	0.000
MDD	2.688	0.24310	2.177	0.17713	6.787	30	0.000

Note: CBE II: Cognitive Behavioral Experiment Two; SVLV: Syntactic variety and lexical variety; SC: Syntactic complexity; DD: The degree of difficulties in pronunciation and use of linguistic units; Mean H: mean value of high-proficiency subject; Mean L: mean value of low-proficiency subject.

The task "*Questions and Answers*" was designed to address the first research question of the current study in **Section 5.3**. The researcher attempted to investigate the subjects' ability to interpret Chinese sentences concerning indirect speech to English from the perspective of fluency, accuracy and complexity. Table 6-7 indicates that the high-proficiency subjects in Group One performed better than the low-proficiency subjects in Group Two in MSVLV, MSC and MDD (p=0.000). This finding shows that the high-proficiency subjects were better at dealing with complexity in the task "*Questions and Answers*". Take the first dialogue for example. With the detailed analysis of the scripts of the subjects' oral production, it has been found that most of the high-proficiency subjects translated "国际展览中心" into English as "the International Exhibition Center" while most low-proficiency subjects preferred to use "the International Show Center". Compared with the word "exhibition", the word "show" is less complex. When asked the reason for the selection of the word "show", the low-proficiency subjects admitted that the word "exhibition" was hard to pronounce. In this case, to retrieve the correct pronunciation of the word "exhibition" was more complex, which involved more attention and time to combine the syllables embedded in the pronunciation of the word "exhibition". This may support the Principle of Least Effort (Zipf, 1972) which postulates that animals, people, even well designed machines will naturally choose the path of least resistance or "effort".

In addition to the finding mentioned above, there are some other findings from the detailed analysis of the scripts of the subjects' oral production. It is found that in most cases, the high-proficiency subjects preferred to use more complex sentence structures or more flexible linguistic units or more complicated words. For example, they preferred to use "exhibition" rather than "show" to express "国际展览中心". The reason for the phenomenon may lie in the fact that the high-proficiency subjects were more familiar with the linguistic units such as the word "exhibition". Though such words were more difficult to pronounce, the familiarity with the words was beneficial to fluency, accuracy and complexity in their pronunciation.

However, it is also found that in some other cases, in order to ensure that their output was grammatically correct in the exercises, the high-proficiency subjects tended to choose less complex sentences or linguistic units. For example, when answering the question in the third dialogue "你骑自行车还是乘公交车上学啊？", most of the high-proficiency subjects chose the simpler sentence pattern "The woman asked the man whether/if he went to school by bike or by bus.". However, four low-proficiency subjects expressed the sentence pattern like 'The woman asked the man whether/if he rided/rode his bike (bicycle) to go to school or took bus/buses to go to school.' The sentence produced by the four low-proficiency subjects was longer than the one that most of the high-proficiency subjects expressed. It is also found that both of the two sentences involve the change of tense of verbs. In the former sentence, the high-proficiency subjects only needed to change the tense of one verb "go" while in the sentence produced by the four low-proficiency subjects, two verbs (i.e., "ride" and "took") were involved in the change of tense.

The reasons for this phenomenon are complex.

On one hand, as to the high-proficiency subjects, one of the obvious reasons is that they were better equipped in terms of familiarized chunks or expressions such as "go to school" and "by bike or by bus", and thus were more fluent and flexible in oral production. Another possible reason is because the high-proficiency subjects were better at using communicative strategies such as reduction strategies (Færch & Kasper, 1983) or avoidance strategies by Tarone (1977), and risk-avoidance strategies by Corder (1983). According to Færch and Kasper (1983), reduction strategies could be phonological, morphological, syntactic and lexical strategies. These strategies may automatize the knowledge of L2 and learners tend to use them either to avoid making errors and/ or to increase their proficiency of oral production. In this case, though they were not needed to communicate with others, the high-proficiency subjects used reduction strategies to avoid errors. It was also a metalinguistic strategy from the perspective of cognitive psychology.

On the other hand, as to the low-proficiency subjects, they were more rigid in the selection of English expressions. When asked to orally produce an English sentence within a short time, they tended to follow the Chinese word order in order to take a safer course. That is to say, the low-proficiency subjects were easily influenced by their first language (L1, i.e., Chinese). The L1 interference is one of the several sources of errors that L2 learners make (Krashen, 1988). In the case of the object clause structure in indirect speech, the existence of L1 interference caused the errors of the low-proficiency subjects in grammar, vocabulary, pronunciation, etc., which was verified in the retrospective interviews made after the experiment. In addition, it was found that the sentences produced by the four low-proficiency subjects included two verbs (i.e., "ride" and "took") which needed the change of tense. According to the principles of information processing, it requires more attention paid to the correct form of past tense of these two verbs. The low-proficiency subjects were not sure about the past tense of the verb "ride" and "take". As a result, the change of tense took much time and influenced fluency and accuracy of their oral production.

Besides, in order to explore the effects of procedural memory on oral production, the correlation between chunks and complexity will be analyzed in **Section 6.3**.

6.3　The Effects of Chunks

Related closely to procedural memory, the use of chunks was explored in oral production in the present study. Meanwhile, because the Chinese subjects in the experiments had mastered a certain knowledge of chunks, chunks used in their oral production can be analyzed, which accorded with the focus of the present study: exploring the type of procedural memory which is parasitic with declarative memory and can be analyzed.

As mentioned in **Section 4.6.2.1**, the present study applied Yuan and Guo's definition of chunks (Yuan & Guo, 2010). In addition, because of the types of tasks in the current study, the present researcher calculated the frequency of chunks by the operational formula: total number of chunks ÷ the number of tested sentences. In this section, the findings will be reported as to the influence of chunks on oral production.

Table 6-8 shows correlation analysis between chunk frequency and the indices of frequency and accuracy in Cognitive Behavioral Experiment One.

Table 6-8   Correlation Analysis between Chunk Frequency and the Indices of Fluency and Accuracy in CBE I

Fluency					Accuracy		
MTRT	MSR	MPTR	MMLR	MALP	MREP	MREULU	
-0.909***	0.858***	0.809***	0.980***	-0.868***	-0.754***	-0.531***	

*** Correlation is significant at the 0.01 level (2-tailed).
Note: CBE I: Cognitive Behavioral Experiment One.

As mentioned in **Section 2.5.2**, chunking is considered a fundamental operation occurring in the human memory (Miller, 1956; Simon, 1974). By using chunks, the number of channels during the input of data can be reduced, so less processing power and less bandwidth will be used (Miller,1956). As Table 6-8 shows, in Cognitive Behavioral Experiment One, chunk frequency had significant correlation with the indices of frequency no matter whether the correlation is positive or negative. This finding supports the view that formulaic sequences or chunks are one of the major causes for the fluent and accurate language output of native-speakers and L2 speakers (Biber et al., 1999; Deng, 2006; Ellis, 1991; Howarth, 1998; Pawley & Syder, 1983; Wei, 2004, 2007; Wei & Wang, 2005). It is also consistent with Zhen's corpus study of the role of chunks in oral production (Zhen, 2009).

Table 6-9 shows correlation analysis between chunk frequency and the indices of fluency, accuracy and complexity in Cognitive Behavioral Experiment Two.

Table 6-9 Correlation Analysis between Chunk Frequency and the Indices of Frequency, Accuracy and Complexity in CBE II

Fluency					Accuracy			Complexity		
MTRT	MSR	MPTR	MMLR	MALP	NC	MREP	MREULU	MSVLV	MSC	MDD
-0.70***	0.77***	0.69***	0.72***	-0.81***	-0.84***	-0.75***	-0.53***	0.94***	0.89***	0.94***

*** Correlation is significant at the 0.01 level (2-tailed).

As Table 6-9 shows, in Cognitive Behavioral Experiment Two, chunk frequency also had significant correlation with the indices of frequency no matter whether the correlation was positive or negative. This finding is consistent with Yuan Ping and Guo Fenrong's corpus study of the positive role of chunks in oral production (Yuan & Guo, 2010).

As discussed in **Chapter Two**, chunking and other formulaic language are closely related to procedural memory. Based on the results of Cognitive Behavioral Experiment One and Cognitive Behavioral Experiment Two, it is found that chunking had strong correlation with the proficiency of oral production in fluency, accuracy and complexity, which supports the studies of chunks (Ding & Qi, 2005; Wray, 2000, 2002; Wray & Perkins, 2000; Yuan & Guo, 2010). In this sense, it is inspired that the increase of chunk frequency will be of great help to L2 learners' oral production.

6.4 Major Factors Influencing Oral Production

As mentioned in **Section 5.5.4** and **Section 5.5.5**, data from retrospective reviews and follow-up questionnaires can reveal some hidden truth about the subjects' major thinking processes and cognitive complexity when they orally produced the object clause structure of indirect speech and the factors which facilitate or constrain the oral production of the object clause structure of indirect speech, thus supplementing the information obtained from the experimental part.

In this section, the factors influencing oral production of the object clause structure of indirect speech and the factors influencing oral production in general are summarized as follows.

6.4.1 Major factors influencing oral production of the object clause structure in indirect speech

The factors influencing oral production of the object clause structure of indirect speech were summarized from the feedbacks of the retrospective and opinion interviews made after the two experiments. In addition, Question 6 and Question 7 in the follow-up questionnaire were also about this aspect. The major results and discussion are presented as follows.

6.4.1.1 Implicit factors

According to the feedbacks, it is found the major implicit factors influencing oral production of the object clause structure of indirect speech include anxiety, self-confidence and the interference of L1.

6.4.1.1.1 Anxiety and self-confidence

These two factors were related to each other in the current study, so the researcher reports and discusses about them together.

On the basis of the retrospective interviews, the researcher finds that the high-proficiency subject felt less anxious than the low-proficiency subjects in both tasks. Within one task, it is also the case. To the low-proficiency subjects, they felt stressed when encountering more difficult tasks such as *"Listen, Judge and Speak"* and *"Questions and Answers"*. According to the feedbacks, when they heard the sentences, they felt confused at what to do with the judgment and correction because they were not familiar with the object clause structure in indirect speech, pronunciation of some words and expressions, the collocations, etc. In this case, they just repeated the incorrect sentences. From the data collected, it was found that some of the low-proficiency subjects spent less time in uttering. However, the ratio of accuracy was unsatisfactory.

In addition, the cognitive complexity increased in dealing with more difficult tasks. In this case, if the subjects did not have any strategies to ease the cognitive complexity, they would feel more anxious. In the present study, it is found that the high-proficiency subjects were better at using chunks, collocations, idioms, etc. which is the major reason for them to feel less anxious when undertaking the tasks.

6.4.1.1.2 The interference of L1

In the light of the feedbacks, the interference of L1 is considered one of the major factors influencing the subjects' oral production, especially to the low-proficiency subjects in the current study.

L1 interference is one of the several sources of errors learners make (Krashen, 1988). Based on the feedbacks from the retrospective interviews, it is found that in the current study, the low-proficiency subjects (second language learners) have accumulated structural entities of the target language (English) while they demonstrated difficulty in organizing the knowledge into appropriate and coherent structures in a fluent way. It appeared to be the most difficult issue that the low-proficiency subjects should encounter. When asked about the reasons, the low-proficiency subjects stated that they were negatively influenced by Chinese, their mother tongue, which caused grammatical interference, lexical interference, phonological interference, etc. especially in the task *"Questions and Answers"*. In this task, the dialogues were made in Chinese while they were asked to answer questions in English. In the case of the object clause structure in indirect speech, the existence of L1 interference might lead to the errors of the low-proficiency subjects in grammar, vocabulary, pronunciation, etc. Therefore, the poorer performance of the low-proficiency subjects could be understandable.

However, to the high-proficiency subjects, the L1 interference was not so serious. When asked about the reasons, the high-proficiency subjects presented the feedbacks which mainly lie in the fact that they had got used to the way of the target language (i.e., English) in organizing the knowledge into appropriate and coherent structures due to intensive practice and training. Meanwhile, they were able to get rid of the negative transfer of L1 in L2 speaking due to the accumulation of chunks, collocations, idioms, etc. From this perspective, the importance of practice is emphasized and hence, the effects of procedural memory are stressed at the same time.

6.4.1.2 Explicit factors

Based on the retrospective interviews, it is found that the major explicit factors influencing oral production of the object clause structure of indirect speech include the familiarity with the object clause structure in indirect speech and with the words, expressions and sentences, the length of the tested sentences as well as frequency of oral practice of the object clause structure in indirect speech. Compared with the high-proficiency subjects, the low-proficiency subjects showed the negative feedbacks in these factors.

Table 6-10 presents the results of the retrospective interviews regarding the familiarity of the subjects with the object clause structure in indirect speech.

Table 6-10 **Familiarity with the Object Clause Structure in Indirect Speech**

		N	Percentage
Familiarity to the OCS in InDS	Unfamiliar	0	0
	A little familiar	20	62.5%
	Familiar	8	25%
	Very familiar	4	12.5%

continued

		N	Percentage
Frequencies of making mistakes	Never	1	3.125%
	Sometime	7	21.875%
	Often	18	56.25%
	Always	6	18.75%

Note: the OCS: the object clause structure; InDS: indirect speech
N: the numbers representing the amount of subject(s) who chose the corresponding option.

Table 6-10 indicates that most students (62.5%) were not so familiar with the object clause structure in indirect speech of oral production though they knew well about the grammatical knowledge of the structure as indicated in **Section 4.6.2.3**. The total number of the subjects who often or always made mistakes in the object clause structure in indirect speech of oral production in the experiments was 24, which occupies 75% among all the 32 subjects.

It is worth mentioning that the length of the sentences tested is influenced by long-term memory. If the speaker does not form a good long-term memory system in his or her brain and make good use of it, it is hard for him or her to memorize longer sentences. In the current study, it is found that due to using more chunks, the high-proficiency subjects were able to memorize the tested sentences more easily while the low-proficiency subjects failed in this aspect. That is why some of the low-proficiency subjects only uttered part of the sentences even in the easier task "*Listen and Repeat*".

As to the frequency of oral practice of the object clause structure in indirect speech, the feedbacks from the low-proficiency subjects were also unsatisfactory, compared with the high-proficiency subjects.

In reality, the factors mentioned above are closely related to procedural memory as introduced in **Chapter Two**. Through the comparison between the high-proficiency and low-proficiency subjects, the effects of procedural memory can be explored.

6.4.2　Factors influencing oral production in general

The factors influencing oral production in general were summarized from the results of the follow-up questionnaire made after the two experiments.

6.4.2.1　Attitudes towards oral English

Table 6-11 reports the results for Question 6 concerning the attitudes towards oral production.

Table 6-11　Attitudes towards Oral Production

Items	N1	N2	N3	N4
Listening	9	11	7	5
Speaking	8	10	9	5
Reading	5	7	8	12
Writing	6	6	7	13

Note: N1 refers to the number of the subjects who thinks the item the least important; N2 refers to the number of the subjects who thinks the item less important; N3 refers to the number of the subjects who thinks the item important; N4 refers to the number of the subjects who thinks the item the most important.

As shown in Table 6-11, it is found that compared with reading and writing, listening and speaking are not considered so important by the subjects from China. In SLA, attitude is an important factor influencing the proficiency of L2 (Ellis, 1999). In the case, we can indirectly find out that the negative attitudes towards speaking may lead to the poorer performance in oral production, compared with reading and writing.

6.4.2.2　Problems of oral production

Table 6-12 reports the results for the difficulties in oral production (See

Question 7).

Table 6-12　The Results for the Difficulties in Oral Production

Items	N	Percentage
Fluency and accuracy of pronunciation	23	71.875%
Fluency and accuracy of words and collocations	23	71.875%
Fluency and accuracy of syntactical structure	21	65.625%
Appropriateness of the communicative strategies	22	68.75%

Note: N: the number of the subjects who chose the item.

Table 6-12 indicates that most subjects had difficulty in pronunciation and the linguistic units like words, chunks and collocations. To retrieve the pronunciation and linguistic units fluently and accurately needs intensive practice and a well- organized memory system to ease the complex processing of brain. Based on the findings of previous studies and the present study, making good use of procedural memory may be one of the approaches to getting through such difficulties.

6.4.2.3　Approaches to improving oral English

Question 10 in the follow-up questionnaires is about the approaches to improving oral English.

According to the feedbacks, the approaches of improving the oral production still focus on oral practice. From the results for the opinions of the improvement of oral production, most subjects recognized the importance of oral practice. Nevertheless, Question 5 reveals the fact that the time for the subjects to practise their oral English is far from being enough. If they spent more time practicing oral English, the proficiency of their oral English would be hopefully improved.

Based on the findings, we can infer the importance of procedural memory which is closely related to practice as mentioned in **Chapter Two**.

In accordance with multiple studies of the adult acquisition of nonlinguistic skills by procedural memory (Mishkin, Malamut & Bachevalier, 1984; Schacter & Tulving, 1994; Squire & Knowlton, 2000), practice should lead to procedural learning and improved performance.

Whether or not a given individual acquires a given set of grammatical knowledge in the procedural system will depend on such factors as the type of grammatical knowledge, the nature of the L2 exposure, and characteristics such as intrinsic procedural learning abilities of the learner. With sufficient experience with L2, the language is expected to become L1-like in its grammatical dependence on the procedural system, with the potential for a high degree of proficiency.

6.5 Summary

This chapter addresses **Question 1** from two angles, followed by the detailed description of the research methodology for the study. The subjects consisted of 32 Chinese tertiary level university students. The instruments included two cognitive behavioral experiments, retrospective interviews and a follow-up questionnaire. The research purposes, principles, the procedures of collecting and analyzing the data are described in detail.

Chapter Seven
RESULTS AND DISCUSSION (2): FEATURES OF NATIVE ENGLISH SPEAKERS AND HIGH–PROFICIENCY NON–NATIVE ENGLISH SPEAKERS

7.1 Introduction

This chapter presents the major results and discussion for the comparative case study of the native English speakers and high-proficiency English speakers among Chinese tertiary non-English majors. The case study was conducted to address the second research question mentioned as follows.

Question 2: Concerning the oral production of the object clause structure in indirect speech, what are the distinctive features of native English speakers and non-native English speakers with high oral proficiency in the application of procedural memory?

2.1 Concerning the oral production of the object clause structure in indirect speech, what are the major similarities and differences between the two groups of subjects as to fluency, accuracy and complexity?

2.2 What are the major effects related to procedural memory on oral production of native-English speakers and non-native English speakers?

Meanwhile, the fourth research question concerning the major factors influencing the application of procedural memory in oral production of the object clause structure in indirect speech and in oral production in general is also explored in this chapter.

The data were obtained from the comparative case study between the native English speakers and the high-proficiency non-native English speakers in **Section 5.6**.

7.2 Similarities and Difficulties between Native English Speakers and High-proficiency Non-native English Speakers

Section 5.6 introduced a comparative case study in which the E-prime experiment was implemented to investigate fluency, accuracy and complexity of the native English speakers and high-proficiency English speakers among Chinese tertiary non-English majors.

This section will report the major results and discussion for fluency, accuracy and complexity in the comparative case study respectively.

7.2.1 Major results and discussion for fluency

In the part of the E-prime experiment, the fluency of the two groups of the subjects (native English speakers and high-proficiency English speakers among Chinese tertiary non-English majors) was explored depending on the time. Hence, the independent variable was the time spent by the subjects in producing each sentence and the dependent variable was fluency. In this case, Speech Rate (SR), Mean Length of Run (MLR), Phonation Time Ratio (PTR), Average Length of Pause (ALP) and the response time (RT) including recognition response time (RRT) and output response time (ORT) were taken into account as the indices of the assessment of fluency. The data of the five indices were collected by the digital recorder and analyzed with Adobe Audition 3.0 software.

The major results for fluency in the case study are reported in two aspects. The first aspect is about the results from the analysis of the sound files collected by the voice recorder during the E-prime experiment. The second aspect deals with the results from the analysis of the E-prime experiment. The discussion will be made after the display of the results.

7.2.1.1 Major results and discussion of the sound files

Four subjects participated in the task of 'The change of the sentence patterns into indirect speech'. Table 7-1 shows the results of the performance in fluency of these subjects. As introduced in **Chapter Five**, among 20 tested sentences shown in **Appendix 7**, 12 sentences concerning the object clause structure in indirect speech were included. The results of the Independent Samples t-Test of the collected data concerning the indices of fluency of the subjects are reported in Table 7-1 (N=24).

Table 7-1 Independent Samples t-Test of Frequency of Native and Non-native English Speakers

Items	Mean NE	Std D	Mean NNE	Std D	t	df	Sig.(2-tailed)
SR (spm)	185.708	49.96127	139.917	32.95177	3.748	39.826	0.001
PTR	0.926	0.12683	0.884	0.09498	1.306	46	0.198
MLR (spr)	9.979	2.78770	8.104	2.13653	2.615	46	0.012
ALP	0.353	0.46613	0.512	0.44053	-1.212	46	0.232

Note: SR: speech rate; MLR: the mean length of run; PTR: phonation time ratio; ALP: average length of pause; spm: syllables per minute; spr: syllables per run; NE: native English speakers; NNE: non-native English speakers.

As shown in Table 7-1, when the comparison was made between nationalities, the following findings were obtained. First, the native English speakers performed much better than the high-proficiency non-native English subjects in SR (speech rate) and MLR (average mean length of run) ($p=0.001$). When averaged, the speech rate (SR) of the native English speakers was 185.708 syllables per minute and that of the high-proficiency non-native English subjects was 139.917 syllables per minute. As to the average mean length of run, the native English speakers had the advantage over the non-native English subjects (9.979 syllables per run and 8.104 syllables per run respectively). This result accords with the similar studies of the native English speakers and non-native English speakers. Second, there did not exist significant differences between the native English speakers and the high-proficiency non-native English subjects in PTR (phonation time ratio) ($p=0.198$) and ALP (average length of pause) ($p=0.232$). It indicates that the native English speakers showed obvious differences in PTR and ALP. With the detailed analysis of the recorded files, it is found that though the speech rate of the native English speakers was faster than Chinese subjects, they paused longer when dealing with the complex tested sentences. For example, Nick had difficulty in dealing with the sentence: " 'Can you tell me how to get to the nearest restaurant?' the man asked the policeman." and he had a very long pause. All the four subjects had much in common when dealing with the complex tested sentences. For another example, when faced with the sentence "'What did Edison do to help the doctor operate on his mother ?' The teacher asked.", all of them spent much pause time. It shows the similarity between the two groups of the native English and non-native English subjects. That is to say, when the task is very difficult, it is possible for the native English speakers to perform unsatisfactorily.

In addition, in order to explore the effects of procedural memory on oral production, the correlation between chunks and accuracy will be analyzed in **Section 7.3**.

7.2.1.2 Major results and discussion of the E-prime experiment

The results of response time (RT) of the 4 subjects who were involved in the task are presented in Table 7-2 (*Note*: The time unit is millisecond in the E-prime program).

Table 7-2 Descriptive Statistics of Response Time

Items	Gender	Subjects	Mean(ms)	*Std.* Deviation	N
ORT	F	NNE	7154.7500	2958.42394	12
		NE	5340.1667	2061.83104	12
		Total	6247.4583	2660.45019	24
	M	NNE	5950.6667	1693.04198	12
		NE	4279.0833	1988.71194	12
		Total	5114.8750	1997.82680	24
	Total	NNE	6552.7083	2436.17838	24
		NE	4809.6250	2053.86945	24
		Total	5681.1667	2396.74870	48
RRT	F	NNE	6889.1667	2374.74836	12
		NE	4855.0000	1914.75876	12
		Total	5872.0833	2351.59561	24
	M	NNE	9089.8333	1332.84411	12
		NE	8342.3333	2616.53356	12
		Total	8716.0833	2066.31863	24
	Total	NNE	7989.5000	2193.19638	24
		NE	6598.6667	2863.61736	24
		Total	7294.0833	2619.29237	48

Note: ORT: output response time; RRT: recognition response time; N: the number of the sentences tested; NE: native English speakers; NNE: non-native English speakers. F: female; M: male; ms: milliseconds.

In Table 7-2, the two types of response time (RT), ORT (output response time) and RRT (recognition response time), are shown in a very clear way. From Table 7-2, we can see the results of these two types of response time (RT) of each subject. These data will help with the analysis of fluency.

For further exploration of the differences and similarities between native speakers and non-native speakers, the Tests of Between-Subjects Effects were carried out with the Repeated Measures in SPSS. The data presented in Table 7-2 were applied. Table 7-3 shows the results of the Tests of Between-Subjects Effects.

Table 7-3   Tests of Between-Subjects Effects

Source	Type III Sum of Squares	df	Mean Square	F	Sig.
Corrected Model	424680677.167(a)	16	26542542.323	9.109	0.000
Intercept	4040570701.500	1	4040570701.500	1386.673	0.000
RT	62436004.167	1	62436004.167	21.427	0.000
nationality	58928602.042	1	58928602.042	20.224	0.000
gender	17573682.042	1	17573682.042	6.031	0.016
nationality * RT	744480.375	1	744480.375	0.255	0.615
gender * RT	94879290.042	1	94879290.042	32.561	0.000
Error	230194879.333	79	2913859.232		
Total	4695446258.000	96			
Corrected Total	654875556.500	95			

a R Squared = 0.648 (Adjusted R Squared = 0.577)

Through the analysis of the Tests of Between-Subjects effects, it is found that there existed very significant main effects in RT (response time) ($F=21.427$, $p=0.000$). As mentioned above, in the present study, RT included output response time (ORT) and recognition response time (RRT). From the analysis of the mean value of ORT and RRT, the time spent in output (Mean of total subjects: 5681.1667 milliseconds) was less than that spent in recognition (Mean of total subjects: 7294.0833 milliseconds). The result may be because the subjects spent more time rereading the tested sentence until they fully understood or memorized it. In the tested sentences, there were no new words to the subjects. Therefore, it may be because the subjects were not familiar with the sentence pattern: the object clause structure in indirect speech. This supposition was verified by the retrospective interviews followed. The retrospective interviews indicated that the subjects were hesitant when they saw the tested sentences appear in the screen and tried to remember these sentences. Most of the time, they had to reread the sentences for better memory. According to Oxford (2006), the student's familiarity with the kind of cognitive operations required is considerably important when he/she actually perceives a given, cognitively complex task to be difficult. In this case, it was most likely that it was because of unfamiliarity with the object clause structure in indirect speech that led to the cognitive complexity of the subjects.

Table 7-3 shows that there existed very significant main effects in nationality ($F=20.224$, $p=0.000$). In the detailed analysis of Table 7-2, it is found that the native speakers spent much less time than the Chinese subjects in sentence output and sentence recognition (ORT: Mean of total native English speakers: 4809.6250 milliseconds; Mean of total Chinese: 6552.7083 milliseconds; RRT: Mean of total native English speakers: 6598.6667 milliseconds; Mean of total Chinese: 7989.5000 milliseconds). The analysis of the data indicates that the native speakers spoke faster than the Chinese subjects though it has already been accepted. It may suggest that the native speakers had the obvious advantages over the non-native English speakers even though these subjects were considered high-proficiency English speakers. As mentioned in the review of literature, oral production is a very complex process which involves physiological motor activities and psychological processes. With the combined action of these activities and processes, the ideas of the speakers can be orally produced. In this sense, it is not hard to understand that these activities and processes influence the oral production of L1 and L2 speakers. L1 speakers performed generally better than L2 speakers because they were better at physiological motor activities and psychological processes to varying degrees. Because the present study focused on procedural memory, it will explore the phenomenon from the procedural memory-based reasons in **Section 7.3**.

As shown in Table 7-3, it is found that there existed no significant interaction effects between RT (including recognition response time and output response time) and nationalities (non-native English speaking country: China; native English speaking countries: the US and Canada) ($F=0.255$, $p=0.615$). In the detailed analysis of Table 7-2, the time spent in recognition was found much longer that that spent in output for both Chinese (non-native speakers) and English native speakers (RRT: Mean of total Chinese: 7989.5000 milliseconds; Mean of total native English speakers: 6598.6667 milliseconds; ORT: Mean of total Chinese: 6552.7083 milliseconds; Mean of total native English speakers: 4809.6250 milliseconds).

From the analysis of response time of the 4 subjects who were involved in the task *"The Change of the Sentence Patterns"*, the major findings concerning the different nationalities are summarized as follows.

1. There existed no significant interaction effects between RT (including RRT and ORT) and nationalities (including Chinese and non-

Chinese) ($F=0.255$, $p=0.615$) (See Table 7-3). In the detailed analysis, it is found that the time spent in recognition was much longer that that spent in output for both Chinese (non-native speakers) and English native speakers. That is to say, both Chinese subjects and the subjects from English speaking countries spent longer time in recognition than in output.

2. Table 7-3 shows that the main effects of nationalities were significant ($F=20.244$, $p=0.000$). That is to say, Chinese subjects spent much more time in RRT and ORT than that of the native English speakers (Mean of total Chinese: RRT: 7989.5000 milliseconds; ORT: 6552.7083 milliseconds; Mean of native English speakers: RRT: 6598.6667 milliseconds; ORT: 4809.6250 milliseconds).

3. Table 7-3 indicates that the main effects of gender were significant ($F=6.031$, $p=0.016$). In detailed analysis, it is found that the time spent by two female subjects in recognition and output was much shorter than that spent by males from China and English speaking countries (Mean of total female subjects: ORT: 6247.4583 milliseconds; RRT: 5872.0833 milliseconds; Mean of total male subjects: ORT: 5114.8750 milliseconds; RRT: 8716.0833 milliseconds). However, because of the limited size of the sample, this finding needs to be verified in further study in the future.

From the findings, a conclusion can be drawn that in the present study, the native English speakers were more fluent than the high-proficiency English speakers in oral production of the object clause in indirect speech. However, some literature holds different opinions. For example, Munro and Derwing (1995) reported that when Mandarin speakers who had been in Canada for 4 years produced English, their utterances were significantly longer than those of native speakers of English. Riggenbach (1991) also reported such rate differences and suggested that L2 speaking rate was faster for more advanced L2 learners (Chakraborty, Goffman & Smith, 2008). The possible reasons for the differences between the research of Munro and Derwing (1995) and Riggenbach (1991) and the present study lie in the following aspects. First, it may be because of the limited size of the sample in the present study. If the size of the subjects was enlarged, the results may be different from the ones of the current study. Second, it may be due to the language environment and practice time. In the English speaking countries, L2 speakers can be immersed in L2 environment, which is beneficial to them to obtain more practice of L2 and may help L2 speakers do better in oral production. To the Chinese subjects in this experiment, they did not have the beneficial English environment for practising English. They still could not surpass the native English speakers though their oral English was better than most Chinese English subjects. In addition, practice time is of great importance. As a matter of fact, the more the L2 speakers could practise their English, the higher their oral English proficiency was.

7.2.2 Major results and discussion for accuracy

In the task of *"The Change of the Sentence Patterns"*, the indices of accuracy mainly included macro assessment including NC (the number of sentences which are correct in sentence builders and sentence patterns) and micro assessment including REP (ratio of errors in pronunciation) and REULU (ratio of errors in use of linguistic units) as indicated in **Section 5.6**.

On the basis of the collected data, the researcher conducted an independent samples *t*-test to explore the differences between native English speakers and non-native speakers. The results are presented in Table 7-4 (N=24).

Table 7-4　Independent Samples t-Test of Accuracy of Native and Non-Native English Speakers

Items	Mean NE	Std D	Mean NNE	Std D	t	df	Sig.(2-tailed)
NC	0.750	0.44233	0.9583	0.20412	-2.095	32.371	0.044
REP	0.000	0.00000	0.3333	0.56466	-2.892	23.000	0.008
REULU	1.417	1.21285	0.8333	0.48154	2.190	30.075	0.036

Note: NC: the number of sentences which are correct in sentence builders and sentence patterns; REP: ratio of errors in pronunciation; REULU: ratio of errors in use of linguistic units; NE: native English speakers; NNE: non-native English speakers.

Table 7-4 indicates that there existed significant differences in NC, REP and REULU ($p<0.05$). However, by further analysis, it is found that the native speakers did better in pronunciation while they did not perform better than the Chinese subjects in sentence builders and sentence patterns (Mean NE: 0.750; Mean NNE: 0.9583) and in use of linguistic units (Mean NE: 1.417; Mean NNE: 0.8333). It indicates that the native English speakers were not as good as the Chinese English speakers at the grammar about the object clause structure in indirect speech. It may be the case that the native English speakers were not systematically trained in grammar about the object clause structure in indirect speech. According to the interviews with the native English speakers, they stated that they acquired the grammatical knowledge from the face-to-face communications with others. They did not pay too much attention to the grammar if their talks were acceptable in communication. They acknowledged that it was not surprising in their countries to find some native English speakers to choose the course "English Grammar" when they were in the university. It is also the case in China. Though Chinese is the mother tongue of Chinese people, not every Chinese knows well about the grammar of Chinese language.

As to the correctness of the answers, it is found that, Li, the

Chinese female subject, did the best in sentence builders and sentence patterns in the task "*The Change of the Sentence Patterns*" while the two native English speakers did not perform well. In detailed analysis of the scripts of the subjects, the native English speakers mostly failed in the change of tense while the Chinese subjects often ignored the change of the adverbials of time and pronouns such as "he" and "she". It shows that it is not always the case that all the native English speakers should be better than non-native English speakers in all the indices of oral production. The native English speakers in the present study were not good at the complex sentence patterns like the object clause structure in indirect speech because they did not often access to such tests.

It is worth noticing that the native English speakers and the Chinese subjects had different answers to the change of the imperative sentence into indirect speech. Take the following sentences for example.

— "Let's go shopping." he said.

The supposed answer was:

— He suggested us going shopping.

The answers of the two Chinese subjects were completely consistent to the supposed answer. However, to the researcher's surprise, the answers of the two native English speakers were similar as follows.

— He said let's go shopping.

According to the requirement of the task, their answer was not ideal. However, as a matter of fact, their answer was acceptable in the face-to-face communication, especially on the occasion when Person A reports Person B's utterance "Let's go shopping" to Person C.

The reason for the phenomenon may lie in the following aspects. As mentioned in **Section 2.5.1**, in China, English teachers tend to teach students to master the grammatical knowledge concerning a certain sentence pattern and then the learners can remember and grasp the sentence pattern by analyzing its grammatical structure and doing many intensive exercises. The teaching and learning approach of this kind depends on the type of procedural memory parasitizing in declarative memory and influencing the automatic processing of its retrieval and application (Chen, 2009). The knowledge they master and the language units such as chunks or idiomatic expressions they produce have been analyzed. However, in the case of the two native English speakers, they acquire language in the native language atmosphere. Because the common way for them to learn the use of a specific sentence pattern is from the face-to-face communication with their parents, teachers, friends and so on, they can use it correctly and acceptably in the face-to-face communication without knowing and analyzing its grammar. From this case, it can be seen that the native English speakers tend to use the first type of procedural memory which is separately stored in the brain and has nothing to do with declarative memory.

From the retrospective interview, the researcher got to know that most native English speakers were not well educated in English grammar when they were very young, which leads to the fact that many native English speakers do not have a good master of grammar even when they are grown up. If the native English speakers are not familiar with some grammatical phenomena in speaking, they would not perform well in the test. In contrast, the high-proficiency subjects from China practice frequently and grasp many skills for memorizing more words, chunks, collocations or idioms. Consequently, they can do better than the native speakers in the rule-based tasks in oral production. This finding may supplement the findings in **Chapter Six** which stress the importance of procedural memory.

7.2.3　Major results and discussion for complexity

In the experiment introduced in **Section 5.6.5.1.3**, the cognitive complexity was explored by comparing the recognition response time (RRT) spent by the subjects. From the length of the recognition time, we may infer the speed and the cognitive complexity of the processing.

The researcher also got a glimpse into the cognitive processing by the retrospective interviews in which she asked some questions about the cognitive processing of the object clause structure in indirect speech.

The analysis of cognitive complexity is the analysis of an aspect of a person's cognitive functioning which at one end is defined by the use of many constructs with many relationships to one another (complexity) and at the other end by the use of few constructs with limited relationships to one another (simplicity) (Pervin, 1984). According to Oxford (2006), cognitive complexity involves a person component (unobservable cognition and observable behavior) and a task structure component. Therefore, in this case study, RRT was analyzed as an index to explore the cognitive complexity.

Then, we can get the mean value of recognition response time of each subject. The data were analyzed by Independent Samples t-Test with SPSS as shown Table 7-5.

Table 7-5 Independent Samples t-Test of Complexity of Native and Non-native English Speakers

Items	Mean NE	Std D	Mean NNE	Std D	t	df	Sig.(2-tailed)
RRT	6598.667	2863.61736	7989.500	2193.19638	-1.889	46	0.065

Note: RRT: recognition response time; NE: native English speakers; NNE: non-native English speakers.

From Table 7-5, it is found that there existed significant differences between the native English speakers and the non-native English speakers (p=0.000). In the detailed analysis, it is found that the native English speakers spent less RRT than the non-native English speakers. It indicates that the native English speakers can reduce the cognitive complexity more quickly than the non-native English speakers. The reason may lie in the fact that English was their mother tongue. The fluent use of mother tongue may help native English speakers reduce the nervousness and the psychological pressure. From the angle of the information processing framework of the present study, if the subject spent less time in the stage of input, he would possibly show some advantages over the peers in total response time. The less time the subject spent in RRT, the less cognitive complexity he experienced. In addition, the retrospective interviews were carried out to investigate the reasons that the native English speakers have less cognitive complexity.

7.3　The Effects of Chunks

As mentioned in **Section 6.3**, the use of chunks was explored in oral production as well. In this section, the findings as to the influence of chunks on oral production will be reported.

Table 7-6 shows the correlation analysis between chunk frequency and the indices of frequency, accuracy and complexity in this case study.

Table 7-6　Correlation Analysis between Chunk Frequency and the Indices of Oral Production

Fluency				Accuracy			Complexity
SR	PTR	MLR	ALP	NC	REP	REULU	RRT
0.353*	-0.028	0.261	0.003	-0.008	-0.108	0.090	0.073

*** Correlation is significant at the 0.01 level (2-tailed).

As Table 7-6 shows, in the task "*The Change of the Sentence Patterns*", chunk frequency did not have significant correlation with the indices of frequency no matter whether the correlation is positive or negative, except for SR which has some correlation with chunk frequency. The reason may be because the chunk frequency of the Chinese high-proficiency subjects and the native English speakers is similar to each other when comparing these subjects no matter whether the produced chunks can be analyzed or not. The frequent use of chunks may help with the improved oral proficiency. This reveals the importance of chunk frequency for the high-proficiency speakers both from native English speaking countries and non-English speaking countries.

7.4 Major Factors Influencing Oral Production of the Object Clause Structure of Indirect Speech

The factors influencing oral production of the object clause structure of indirect speech were summarized from the feedbacks of the retrospective and opinion interviews made after the E-prime experiment. The results are reported in Table 7-7.

Table 7-7　Feedbacks of the Retrospective Interview

NEs	Implicit factors	nervousness
	Explicit factors	the difficulty of the task, the length of sentences tested, the familiarity to the words (meaning and pronunciation)
NNEs	Implicit factors	Anxiety, self-confidence, L1 interference
	Explicit factors	the difficulty of the task, the length of sentences tested, the familiarity to the words (meaning and pronunciation)

Note: NEs: the native English speakers; NNEs: the non-native English speakers.

From Table 7-7, we can see that the native English speakers were mostly influenced by the explicit factors such as the difficulty of the task, the length of sentences tested, the familiarity to sentence patterns while the non-native English speakers were influenced by both implicit and explicit factors. As to the implicit factor, the researcher found Kate was somewhat nervous at the beginning of the E-prime experiment. When asked about the reason, Kate explained that the phenomenon was very common at the beginning of any tests because she was a little scared of tests. To the non-native English speakers, they sometimes had the similar problem like Kate. Therefore, it is suggested that the subjects should be psychologically well prepared for the purpose of avoiding the invalid results. However, in the current study, the unsatisfactory emotion did not influence the data and the results significantly because Kate managed to adapt herself to the test very soon.

The discussion of the implicit and explicit factors of the non-native English speakers can be referred to **Section 6.5.1**.

7.5 Summary

This chapter presents the results and discussion for the research questions as to the similarities and differences between the native-English speakers and non-native English speakers in the object cause structure in indirect speech in the aspects such as fluency, accuracy and complexity as well as the effects of procedural memory on their oral production.

Chapter Eight
RESULTS AND DISCUSSION (3): THE EFFECTS OF THE PRINCIPLES OF PROCEDURAL MEMORY ON ORAL PRODUCTION

8.1 Introduction

This chapter reports the major results and discussion for the longitudinal case study and the cross-comparative case study conducted in **Section 5.7** and **Section 5.8**. This general question is addressed by finding answers to the following two specific questions:

Question 3: What are the effects of procedural memory on the improvement of oral production of the object clause structure in indirect speech?

1. What progress does the low level L2 subject make with the scientific oral training approaches in light of the principles of procedural memory?

2. If the oral training approaches in light of the principles of procedural memory have effects on oral production, what aspects of oral production (for example, pronunciation, use of linguistic use, etc.) will benefit most in the case of the oral production of the object clause structure in indirect speech?

Meanwhile, the fourth research question concerning the major factors influencing the application of procedural memory in oral production of the object clause structure in indirect speech and in oral production in general is also addressed in this chapter.

The results for fluency, accuracy and complexity of the two tasks (Task One: *The Change of Sentence Patterns*; Task Two: *Questions and Answers*) are presented in **Section 8.2**, **Section 8.3** and **Section 8.4** respectively. The possible reasons or the significance of the findings will be discussed in each section. **Section 8.5** reports the major findings and discussion for retrospective interviews made with Jun, the subject in the longitudinal case study.

Some other findings are reported and discussed in **Section 8.6** since they have some relevance to procedural memory, oral production and so on.

8.2 Major Results and Discussion for Fluency

As introduced in **Section 5.7**, a longitudinal case study was made in order to explore fluency of Jun. In this case study, Jun took three times of oral tests concerning Task One: *The Change of the Sentence Patterns*, and other three times of oral tests concerning Task Two: *Questions and Answers*. The data were collected from these oral tests. In addition, the data of Gang and Li, two Chinese high-proficiency English speakers participating in the previous comparative study, as well as the data of 16 high-proficiency subjects participating in the previous cross-sectional study were utilized for the further exploration of Jun's progress during the three months.

8.2.1 Major results and discussion for fluency in Task One: The Change of the Sentence Patterns

In the longitudinal case study, the indices of fluency include Speech

Rate (SR), Mean Length of Run (MLR), Phonation Time Ratio (PTR) and Average Length of Pause (ALP) (See **Section 8.2.1.1**). Just as how the researcher dealt with the comparative case study in the previous chapter, the total response time (TRT) was used as another index to assess fluency since fluency is closely related to time. The response time (RT) is an important index in this temporal analysis, which includes recognition response time (RRT) and output response time (ORT). The results and discussion for response time will be reported in **Section 8.2.1.2**.

8.2.1.1 Major results and discussion for SR, PTR, MLR and ALP in Task One

As introduced in **Section 5.7.5**, with the SPSS file, univariate analysis was employed for descriptive analysis to investigate the tendency of the two types of response time: output response time (ORT) and recognition response time (RRT).

Table 8-1 shows the results of univariate analysis of the indices such as SR, PTR, MLR and ALP in fluency of Jun's performance in three times of oral tests concerning Task One. In addition, the result of chunk frequency is also listed to explore the change of the use of chunks of Jun during the oral training.

Table 8-1 Univariate Analysis of Frequency and Chunks of Task One

			Jun			Gang	Li
Items	F	p	Mean 1	Mean 2	Mean 3	Mean 4	Mean 5
SR	10.740	0.000	93.000	119.750	117.750	148.830	131.000
PTR	3.229	0.052	0.742	0.786	0.841	0.866	0.890
MLR	20.096	0.000	4.267	6.103	6.367	7.833	8.375
ALP	11.976	0.000	1.307	0.722	0.671	0.459	0.565
CF	11.000	0.000	1.500	2.333	2.333	2.417	2.417

Note: SR: speech rate; PTR: phonation time ratio; MLR: the mean length of run; ALP: average length of pause; CF: chunk frequency; The values of F and p in the table were obtained through the univariate analysis of Jun's three oral tests.

As shown in Table 8-1, Jun made progress in SR, PTL, MLR and ALP in different degrees. In the detailed analysis, his progress in SR, MLR, ALP was very obvious ($p=0.000$). From the mean speech rate in each oral test it is found that after the three-month training, he spoke faster and meanwhile the time for pauses was reduced. As to PTR (phonation time ratio), the change was not statistically significant ($p=0.052$) while by further analysis it is found that he also made some progress in PTR (Mean 1:0.742; Mean 2:0.786; Mean 3:0.841). As introduced in **Chapter Four**, phonation time ratio is defined as total time spent speaking divided by total time to produce speech sample. From the results of PTR, it can be seen that in Jun's total response time, he did not spend all the time speaking. The pause time he spent was longer than that of Gang and Li, these two Chinese high-proficiency English speakers. From this case, it is found that pause time is one of the influential factors influencing the speakers' fluency. The reason for the disfluent subject to have longer pause time may lie in the fact that though through three-month training, Jun was not as familiar as Gang and Li with the object clause structure in indirect speech. In this case, he needed more practice of such sentence pattern to achieve an ideal result.

In order to further explore Jun's changes during the oral training, the researcher reported the results of Post Hoc Tests with Turkey HSD of the indices in three times of oral tests. Meanwhile, each index of Gang and Li was applied to make a comparison with Jun's changes (See Table 8-2). Take SR for example.

Table 8-2 Pairwise Comparison of SR

Dependent Variable: SR

(I) Subjects	(J) Subjects	Mean Difference (I-J)	*Std.* Error	*Sig.*(a)
2.00	1.00	26.750(*)	9.732	0.008
	3.00	2.000	9.732	0.838

Chapter Eight
RESULTS AND DISCUSSION (3):THE EFFECTS OF THE PRINCIPLES OF PROCEDURAL MEMORY ON ORAL PRODUCTION

continued

(I) Subjects	(J) Subjects	Mean Difference (I-J)	Std. Error	Sig.(a)
3.00	1.00	24.750(*)	9.732	0.014
	2.00	-2.000	9.732	0.838
4.00	1.00	55.833(*)	9.732	0.000
	2.00	29.083(*)	9.732	0.004
	3.00	31.083(*)	9.732	0.002
5.00	1.00	38.000(*)	9.732	0.000
	2.00	11.250	9.732	0.253
	3.00	13.250	9.732	0.179
	4.00	-17.833	9.732	0.072

* The mean difference is significant at the .05 level.
 a Adjustment for multiple comparisons: Least Significant Difference (equivalent to no adjustments).
Note: 1: Time 1 of Jun's oral test; 2: Time 2 of Jun's oral test; 3: Time 3 of Jun's oral test; 4:Gang; 5:Li

From Table 8-2, it is found that as to SR (speech rate), there existed significant differences between the first and second oral tests and between the first and third oral tests of Jun ($p<0.05$). It indicates that after a period time of oral training, Jun made progress in SR. Though between the second test and the third test, the researcher did not arrange any special tasks for Jun to take, he still performed better than the first time. From this view, it is found that after being trained Jun was influenced by the approaches based on the principles of procedural memory, which can be verified by the increasing chunk frequency. With enough practice, proceduralization and reconstructuring of the procedural knowledge may gradually develop, which may play a decisive role in implicitizing the learners' implicit representation and improving the efficiency of the application of language (Wu, 1999).

As shown in Table 8-2, Jun did make much progress in SR while compared with Gang and Li, he did not surpass them in the performance of SR. The possible reasons for this phenomenon lie in the following aspects.

(1) The time of oral training was not long enough, so during this period, Jun could not speak as well as those high-proficiency subjects. From the interviews made with Gang and Li, the possible reason can be verified. Gang and Li stated that they often spoke English to other people or read aloud or recited many English texts. These approaches were very effective to improve their oral English as a whole.

(2) The use of chunks was not as frequent as Gang and Li. As indicated in Table 8-1, the chunk frequency of Jun (Mean value of the third time: 2.333) is not as satisfactory as that of Gang and Li (Mean value: 2.417). The feasible approach for Jun to improve his oral English is to practice the use of chunks in order to develop more schematic information in his mind, since the use of chunks is often influenced by the length of practice, the familiarity with more fixed phrases or expressions and so on.

(3) Age may be another factor influencing the effects of Jun's oral training. According to the Critical Period Hypothesis (Krashen, 1982; Singleton, 2002), during this critical period, typically early in life, there is a (heightened) sensitivity to stimuli that are necessary for the development of the first or second language acquisition while after this period, there is a non-linear decline in sensitivity. Since Jun was 24 years old when he took part in the oral training, it was very difficult for him to obtain an ideal effect within three months. However, the window for adults to learn a second language never completely closes and Jun still needs more practice in oral English.

By Pairwise Comparisons, it is found that Jun made much progress in the indices of fluency such as SR, MLR and ALP ($p<0.05$). It is worth mentioning that from Table 8-1, it is found that Jun's performance in

PTR was not statistically different ($p=0.052$) while by further exploration of the results of Pairwise Comparisons, it is found that the difference between the first time and the third time is significant ($p=0.014$). Besides, there is no significant difference between Time 3 and Time 4 ($p=0.838$) and between Time 4 and Time 5 ($p=0.072$). It indicates that the performance of Jun in the third oral test can be considered almost as good as Gang and Li. This finding confirms the effect of procedural-memory-based principles in one's oral proficiency. As introduced in **Chapter Two**, the procedural memory system is rooted in portions of the frontal cortex (including Broca's area and the supplementary motor area), the basal ganglia, parietal cortex and the dentate nucleus of the cerebellum. Once these regions of one's brain are activated, they will do a favor for the learner in memorizing procedural knowledge or skills. Meanwhile, since procedural memory is also related to motor skills and habits, intensive practice will inevitably lead to automaticity. That is why Jun improved in the performance of the indices of fluency. In addition, it is worth mentioning that though there were no special training plans for Jun between the second test and the third test, the results of the third test shows Jun's performance was still satisfactory. It may be because the procedural memory system is implicitly developed in the learning of new and in the control of the long-established, motor and cognitive skills and habits, especially those involving sequences (Aldridge & Berridge, 1998; Mishkin, Malamut & Bachevalier, 1984; Schacter & Tulving, 1994; Squire & Knowlton, 2000; Willingham, 1998; Ullman, 2005). Once procedural memory has developed, the effects of it are not easy to disappear due to the influence of proceduralization which undertakes the transition of knowledge from declarative knowledge to procedural knowledge by practice and reconstructuring of the procedural knowledge (Wu, 1999). It is the same story as the example in which once a person has learned how to ride a bicycle, he can ride the bicycle well even after many years. In addition, schema theory may be employed to explain this phenomenon as well. According to schema theory, the knowledge stored in memory is organized as a set of schemata or mental representations, each of which incorporates all the knowledge of a given type of object or event that we have acquired from past experience. The prior knowledge can be retrieved when the schemata are activated (Driscoll, 2000).

8.2.1.2 Results and discussion for the response time

Response time (RT) was another index of fluency in this study. RT includes the two types: recognition response time (RRT) and output response time (ORT). The results of the change of the response time of Jun in Task One are shown in Table 8-3. Meanwhile, the data of Gang and Li are also displayed for comparison (***Note***: The time unit of response time is ms, short for millisecond).

Table 8-3   Univariate Analysis of RT: Jun's Three Oral Tests vs. Gang & Li

Items	Jun					Gang	Li
	F	p	Mean 1	Mean 2	Mean 3	Mean 4	Mean 5
RRT	74.374	0.000	10886.750	5054.667	5426.750	9089.833	6889.167
ORT	2.914	0.068	10031.080	8239.667	8527.417	5950.667	7154.750
RRT*ORT	30.846	0.000					

Note: RRT: recognition response time; ORT: output response time.
The values of F and p in the table were obtained through univariate analysis of Jun's three oral tests.

As indicated in Table 8-3, the mean time of RRT (recognition response time) from the first oral test to the third is 10886.750 milliseconds, 5054.667 milliseconds and 5426.750 milliseconds respectively. These data indicate that during the three-month training, Jun made much progress in the RRT (p=0.000). In the first and second

Chapter Eight
RESULTS AND DISCUSSION (3):THE EFFECTS OF THE PRINCIPLES OF PROCEDURAL MEMORY ON ORAL PRODUCTION

oral tests, the change was obvious. It may be due to the guidance of the oral training on the basis of the principles of procedural memory. According to Anderson's ACT theory, during the development of automatic skills, conscious representations are gradually transformed into unconscious ones. The theory proposed that human cognition arose as an interaction between declarative and procedural knowledge structures. Learning a language, like any other type of skill learning (for example, driving a car or playing tennis), involves the development of procedures that transform declarative knowledge into a form that makes for easy and efficient performance. This transition of declarative to procedural knowledge takes place in three stages: the cognitive stage, the associative stage and the autonomous stage. In the third stage, performances become more or less totally automatic and errors disappear. The learner relies less on working memory and performance takes place below the threshold of consciousness. Therefore, in the present study, after being orally trained, Jun's performance may be in the third stage, which was indicated by the less RRT.

In the further exploration of Jun's changes in RRT during the oral training, with the Post Hoc Tests, it is found that by Pairwise Comparisons, Jun's RRT decreased obviously in the second oral test ($p=0.000$) while there is no significant difference between the two and third times of oral tests ($p=0.568$). It can be verified by the mean values of Time 2 and Time 3 (Mean 2: 5054.667 milliseconds; Mean 3: 5426.750 milliseconds). It is found that in the third oral test, Jun's RRT increased slightly, which shows that Jun retrogressed in RRT. The increase of Jun's RRT may be because of lack of practice during the second and third times of oral tests. Though he spent more RRT in the third time than that in the second time, his progress was encouraging. With the Pairwise Comparison, We also find there were significant differences between Jun's second time of oral test and Gang, between his second time of oral test and Li, between his second time of oral test and Gang and between his second time of oral test and Li (p=0.000). Table 8-3 also indicates that in these two times of oral tests, Jun spent much less RRT than Gang and Li. This finding significantly supports the approaches based on the principles of procedural memory, in which the use of chunks can help reduce the number of channels during the input of data and so less processing power and less bandwidth will be used (Miller, 1956). Thus, it can save much time of planning and processing during oral production. Meanwhile, it shows that Jun was more familiar with the object clause structure in indirect speech in oral production, and that is why he spent less time for sentence processing. This finding supports Oxford's statement in cognitive complexity that the student's familiarity with the kind of cognitive operations required is considerably important when he/she actually perceives a given, cognitively complex task to be difficult (Oxford, 2006).

In Table 8-3, the changes in ORT (output response time) were not statistically significant ($p=0.068$). That result is because the comparison was made among the three times of oral tests. However, based on the data with the Post Hoc Tests, the following significant findings have been obtained.

First, Jun's ORT reduced obviously in the second oral test ($p=0.046$), which shows that Jun's oral English was more fluent compared with his first time of oral test. As mentioned above, during the development of automatic skills, this transition from declarative knowledge to procedural knowledge takes places in three stages: the cognitive stage, the associative stage and the autonomous stage (Anderson, 1976). In the present study, after being orally trained with the principles of procedural memory, Jun's performance may be in the third stage, which was featured by being automatic. In this case, automaticity was indicated by the less ORT.

Second, there was no significant difference between the second and third times of oral tests ($p=0.744$). Table 8-3 indicates that Jun's ORT increased slightly from the second time to the third time but the change was not so obvious. This phenomenon may be because of lack of practice during the second half of the longitudinal study. As we know, practice plays an important role in the development of procedural memory. According to Anderson (1976), O'malley, Chamot and Walker (1987) and so on, learning begins with declarative knowledge which slowly becomes proceduralized, and that the mechanism by which this takes place is practice.

Third, with univariate analysis, it is also found that the types of response time have significant main effect ($F=30.846$, $p=0.000$). It indicates that the intensive practice is a main factor influencing the effect of training.

Graph 8-1:

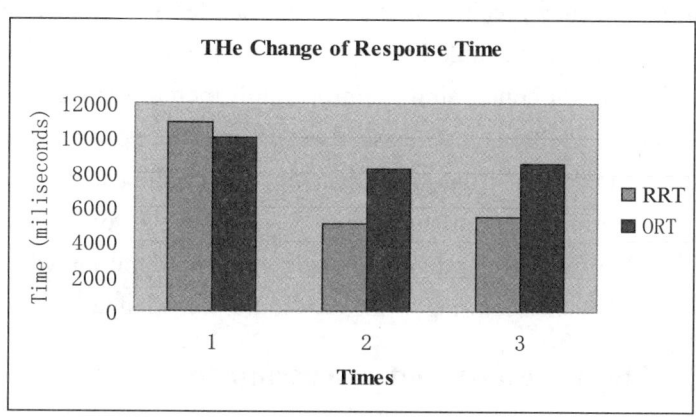

Note: RRT: recognition response time; ORT: output response time

Graph 8-1 shows the changes of output time and recognition time in Task One more clearly. From Graph 8-1, we can easily find the progress made by Jun in the process of the training of oral production.

Meanwhile, in Task One, it is found that the response time of recognition and output in the third oral test were somewhat longer than that of the second time, which may be because of the fact that the subject was asked to do nothing at the interval between the second and the third oral tests and therefore the lack of practice might lead to such retrogress. However, compared with what Jun performed in the first test, it can still be concluded that after a period of training, Jun, the low-proficiency subject, made much progress in RRT and ORT, which confirms the effects of procedural memory in oral training. According to Ullman and other researchers (Aldridge & Berridge, 1998; Mishkin, Malamut & Bachevalier, 1984; Schacter & Tulving, 1994; Squire & Knowlton, 2000; Willingham, 1998; Ullman, 2005), the procedural memory system is an implicit system, which is related to the control of long-established, motor and cognitive skills and habits, especially those involving sequences. Once procedural memory has developed through repetition, rehearsal, recitation and so on, the effects of it cannot easily disappear. Jun's case should be employed as a good example to support Ullman's opinion concerning the procedural memory system and his DP model. In addition, Jun's case also supports the positive influence of proceduralization in language learning. According to Wu (1999), proceduralization is important because it is beneficial to the transition of knowledge from declarative knowledge to procedural knowledge by practice and reconstructuring of the procedural knowledge.

8.2.2 Major results and discussion for fluency in Task Two

Table 8-4 shows the results of univariate analysis of the indices such as SR (speech rate), PTR (phonation time ratio), MLR (mean length of run) and ALP (average length of pause) in fluency of Jun's performance in three times of oral tests concerning Task Two. Meanwhile, the result of

Chapter Eight

chunk frequency is also listed for the exploration of the change of the use of chunks of Jun during the oral training.

Table 8-4   Univariate Analysis of Fluency and Chunks in Task Two

Items	Jun					HPs
	F	p	Mean 1	Mean 2	Mean 3	Mean 4
SR	9.256	0.002	145.667	180.833	179.000	187.667
PTR	6.588	0.009	0.600	0.831	0.805	0.845
MLR	3.577	0.054	5.737	7.638	8.122	11.068
ALP	1.858	0.190	1.271	0.803	0.716	0.619
CF	9.800	0.002	1.500	2.667	2.667	2.895

Note: SR: speech rate; PTR: phonation time ratio; MLR: the mean length of run; ALP: average length of pause; CF: chunk frequency; HPs: 16 high-proficiency students who participated in the cognitive behavioral experiments in **Chapter Four**; Mean 4: Average value of each item of these 16 high-proficiency students. The values of F and p in the table were obtained through the univariate analysis of Jun's three oral tests.

As shown in Table 8-4, compared with the first oral test, Jun made progress in the indices such as SR, PTR, MLR and ALP in different degrees. It is found that Jun made much progress in SR and PTR ($p<0.05$) and the changes of MLR and ALP are not of significant difference ($p>0.05$). This result may be due to the way of analysis applied in the longitudinal study. It can only analyze the data of the three oral tests as a whole. In order to further explore Jun's changes during the oral training, the researcher reports the results of Post Hoc Tests with Turkey HSD of the indices of three oral tests. Meanwhile, average value of each index of 16 high-proficiency subjects was applied to make a comparison with Jun's changes (See Table 8-4).

By Pairwise Comparisons, compared with the first oral tests, it can be found that Jun made much progress in SR, PTR and MLR ($p<0.05$) in the second and third oral tests. From Table 8-4, it can be found that Jun's ALP was not statistically different ($p=0.190$), which indicates the pause time did not reduce obviously. However, by further exploration of the results of Pairwise Comparisons, it is found that the difference between the first time and HPs is significant ($p=0.029$) while there was no significant difference between Time 2 and HPs ($p=0.515$) and between Time 3 and Time of HPs ($p=0.732$). It indicates that the pause time of Jun still decreased compared with the first oral test. In this sense, it can be concluded that Jun's oral production in the object clause structure in indirect speech was more fluent compared with the first oral test.

In addition, chunk frequency increased obviously ($p=0.002$). It is consistent with the findings of the studies of chunks in which chunks are relevant to fluency (Howarth, 1998; Yuan & Guo, 2010). The finding is very significant in the emphasis on the importance of the procedural memory-based oral training approaches. According to the review of formulaic language in **Chapter Two**, several theories of cognition can be integrated with knowledge about formulaic language and formulaic sequences to produce models of language production, including controlled and automatic processing (McLaughlin, Rossmann & McLeod, 1983), declarative and procedural knowledge (Anderson, 1983c; Levelt, 1989), etc. It can be said that formulaic language and formulaic sequences are related to "how-to-do" (procedural) knowledge. As part of formulaic language, chunking is a fundamental operation occurring in the human memory. By using chunking, we reduce the number of channels during the input of data (for instance, acquisition of a new language, chess playing, memorizing a phone number), so we use less processing power and less bandwidth (Miller, 1956). In other words, chunking can help with the development of automatic processing and hence the time spent in response can be reduced.

Chapter Eight
RESULTS AND DISCUSSION (3):THE EFFECTS OF THE PRINCIPLES OF PROCEDURAL MEMORY ON ORAL PRODUCTION

8.3 Major Results and Discussion for Accuracy

This section includes the results and discussion for accuracy in oral production of Jun, who took three oral tests concerning Task One: *The Change of the Sentence Patterns* and the other three times of oral tests concerning Task Two: *Questions and Answers*. The data were collected from these oral tests. Besides, in order to make a comparison with the high-proficiency speakers in China, the data of Gang and Li as well as of the 16 high-proficiency subjects were applied.

8.3.1 Major results and discussion for accuracy in Task One

In the longitudinal case study, the indices of accuracy include NC (the number of sentences which are correct in sentence builders and sentence patterns), REP (ratio of errors in pronunciation) and REULU (ratio of errors in use of linguistic units).

Table 8-5 Univariate Analysis of Jun's Three times of Accuracy in Task One

	Jun					Gang	Li
Items	F	p	Mean 1	Mean 2	Mean 3	Mean 4	Mean 5
NC	1.978	0.154	0.417	0.750	0.750	0.917	1.000
REP	10.684	0.000	1.667	0.583	0.583	0.250	0.417
REULU	9.434	0.001	2.000	0.583	0.750	0.917	0.750

Note: NC: the number of sentences which are correct in sentence builders and sentence patterns; REP: ratio of errors in pronunciation; REULU: ratio of errors in use of linguistic units. The values of *F* and *p* in the table were obtained through univariate analysis of Jun's three oral tests.

As shown in Table 8-5, Jun's REP and REULU reduced obviously ($p<0.05$). It indicates that, with the oral training, Jun made fewer errors in pronunciation and the use of linguistic units. As mentioned in **Chapter Four**, the conceptual framework of the present study emphasizes the role of errors in oral production. In the field of psycholinguistics, speech error data have been used the research on linguistic mental processes, providing empirical evidence for testing hypotheses about language and language behavior (Jiang, 2001). The reduction of REP and REULU of Jun can be employed as evidence for the improvement in accuracy.

In order to further explore Jun's changes in REP and REULU during the oral training, with the Post Hoc Tests, it is found that according to Pairwise Comparisons, Jun's REP and REULU in the second and third oral tests were the same, which were both less than that in the first oral tests. Compared with Gang and Li, there was no significant difference between Time 2 and Gang, between Time 2 and Li, Time 3 and Gang and between Time 3 and Li ($p>0.05$). It can also prove that Jun made much progress in pronunciation and the use of linguistic units. As to NC, from Table 8-5, it is found that there is no significant difference ($p=0.154$) while by further exploring of the results of Pairwise Comparisons, it is found the differences between Time 1 and Time 2, between Time 1 and Time 3, between Time 1 and Gang, and between Time 1 and Li are all significant ($p<0.05$). In this sense, it can be concluded that Jun improved in the performance of NC during the three oral tests.

Table 8-1 shows that chunk frequency increased obviously ($p=0.000$). It is consistent with the findings of the studies of chunks in which chunks are relevant to accuracy (Yuan & Guo, 2010; Zhen, 2009). It indicates that with the help of procedural memory-based oral training approaches, Jun was better at the use of chunks, which helped improve accuracy in the grasp of the object clause structure in indirect speech and the use of linguistic units. This finding also supports the role of chunks in language learning mentioned in **Section 2.5.2.3**.

It is worth noticing that is an effective way to orally train Jun by constantly changing the linguistic units within the sentence structure. During the oral training of the use of the object clause structure in indirect speech, the present researcher asked Jun to spend at least one hour practising reading the 20 sentences used in *Listen and Repeat* by changing the subjects, verbs, adverbials of each sentence.

For example, the original sentence is 'She said Jacky would be busy with his study.'

The subject should practice like:

—He said Jacky would be busy with his study.

—He said Mary would be busy with her study.

—Mom said Jacky would be busy with his study.

By constant practice, Jun was able to deal with various sentences generated from the same sentence structure and performed satisfactorily in accuracy. It indicates that during the oral training of Jun in use of the object clause structure in indirect speech, syntagmatic relations helped with the formation of procedural memory and were beneficial to the improvement of oral proficiency, especially in accuracy. The finding supports the view of Lyons (2002) and Zhang (2009) on the important role of syntagmatic relations.

8.3.2 Major results discussion for accuracy of Task Two

As analyzed in Task One, the indices of accuracy in second task also include NC, REP and REULU. Table 8-6 shows univariate analysis of Jun's three times of accuracy in Task Two.

Table 8-6 Univariate Analysis of Jun's Three times of Accuracy in Task Two

Items	Jun					HPs
	F	p	Mean 1	Mean 2	Mean 3	Mean 4
NC	2.500	0.116	0.500	1.000	0.833	0.867
REP	11.327	0.001	2.333	0.667	0.500	0.178
REULU	24.571	0.000	2.500	0.167	0.500	0.145

Note: NC: the number of sentences which are correct in sentence builders and sentence patterns; REP: ratio of errors in pronunciation; REULU: ratio of errors in use of linguistic units. The values of F and p in the table were obtained through the univariate analysis of Jun's three oral tests.

As shown in Table 8-6, Jun's REP and REULU decreased obviously ($p<0.05$). It indicates that, with the oral training, Jun made fewer errors in pronunciation and the use of linguistic units in Task Two. According to the conceptual framework of the present study in **Chapter Four**, the investigation of errors is of great significance in oral production because the data of speech errors can be employed to explore linguistic mental processes. In this sense, the reduced ratio of Jun in accuracy may prove his progress in pronunciations and the use of linguistic units in Task Two.

For further exploration of Jun's changes in REP and REULU during the oral training, with the Post Hoc Tests it is found that there were significant differences in Jun's REP and REULU between Time 1 and Time 2 and between Time 1 and Time 3 ($p<0.05$). Compared with high-proficiency subjects, there is no significant difference between Time 2 and Time 3, between Time 2 and HPs and between Time 3 and HPs ($p>0.05$). It can prove that Jun made much progress in pronunciation and the use of linguistic units. As to NC, from Table 8-6, it is found that there is no significant difference ($p=0.116$). However, by further exploration of the results of Pairwise Comparisons, it is found that the difference between Time 1 and Time 2 is significant ($p=0.020$). In this sense, it can be concluded that, to Jun, the number of sentences which were correct in sentence builders and sentence patterns increased. In other words, Jun improved in the performance of NC during the three oral tests.

Chunk frequency increased obviously ($p=0.000$) in Task Two (See Table 8-1). It is consistent with the findings of the studies of chunks in which chunks are relevant to accuracy (Yuan & Guo, 2010). The finding is of great significance because it indicates the importance of the procedural memory-based oral training approaches. As Ullman's DP model implies, procedural system subserves aspects of mental grammar (Pinker & Ullman, 2002). Because the focus of the present study was about syntax, it was a good case to be employed to show the effect of procedural memory. That is why during the three-month training, the progress of Jun was positive. In addition, Anderson's ACT model (Anderson, 1983b, 1983c) proposed that human cognition arose as an interaction between declarative and procedural knowledge structures. According to Chen (Chen, 2009), procedural memory can parasitize in declarative memory and influence the automatic processing of its retrieval and application. From this angle, the role of declarative memory is equally important. As **Appendix 8** shows, the training plans were made on the basis of procedural memory. Jun had already mastered sufficient declarative knowledge about the object clause structure in indirect speech, which was verified by the written test of his grammar. The good mastery of declarative knowledge helped Jun with the improvement of his oral proficiency. If he had not had grasped sufficient declarative knowledge and had been trained according to the same training plans, the results might not have been so satisfactory.

8.4　Major Results and Discussion for Complexity

In the longitudinal study, Jun took three oral tests concerning Task One: *The Change of the Sentence Patterns* and the other three oral tests concerning Task Two: *Questions and Answers*. As introduced in **Section 5.7.5.3**, the indices of complexity include response time in Task One, and language structure and cognitive complexity in Task Two. The data were collected from these oral tests.

This section includes the results and discussion for complexity in this longitudinal study. In addition, in order to make a comparison with the high-proficiency speakers in China, the data of Gang and Li participating in the comparative study as well as of the 16 high-proficiency subjects participating in the cross-sectional study were employed.

8.4.1　Major results and discussion for complexity in Task One

The assessment of complexity included complexity in language structure and cognitive complexity.

In Task One "*The Change of the Sentence Patterns*", the researcher assessed the cognitive complexity by comparing the recognition response time (RRT), which indicated the time for the subjects to plan and organize the utterances in order to test the familiarity of the subjects with the object clause structure in indirect speech.

In Task One, the index of complexity is RRT as shown in Table 8-7.

As mentioned in **Section 8.2.1.2**, during the three-month training, Jun's RRT decreased obviously ($p=0.000$). With the Post Hoc Tests it is found that Jun's RRT reduced obviously in the second oral test ($p=0.000$) while there was no significant difference between Time 2 and Time 3 ($p=0.568$). Though he spent more RRT in Time 3 than that in Time 2, his

Chapter Eight
RESULTS AND DISCUSSION (3):THE EFFECTS OF THE PRINCIPLES OF PROCEDURAL MEMORY ON ORAL PRODUCTION

progress was encouraging. By Parewise Comparison, it is also found that there were significant differences between Time 2 and Gang, between Time 2 and Li, between Time 3 and Gang and between Time 3 and Li ($p=0.000$). From Table 8-8, it is found that Jun even spent less RRT than Gang and Li. These findings can demonstrate Jun's improvement of oral proficiency.

Table 8-7 Univariate Analysis of Jun's Three Times of Complexity in Task One

			Jun			Gang	Li
Items	F	p	Mean 1	Mean 2	Mean 3	Mean 4	Mean 5
RRT	74.374	0.000	10.887	5.055	5.427	9089.833	6889.167

Note: RRT: recognition response time. The values of F and p in the table were obtained through the univariate analysis of Jun's three oral tests.

Table 8-7 indicates that Jun's RRT was reduced. From the perspective of complexity, it may be because of Jun's familiarity with the object clause structure in indirect speech. With intensive oral training, Jun became more and more familiar with the structure. Meanwhile, from the perspective of information processing, the use of chunks is beneficial to the development of the automatic processing and helps save much planning and processing time before oral production. Hence, this finding supports the effects of procedural memory in L2 oral training.

8.4.2 Major results for complexity in Task Two

This section reports complexity in Task Two from the following two aspects: complexity in language structure and cognitive complexity. The former include SVLV (syntactic variety and lexical variety), SC (syntactic complexity) and DD (the degree of difficulties in pronunciation, words, phrases and sentence patterns). The latter was explored by the questions in the three retrospective interviews after each oral test concerning Task Two.

8.4.2.1 Complexity in language structure

As introduced in **Section 4.6.2.3** and **Section 5.7.5.3**, complexity in language structure included three indices: SVLV (syntactic variety and lexical variety), SC (syntactic complexity) and DD (the degree of difficulties in pronunciation and use of linguistic units) in Task Two. The results of the performance of the subjects in the indices of complexity are displayed in Table 8-8. As mentioned in **Chapter Five**, in Table 5-8, the degrees of each item were divided into four ranks. The researcher ranked the performance of each subject and calculated all the subjects' performance according to her judgment.

Table 8-8 Univariate Analysis of Jun's Three Times of Complexity in Task Two

Items	Jun					HPs
	F	p	Mean 1	Mean 2	Mean 3	Mean 4
SVLV	40.000	0.000	1.667	3.000	3.000	3.417
SC	49.000	0.000	1.833	3.000	3.000	3.460
DD	1.000	0.391	1.833	2.000	2.000	2.543

Note: SVLV: syntactic variety and lexical variety; SC: syntactic complexity; DD: the degree of difficulties in pronunciation and use of linguistic units. The values of F and p in the table were obtained through the univariate analysis of Jun's three oral tests.

As shown in Table 8-8, Jun's SVLV and SC increased obviously ($p=0.000$). It indicates, with the oral training, Jun made much progress in SVLV and SC in Task Two. In the further exploration of Jun's changes in SVLV and SC during the oral training, with the Post Hoc Tests it was found that by Pairwise Comparisons, there were significant differences in Jun's SVLV and SC between Time 1 and Time 2 and between Time 1 and Time 3 ($p=0.000$). Compared with high-proficiency subjects, there were significant differences between Time 2 and HPs and between Time 3 and HPs ($p<0.05$). It indicates that though Jun made much progress in SVLV and SC, he still needed to practice his oral English in order to catch up with HPs. From Table 8-8, no significant difference was found ($p=0.391$) as to DD. By further exploration of the results of Pairwise Comparisons, the differences between Time 1 and HPs, between Time 2 and HPs, and between Time 3 and HPs were found significant ($p<0.05$). In this sense, it can be concluded that Jun did not make much progress in DD in the three oral tests. This may be because of the limited training time during which Jun could not solve all the problems in pronunciation and in use of linguistic units.

8.4.2.2 Cognitive complexity

In Task Two, cognitive complexity was explored by the questions in the three retrospective interviews after each oral test concerning Task Two. The questions were about the psychological issues such as anxiety, and the cognitive causes of hesitation, self-repairs during the process of language utterances.

From the retrospective interviews, the subject was found most anxious in the first oral test. In the second oral test, he felt more confident. In the third oral test, he felt somewhat anxious again. When asked about the causes of anxiety, Jun thought that the task difficulty influenced most. In Task Two, he had to answer the questions from the perspective of the object clause structure in indirect speech which involved many changes in the structure such as the changes of subjects, predicates, objects and adverbials. The second cause of anxiety was due to the fear of making mistakes. Every time, he tried his best to perform in the task. However, he was not confident about his answers, which caused his anxiety. The third cause was due to the requirement of the Task Two. In Task Two, Jun was asked to answer the question in each dialogue in English and the dialogue was made in Chinese. Jun had to transfer L1 to L2 and during this process more issues arose. In this sense, the task was cognitively complex.

As to Jun, the cognitive causes of hesitation, self-repair, etc. included the familiarity with the object clause structure in indirect speech. As mentioned above, though Jun got full scores in Multiple Choices concerning the object clause structure in indirect speech, he was not familiar with the structure in oral English. In addition, the length of sentences tested and the familiarity to the words, expressions and sentences (meaning and pronunciation) also influenced his fluency. In the first interview, he admitted that he seldom spent time practicing this structure. However, with the oral training, in the second interview, he stated that the increasing practice of the object clause structure in indirect speech and pronunciation of difficult words as well as the use of chunks helped reduce the time and times of hesitation and self-repair. This finding also supports Oxford's view of familiarity with the task (Oxford, 2006).

8.5 Results and Discussion for the Interviews

This case study included six interviews which were made after each oral test to explore the research questions concerning the effects of the principles of procedural memory on oral production of object clause structure in indirect speech as well as the implicit and explicit factors influencing the change of sentence patterns concerning indirect speech in oral production.

The results are presented in Table 8-9.

Table 8-9 Major Feedbacks from the Retrospective Interviews

	Feedbacks from the Retrospective Interviews
Implicit factors	anxiety, confidence; the interference of L1, etc.
Explicit factors	the difficulty of the sentence type, the length of sentences tested, the familiarity to the words, expressions and sentences (meaning and pronunciation)

The discussion for cognitive complexity can be referred to **Section 8.4.2.2**.

It is worth mentioning that because of the task difficulty, compared with Task One, Jun felt more anxious and had more hesitations and self-repairs in the oral production of Task Two. For example, Jun paused for a long time before he answered the question of the first dialogue in the first oral test. When he attempted to express "exhibition center" for "展览中心", he paused again because he was not sure about the pronunciation of the word "exhibition". The pause and hesitation cost him much time and led to the disfluency of his oral production. Following the training plans, he spent much time practicing the pronunciations of the complex words, especially those with more than three syllables. That is why in the second oral test, Jun was more confident about the pronunciations of such complex words as "exhibition" and "graduated".

This finding supports Pica et al.'s views of the influence of task types on the performance of tasks (Pica, Kanagy, & Falodun, 1993). In the case of Jun, the performance was better in the easier or more familiar tasks (such as Task One). It shows that when doing such task, Jun did not spend many efforts and time in cognitive familiarity and cognitive processing. As to the cognitive problems occurring during the performance of the more difficult tasks, it is found that in the case of Jun, practice can help solve such problems caused by cognitive complexity. From the perspective of the information processing framework of the present study, practice is emphasized for its effects on proceduralization and on L2 learning (Wu, 1999). In addition, O'malley, Chamot and Walker (1987) supported Anderson's ACT models concerning declarative knowledge and procedural knowledge by claiming that learning begins with declarative knowledge which slowly becomes proceduralized, and that the mechanism by which this takes place is practice.

In terms of the development of cognitive structures, we can use schema theory to explain this type of progress. As we know, in the field of cognitive science, the importance of schemata has been acknowledged widely (Bartlett, 1932; Piaget, 1985; Rumelhart, 1997). According to these views, schemata can be developed and employed in L2 learning of listening, speaking, reading and writing (Chen, 1988, 2000, 2001, 2002; Liu,1996; Ni, 2004; Wu & Wei, 2009; Yang & He, 2007; Zi, 2004). They can grow and change as new information is acquired, relieve the cognitive load, enhance the speed of comprehension process, simplify the memory process and hence increase the rate of retrieving knowledge (Rumelhart, 1997).

In the current study, schemata were of great benefit to Jun in memorizing the meaning and pronunciations of the complex words, especially those with three or more than three syllables. In addition, schema theory stressed the impact of prior knowledge on learning new information and the importance of self-regulatory skills in learning. In this sense, it can be concluded that the development and functioning of schemata played an important part in the exploration of the effects of procedural memory in the oral production in Jun's case.

8.6 Other Findings and Discussion

Some other findings were also obtained in the present study. Though they are not about the focus of the present study, these findings are related to the previous studies of procedural memory to some extent and are of significance in the research on procedural memory.

8.6.1 The correlation of procedural memory to lexical processing

From the analysis of the recorded files, it is found that the pronunciation of the words, the selection of words, etc. (See **Appendix 7**) often influenced fluency, accuracy and complexity of oral production. Referring to the findings, we may conclude that in L2 speaking, procedural memory may have the correlation to both lexical and grammatical processing rather than only to grammatical processing held in Ullman's DP model.

This finding can be explained on the basis of the following facts:

(1) As a part of linguistic units, words themselves entail smaller linguistic units such as morphemes and syllables. In each word, there are several smaller linguistic units which are combined together and form into a word module. Only by frequent practice can the word module become a chunk. In this sense, a word can be considered as a chunk. To high-proficiency speakers including native English speakers and non-native English speakers, the reason for them to be very frequent in oral English may partly lie in fluency in the production of smaller linguistic units in each word or chunk. As we know, words in a sentence serve as the bricks of a building (speech). It is understandable that one can be more fluent that others if he or she is more fluent in the production of smaller linguistic units in each word or chunk.

(2) In oral production, form and meaning are a pair of key terms. On the basis of L1, Saussure states that language form and meaning are two sides of a mental reality, just like the two sides of a coin. However, to a second language learner, it is a different case (Stern, 1983). The harmonious fusion of form and meaning in the first language does not work well in a second language. In other words, second language forms, to begin with, are meaningless to the second language learners, especially to those who are at the preliminary stage, and appear at first arbitrary and sometimes even unnatural and peculiar. In this case, it is common for less proficient L2 speakers to tend to separate the form from the meaning that they want to convey.

The possible reason for the poor proficiency of oral production may lie in the lack of proceduralization of the associated relations between form and meaning. Associative properties of lexical memory may lead to productivity in L2 (Hartshorne & Ullman, 2006; Pinker, 1999; Prasada & Pinker, 1993).

8.6.2 The effect of gender

According to Ullman (2004), women could tend to show a faster learning rate than men during early stages of L2 learning (due to females' superior declarative memory abilities), men may show an advantage in later stages (due to a possible male advantage at procedural memory). That means the male subjects are possible to do better than the female subjects in the tasks related to procedural memory (Here the subjects are grown up and not in their teens.). However, this present study did not support the opinion.

By the analysis of the correlations between gender and the level of oral production in the object clause structure in indirect speech, the following findings have been found.

First, the time spent both in recognition and in output by the Chinese female the American female was similar while to the males the time spent in recognition was much longer that that spent in output.

Second, the time spent by the two female subjects in recognition and output was much shorter than that spent by males from China and English speaking countries.

Third, male subjects spent longer time in sentence recognition and output than female subjects.

The reasons for the findings mentioned above may be presented as follows. First of all, it may be because the male subjects reread the sentence tested until they were sure that they had memorized it. This took them more time in recognition, compared with the female subjects.

It needs further exploration of the factors which caused the longer recognition of the males. In addition, compared with the females, the males may be not familiar with such complex grammatical structure as the object clause structure in indirect speech in oral production.

These findings were obtained on the basis of the limited number of the subjects, and therefore they cannot be applied to verify Ullman's view of the difference between the genders as far as declarative memory and procedural memory are concerned. In this sense, further study is needed on this aspect.

8.7 Summary

In this chapter, the answers to the third and fourth research question and other relevant questions are presented with the major findings and discussion for them.

In addition, other findings are exhibited and discussed because they are connected to procedural memory and oral production.

Chapter Nine
CONCLUSION

9.1 Introduction

Motivated by the problems in oral production of Chinese tertiary non-English major students, the present study explored L2 oral proficiency of Chinese university students from the perspective of an information-processing framework. It specifically focused on the effects of procedural memory on L2 oral proficiency and, to make the task more tangible, it selected the object clause structure in indirect speech as the linguistic object of study.

This chapter concludes the present study concerning effects of the principles of procedural memory on oral production from the perspective of the object clause structure in indirect speech. It begins with the summary of the major findings and then moves to the practical implications for instruction in the local EFL educational environment, followed by limitations of this study and suggestions for further research.

9.2 Major Findings

As outlined in **Chapter Four**, the present study is intended to address four research questions concerning the research focus of the present study. The major findings have been obtained from the current research as follows.

9.2.1 Major findings concerning the features of high-proficiency and low-proficiency L2 speakers

As a whole, there exist significant differences between high-proficiency and low-proficiency English speakers in fluency, accuracy and complexity in the object clause structure in indirect speech. Under the equivalent condition of the mastery of declarative knowledge, the indices in oral production are related to the application of procedural memory. The major differences between high-proficiency and low-proficiency L2 English speakers lie in the following aspects.

(1) In general, when compared between levels and between groups, the high-proficiency subjects performed better in fluency, accuracy and complexity than the low-proficiency subjects in oral production of the object clause structure in indirect speech. For example, when undertaking the tasks with different difficulties such as Task One *"Listen, Judge and Speak"* and Task Two *"Listen and Repeat"* in Cognitive Behavioral Experiment One, the high-proficiency subjects in both tasks performed better than the low-proficiency subjects in the three indices (i.e., fluency, accuracy and complexity) of oral proficiency (See **Chapter Six**). The major reasons for this phenomenon may be because they were better equipped in terms of grammatical rules, lexical knowledge, exemplar storage, four-channel mental representation of language, encyclopedia knowledge and pronunciation procedures. In addition, they may be more familiar with the retrieval and the use of procedural knowledge.

(2) It is found that in their use of the object clause structure in indirect speech, compared with the low-proficiency English speakers, the high-proficiency English speakers more frequently applied the chunks which are closely related to procedural memory. It indicates that

as one of the factors influencing oral proficiency, procedural memory has impact on the skill-based knowledge. This finding has been verified by the retrospective interviews and follow-up questionnaires made with the subjects in **Chapter Five** and **Chapter Six**.

(3) It is worth mentioning that generally speaking, the high-proficiency subjects performed better in accuracy and complexity than the low-proficiency subjects. However, the accuracy of the high-proficiency subjects declined when the difficulty of the tasks increased to a certain degree. This phenomenon was possibly because they overstressed fluency, compared with accuracy.

(4) In some cases (for example, in Cognitive Behavioral Experiment Two: Questions and Answers in **Chapter Five**), in order to ensure their output was grammatically correct, the high-proficiency subjects tended to choose less complex sentences or linguistic units, which made the difference between the high-proficiency subjects and the low-proficiency subjects statistically insignificant. The reason for the phenomenon may be because the high-proficiency subjects were better at using some communicative strategies such as reduction strategies to avoid errors in their oral production and obtain automaticity in L2 output (Færch & Kasper, 1983). To the low-proficiency subjects, they were more rigid in the selection of English expressions and tended to follow the Chinese word order in order to take a safer course. This may be due to the L1 interference.

9.2.2 Major findings concerning the features of the native English speakers and high-proficiency L2 speakers

In their use of object clause structure in indirect speech, the native English speakers performed much better in fluency measured by response time due to the language environment and the production of the internal

Chapter Nine
CONCLUSION

grammar embedded in their brain. But it is worth noticing that because they sometimes lacked explicit grammatical knowledge, the native English speakers did not uniformly perform better than the high-proficiency L2 speakers from China in accuracy and complexity in the object clause structure in indirect speech. It indicates that under the condition of sufficient practice, Chinese high-proficiency English speakers can do as well as or even better than the native English speakers at proceduralized knowledge or skills. This finding establishes the importance of practice of the high-proficiency L2 English speakers from China. In this case, the role of procedural memory is emphasized.

It is worth mentioning that based on the results of the experiment in the current study, it is found that the native English speakers and L2 speakers from China tended to use different types of procedural memory. The native English speakers tended to use the type of procedural memory which is separately stored in the brain and has nothing to do with the declarative memory. The linguistic units such as chunks influenced by this procedural knowledge have not been analyzed by the native English speakers before they speak. To the L2 speakers from China, they tended to use the type of procedural memory parasitizing in declarative memory and influencing the automatic processing of its retrieval and application (Chen, 2009). The linguistic units the L2 speakers produce have been analyzed by them and proceduralized and are therefore beneficial to the functioning of the working memory in terms of speed and storage capacity.

9.2.3 Major findings concerning the major effects of procedural memory on oral production of the object clause structure in indirect speech

The major effects of procedural memory on oral production of the object clause structure in indirect speech are based on the research on the major differences between high-proficiency and low-proficiency L2 English speakers, on the similarities and differences between the native English speakers and high-proficiency L2 English speakers from China and on Jun's longitudinal case study.

First, in Cognitive Behavioral Experiment Two: Questions and Answers in **Chapter Five**, the high-proficiency subjects tended to use procedural memory more frequently in lexical, grammatical issues as well as the composition of linguistic units. Compared with the low-proficiency subjects, the high-proficiency subjects used more chunks in their oral production.

Second, the oral proficiency of Jun, the subject in the longitudinal case study, was improved by constantly changing the linguistic units such as the subjects and the predicative verbs within the sentence structure. This indicates that procedural memory exists and functions in the mental storage of linguistic units of different levels and sizes. In addition, practice matters in the formation of proceduralization of procedural knowledge and procedural memory. Meanwhile, it also demonstrates that syntagmatic relations played an important role in training low-proficiency L2 speakers like Jun as they were beneficial to the formation of procedural memory.

Third, with the retrospective interviews and the follow-up questionnaires, it is found that the development and functioning of schemata played an important part in the exploration of the effects of procedural memory in the oral production. It is because the schemata can increase the rate of retrieving knowledge by relieving the cognitive load, enhancing the speed of comprehension process and simplifying the memory process (Rumelhart, 1997).

Fourth, the findings obtained in the longitudinal study are theoretically connected with the views of Ullman and Chen's. (1) The findings are consistent with Ullman's DP model (Ullman, 2001) in the relationship between the grammatical storage and procedural memory. For example, Jun's improvement in the oral production of the object clause structure in indirect speech proves that the grammatical storage is related to procedural memory. (2) It is found that Jun's pronunciation of words was improved during the oral training, especially in fluency and accuracy. This finding can enrich Ullman's DP model as to the fact that procedural memory has the correlation to lexical processing as well. (3) Jun's improvement in the oral production of the object clause in indirect speech also supports the new views on linguistic competence of Chen's as far as the importance of procedural memory is concerned.

9.2.4 The findings concerning the major factors influencing L2 oral proficiency in the light of procedural memory

According to the interviews and questionnaires made in the study, in the case of the object clause structure in indirect speech, the major factors influencing L2 oral production proficiency in the light of procedural memory include both implicit and explicit ones. The former mainly include anxiety, confidence, the anti-interference of L1, the ability to restructure the sentence structures, reduction strategies, etc. The latter mainly include the difficulty and the length of the sentences tested and their linguistic units, familiarity to the grammatical structures and linguistic units, the frequency of oral practice, etc. But as indicated in the case of Jun, the subject in the longitudinal case study, with the emphasis on the principles of procedural memory in the oral training, L2 oral proficiency can be improved by reducing anxiety and increasing speaking confidence.

9.3 Implications

The implications of the findings of the current studies are presented from the perspectives of theory, methodology and pedagogy. They are presented as follows.

9.3.1 Theoretical implications of the study

9.3.1.1 To base the linguistic study on the findings of memory studies from across disciplines

This dissertation reviewed and introduced major memory classifications in the light of their importance in memory research. It contributes to the understanding of oral production from the psycholinguistic perspective, and to the theoretical study of procedural memory in China. From the literature review of the study, it is found that the development of memory studies from traditional memory models to the DP model in multiple memory models is accompanied by the development of disciplines like psychology, cognitive neuroscience, cognitive psychology, psycholinguistics and so on. In turn, the development of memory studies accelerates the development of such disciplines. It can be said that without the development of cognitive science, the present study of oral production could not have come into reality. The combination of the theories from across disciplines will benefit the research on linguistic issues.

However, the emphasis on the disciplines like psychology, cognitive neuroscience, cognitive psychology, psycholinguistics and so on does not reduce or negate the contribution by such masters as Chomsky and Bloomfield in the field of linguistics. Chomsky refers to the ability to produce an infinite number of sentences never spoken before and to understand sentences never heard before as the "creative aspect" of language use (Chomsky, 1957, 1965, 1968). For Bloomfield, his structural linguistics maintains that all linguistic structures could be determined by the application of analytic procedures starting with the smallest units which combine sound and meaning (Bloomfield, 1926, 1933). The present study emphasizes the psychological issues like linguistic units, which more or less is consistent with the Bloomfield's views. The present study was aimed to integrate these theories with the cognitive theories because these theories can play an important role in different situations. For example, in the immediate speech, the use of chunks may show their advantages in fluency or accuracy of language while in prepared speeches, Chomsky's view on creativity in language use may occupy a dominant position. In a word, the present study can be thought to enrich the linguistic theories.

9.3.1.2 To establish an information–processing conceptual framework for probing the relationship between procedural memory and L2 oral proficiency

This study investigated the correlation between procedural memory and L2 oral proficiency by establishing an information-processing conceptual framework for probing issues of procedural memory such as the definitions, forms and functions. The information-processing conceptual framework is influenced by the cognitive models which are most closely related to procedural memory, including schema theory, Anderson's ACT models and Ullman's declarative/procedural model. Meanwhile, this conceptual framework has theoretically served the empirical studies by providing important principles for the research design. In turn, the results of the designed empirical studies have supplemented and enriched the contents of the theoretical framework. In addition, the exploration of the effects of chunks on the indices of L2 oral proficiency in **Chapter Six** has enriched the theoretical framework concerning the correlation between procedural memory and L2 oral proficiency. It can be said that with the information-processing conceptual framework, the study of oral production and procedural memory has become systematic and scientific. The information-processing conceptual framework can hopefully provide an overall theoretical view on the similar studies of oral production and procedural memory.

9.3.1.3　To enrich the theories of linguistic competence

The theories of linguistic competence are essential in the assessment of one's abilities in oral production. The present study theoretically supports Chen's proposal of linguistic competence from the cognitive perspective with detailed illustrations and enriches the concept of linguistic competence by emphasizing the importance of procedural memory and automaticity. Compared with the popularly accepted views on linguistic competency such as Hymes' communicative competence, Chen's view of linguistic competence emphasizes the mechanism of language processing from the cognitive perspective and hence it is more scientific to be applied in the assessment of language proficiency. Because of the complexity of oral production, it is implicated that the scientific assessment of the proficiency of oral production should be influenced not only by the communicative concepts of linguistic competence but also by the cognitive perspective of language production.

9.3.1.4　To enrich the content of Ullman's DP model

Ullman's declarative/procedural (DP) model claims that the mental lexicon of memorized word-specific knowledge depends on declarative memory while the mental grammar depends on the procedural memory system (Ullman, 2004). Based on the results of the experiments, the present study revealed the improvement of Jun's pronunciation of words during the oral training, especially in fluency and accuracy. The words are part of linguistic units and within a word there are smaller linguistic units such as syllables. Therefore, it can be held that this finding enriches the content of Ullman's DP model because it demonstrates the correlation of procedural memory to lexical processing in L2 speaking.

9.3.2 Methodological implications of the study

The study was conducted in a multi-disciplinary way which offered an all-round approach to language research. For example, in the present study, the design of the cognitive behavioral experiments as well as the data collection and data analysis depended on the principles in psychology and cognitive neuroscience. Compared with the methods applied in linguistics, there is no doubt that the methods applied in the present study have their obvious advantages in logicality, validity and scientificity.

In addition, systematical methodologies are still not included on this topic though an increasing number of researchers study the correlation between memory and language learning from across disciplines. The present research designed the studies in such a way that its methodologies can be used by future researchers. For example, the diagnostic study was conducted when the subjects were screened. In addition, the cross-sectional study, the comparative study and the longitudinal study were carried out in the main parts of the present study. These studies are logically related to each other. Each study consisted of the quantitative and qualitative parts in which quantitative and qualitative analyses were also applied. By doing so, the current research can hopefully offer a comparatively systematic survey and ensure its reliability and validity in methodology.

9.3.3 Pedagogical implications of the study

On the basis of the experimental studies and newly-forwarded linguistic theory, this study has established new indices for evaluating one's L2 oral production, which theoretically supports the views of other researches on L2 oral production (Oxford, 2006; Yuan & Guo, 2010). The pedagogical implications of the study are as follows.

First, from the perspective of the principles of procedural memory, the current study will help L2 teachers and learners adjust their ways of training L2 speaking abilities. For example, this study adds automaticity as a factor into fluency, an index for evaluating one's L2 oral production, which stresses the importance of psychological issues in teaching and learning L2 oral production. For another example, it expounded two types of procedural memory and stressed the analyzed and proceduralized production of linguistic units such as chunks, idioms and collocations because the learning approach in China largely depends on the type of procedural memory parasitizing in declarative memory and influencing the automatic processing of its retrieval and application (Chen, 2009). The present study has established the important role of the analyzed chunks in L2 oral production of Chinese subjects with high oral proficiency. Therefore, in L2 oral training, it is important for teachers to encourage the learners to use more formulaic language in order to improve fluency, accuracy and complexity in oral production. However, the learners should not overuse such kind of chunks because the overuse may lead to loss of creativity. In addition, the emphasis on chunks or idioms does not mean ignoring communicative strategies in oral training. As a matter of fact, communicative strategies in oral production are still very important though they are easier to acquire compared with chunks. For instance, in Cognitive Behavioral Experiment Two, the high-proficiency subjects tended to choose less complex sentences or linguistic units in order to ensure that their output was grammatically correct in the experiment. This phenomenon can be explained by the reduction strategies in communication. Therefore, it is implicated that both cognitive and communicative strategies should be stressed in the teaching and learning of L2 oral production.

Second, in the case of Jun, the subject in the longitudinal study as well as in the cases of the other Chinese subjects in the interviews and questionnaires, this study has reproved that traditional skill training methods like recitation, retelling and rehearsal are still of great importance in improving L2 oral production. The reason is because repeated and intensive practice is beneficial to the formation of proceduralization of procedural knowledge and procedural memory, which will help form the real proceduralization and enrich the productive system. The real proceduralization is manifested in internal activities and external representations like motor activities and habits, which will prolong the memory of knowledge and procedures in motor and cognition. But it is worth noticing that the proceduralization of oral production is different from that of listening, writing or reading because the proceduralization for different skills involves different factors. According to Chen's view on four-channel mental representation of language (Chen, 2009), while the proceduralization for all the skills are related to linguistic chunks, speaking needs procedualization in pronunciation and related activities, which are different from the mental or motor activities in listening, writing or reading. Therefore, on one hand, in the oral training, the teachers may encourage the learners to apply the traditional methods like recitation, retelling and rehearsal and, on the other hand, in different tests such as oral tests and listening tests, the teachers should apply different training methods.

Third, the teachers of L2 speaking should pay due attention to the problems in the L2 oral production of their students. For example, in Cognitive Behavioral Experiment Two, the high-proficiency subjects did not perform satisfactorily in accuracy because they overstressed fluency while the low-proficiency subjects were negatively interfered by L1 in their oral production. When such problems appear among their students, the teachers of L2 speaking had better roundly analyze the factors of such problems in order to find some effective ways to solve them. These ways may include the use of chunks, idiom and collocations, the use of schemata, etc.

Fourth, it is worth noticing that it is an effective way to orally train the subject by constantly changing the linguistic units within the sentence structure. That is to say, in training low-proficiency L2 speakers, syntagmatic relations play an important role in the formation of procedural memory. Therefore, the teachers may help the L2 learners improve their oral proficiency by teaching them how to "fish" (i.e. by changing the linguistic units within a certain sentence structure) rather than by giving them fish.

As a result, this study is of great instructive significance to the reform of the learning methods, teaching methods, teaching material compilation and so on of L2 speaking in China.

9.4 Limitations

Research on memory and oral production is hard to conduct since both of them are closely related to psychological and cognitive issues.

The limitations of the present study are displayed in the following aspects.

(1) The research setting. This study is limited because it was carried out in a semi-experimental setting (i.e., in a language lab). This limitation may negatively influence the validity and reliability of the study since we know it is in the real communication that a person's proficiency of oral production can be fairly revealed and assessed.

(2) The research focus. This study was conducted from the perspective of the object clause structure in indirect speech. This

research focus is limited to the object clause structure in indirect speech though this grammatical phenomenon is very typical in oral production. Besides, the researcher chose the tasks which were only about sentence patterns among separate sentences rather than in texts or passages, which more or less influenced the validity of the present study.

(3) The selection of the subjects. The study is limited in the selection of the subjects. In this study, the Chinese subjects were selected from part of departments and schools in Southeast University, whose proficiency of L2 oral production is relatively high and cannot represent the overall situation of all the university tertiary students. So if conducted in different universities and colleges in China, the results of the study may be different from the present ones. In addition, the sample size was limited because of the researcher's time and energy. Besides, because of the researcher's time and other reasons, the selection of the two native English speakers was not so strict. All of the mentioned issues may influence the generality of the findings.

(4) Data collection methods. The data collection methods were limited in the fact that although the researcher carried out the study in a series of research methods such as cognitive behavioral experiments, questionnaires and retrospective interviews and cases studies, other cross-disciplinary research methods should be applied since memory and oral production are both closely related to psychological and cognitive processes.

9.5 Suggestions for Future Research

Suggestions for further research are based on the findings and the limitations of the present study and they are as follows.

(1) More further theoretical studies on the proficiency of oral production by combining with the theories and application of cognitive

science are called for to validate and strengthen the theoretical framework of the present study.

(2) More cross-disciplinary researches on oral production of L2 learners should be carried out by adopting FMRI (the Functional Magnetic Resonance Imaging), ERP (Event-related potential), EEG (Electroencephalogram) and other advanced instruments and technologies which are commonly applied in cognitive science. These instruments and technologies will help with the judgment and verification of the phenomena in the area of L2 oral production by presenting the visual graphs and data.

(3) The contents of the study may be enriched at least in the following three aspects. First, further studies may explore the relationship between procedural memory and other kinds of memory and age, gender and other personal differences which may be the factors influencing the proficiency of oral production. Second, the investigation of the object clause structure in indirect speech may be carried out with the texts, passages, etc., instead of separate sentences. Third, other grammatical structures and forms of oral production may be probed into, such as pronunciation, lexicon, chunks, discourse etc.

(4) The pool of samples may be expanded by introducing more university students with various academic backgrounds, language proficiency levels, gender mixtures, nationalities, grouping patterns (such as group size and proficiency matching), etc. to further ensure the validity and reliability of the study and clarify the effects of procedural memory on oral production.

9.6 Summary

This chapter concludes the present study by summarizing the major findings and discussing the implications from the theoretical, methodological and pedagogical perspectives. It also points out the limitations of the present study and makes some suggestions for future research on the basis of the limitations.

From the perspective of the information processing framework, especially the principles of procedural memory, it can be claimed that the present study has to some degree succeeded in revealing the relevant psychological mechanisms in oral production and providing feasible solutions to the problems such as disfluency and inaccuracy in L2 oral production. However, because of the complexity of the psycholinguistic research and the existing limitations, more all-round and multi-disciplinary approaches are called for to perfect the study of the effects of procedural memory on oral production.

REFERENCES

Aldridge, J. W., & Berridge, K. C. (1998). Coding of serial order by neostriatalneurons: A "natural action" approach to movement sequence[J]. *Journal of Neuroscience, 18*, 2777–2787.

Anderson, J. R. (1976). *Language, memory, and thought*[M]. Hillsdale, NJ: Erlbaum.

Anderson, J. R. (1982). Acquisition of cognitive skill[J]. *Psychological Review, 89*, 369-403.

Anderson, J. R. (1983a). A general learning theory and its application to the acquisition of proof skills in geometry[A]. In R. Michalski, J. Carbonell, and T. Mitchell (Eds.), *Machine Learning: An Artificial Intelligence Approach*[C]. Palo Alto, CA: Tioga Publishing.

Anderson, J. R. (1983b). A spreading activation theory of memory[J]. *Journal of Verbal Learning and Verbal Behavior, 22*, 261-295.

Anderson, J. R. (1983c). *The architecture of cognition*[M]. Cambridge, MA: Harvard University Press.

Anderson, J. R. (1983d). Retrieval of information from long-term memory[J]. *Science, 220*, 25-30.

Anderson, J. R. (1995). *Learning and memory: An integrated approach*[M]. New York: Wiley.

Anderson, J. R. (2005) Human symbol manipulation within an integrated cognitive architecture[J]. *Cognitive Science, 29*(3), 313-341.

Anderson, J. R., & Bower, G. H. (1973). *Human associative memory*[M]. Washington: Winston and Sons.

Anderson, J. R., & Lebiere, C. (1998). *The atomic components of thought*[M]. Mahwah, NJ: Erlbaum.

Anderson, R. C., & Pearson P. D. (1984). A schema theoretic view of basic process in reading comprehension[A]. *Handbook of reading research*[C]. New York: Longman.

Applecate, J. L., Kline, S.L., & Delia, J. G. (1991). Alternative measures of cognitive complexity as predictors of communication performance[J]. *Journal of Constructivist Psychology*, *4*(2), 193-213.

Arnold, J., Wasow, T., Losongco, A., & Ginstrom R. (2000). Heaviness vs. newness: The effects of structural complexity and discourse status on constituent ordering[J]. *Language*, *17*(1), 28-55.

Atkinson, R. C., & Shiffrin,R. M. (1968). Human memory: A proposed system and its control processes[A]. In K. W. Spence & J. T. Spence (Eds.), *The psychology of learning and motivation: Advances in research and theory*[C], Vol. 2. New York: Academic Press.

Baddeley, A. D., & Hitch, G. J. (1974). Working memory[A]. In G. A. Bower (Eds.), *Recent advances in learning and motivation*[C] (Vol. 8). New York: Academic Press.

Baddeley, A. D. (2000). The episodic buffer: a new component of working memory?[J]. *Trends in Cognitive Science*, *4*, 417-423.

Bargh, J. A. (1989). Conditional automaticity: Varieties of automatic influence in social perception and cognition[A]. In J. A. Bargh & J. Ullman (Eds.), *Unintended thought* [C] (pp. 3-51). London: Guilford Press.

Bargh, J. A. (1992). The ecology of automaticity: Towards establishing the conditions needed to produce automatic processing effect[J]. *American Journal of Psychology*, *105*, 181-199.

Bartlett, F. C. (1932). *Remembering: An experimental and social study*[M]. Cambridge: Cambridge University Press.

Bates, E., & MacWhinney, B. (1989). Functionalism and the

competition model[A]. In B. MacWhinney & E. Bates (Eds.), *The crosslinguistic study of sentence processing* [C] (pp. 3-73). Cambridge: Cambridge University Press.

Biber, D., Johansson, S., Leech, G., Conrad, S., & Finegan, E. (1999). *Longman grammar of spoken and written English*[M]. Beijing: Foreign Language Teaching and Research Press.

Bloomfield, L. (1926). A set of postulates for the science of language[J]. *Language, 2,* 153-164.

Bloomfield, L. (1933). *Language*[M]. New York: Henry Holt.

Bolinger, D. (1961). Contrastive accent and contrastive stress[J]. *Language, 37,* 83-96.

Bolinger, D. (1976). Meaning and memory[J]. *Forum Linguisticum, 1,* 1-14.

Borden, G. J., Harris, K.S., & Raphael, L. J. (1994). *Speech science primer: physiology, Acoustics and perception of speech*[M]. Philadelphia: Lippencott Williams & Wilkins.

Brown, G. (1977). *Listening to spoken English*[M]. London: Longman Group Ltd.

Cai, J. G. (蔡基刚), 2002, 如何评价大学生的英语口语能力[J]. 外语界, (1):64-67.

Campbell, B., & Spear, N. (1972). Ontogeny of memory[J]. *Psychological Review, 79,* 215-236.

Carr, T. H. (1992). Automaticity and cognitive anatomy: Is word recognition automatic [J]. *American Journal of Psychology, 105,* 201-237.

Carr, T. H., & Curren, T. (1994). Cognitive factors in learning about structured sequences: applications to syntax[J]. *Studies in Second Language Acquisition, 16,* 205-230.

Carroll, D. W. (2000). *Psychology of language*[M]. Beijing: Foreign Language Teaching and Research Press.

Cermak, L. S., Lewis, R., Butters, N., & Goodglass, H. (1973). Role of verbal mediation in performance of motor tasks by Korsakoff patients[J]. *Perception and Motor Skills, 37*, 259-263.

Challis, B. H., & Brodbeck, D. R. (1992). Levels of processing affects priming in word fragment completion[J]. Journal of Experimental Psychology: *Learning, Memory and Cognition, 18*, 595–607.

Chakraborty, R., Goffman, L., & Smith, A. (2008). Physiological indices of bilingualism: oral-motor coordination and speech rate in Bengali-English speakers[J]. *Journal of Speech, Language, and Hearing Research, 51*(2), 321-32.

Chang, X. (常欣), 2009, 认知神经语言学视野下的句子理解[M]. 科学出版社.

Chen, K.S. (陈开顺), 1988, 听话过程中的心理活动方式与听力的构成[J]. 外语教学与研究,(2):31-35.

Chen, K.S. (陈开顺), 2000, 语言心理研究[M]. 北京: 华艺出版社.

Chen, K.S. (陈开顺), 2001, 言语知觉和理解中的心理模式[J]. 外语研究,(3): 31-35.

Chen, K.S. (陈开顺), 2002a, 重新认识自动性在语言能力中的地位[J]. 解放军外国语学院学报, (3):16-19.

Chen, K.S. (陈开顺), 2002b, 从认知角度重新探讨语言能力的构成与表征[J]. 外语研究, (3):16-21.

Chen, K.S. (陈开顺), 2002c, 语言能力与认知模式自动性[M]. 军事谊文出版社.

Chen, K.S. (陈开顺), 2009, 从多重记忆系统看外语能力与学习浅谈[J]. 外语研究, (2): 63-66.

Chomsky, N. (1957). *Syntactic structures*[M]. The Hague: Mouton.

Chomsky, N. (1965). *Aspects of the theory of syntax*[M]. Cambridge: MIT Press.

Chomsky, N. (1968). *Language and mind*[M]. New York: Harcourt,

Brace & World.

Clark, H. H., & Clark, E.V. (1977). *Psychology and language: An introduction to psycholinguistics*[M]. New York: Harcourt Brace Jovanovich, Inc.

Cohen, N. J., & Squire, L. R. (1980). Preserved learning and retention of pattern analyzing skill in amnesia: Dissociation of knowing how and knowing that[J]. *Science, 210*, 207–209.

Cohen, N. J. (1984). Preserved learning capacity in amnesia: Evidence for multiple memory systems[A]. In L. R. Squire & N. Butters (Eds.), *Neuropsychology of Memory*[C] (pp. 83-103). New York: Guilford Press.

Cohen, N. J., Eichenbaum, R., Decedo, J.C., & Corkin, S. (1985). Preserved learning capacity in amnesia: Evidence for multiple memory systems[A]. In L.S. Squire and N Butters (Eds.), *Neuropsychology of Memory*[C]. New York: The Gilford Press.

Conklin, K., & Schmitt, K. (2008). Formulaic sequences: Are they processed more quickly than nonformulaic language by native and nonnative speakers?[J]. *Applied Linguistics, 29*,72-89.

Corder, S. P. (1967). The significance of learner's errors[M]. *International Review of Applied Linguistics, 9*, 149-159.

Corder, S. P. (1983). Strategies of communication[A]. In C. Færch, & G. Kasper (Eds.), Strategies in interlanguage communication[C] (pp.56-77). London: Longman.

Corkin, S.(1968). Acquisition of motor skill after bilateral medial temporal-lobe excision[J]. *Neuropsychologia, 6*, 255-265.

Corkin, S. (1984). Lasting consequences of bilateral medial temporal lobectomy: clinical course and experimental findings in H.M.[J]. *Seminars in Neurology, 4*, 252-262.

Coward, L. A., & Sun, R. (2004). Criteria for an effective theory of consciousness and some preliminary attempts[J]. *Consciousness and*

Cognition,13, 268–301.

Craik, F. I. M. (2002). Levels of processing: Past, present and future[J]. *Memory, 10,* 305-318.

Craik, F. I. M., & Lockhard, R.S. (1972). Levels of processing: A framework for memory research[J]. *Journal of Verbal Learning and Verbal Behavior, 11,* 671-684.

Crookes, G. (1989). Planning and interlanguage variation[J]. *Studies in Second Language Acquisition, 11,* 367-383.

Crowder, R. G., & Morton, J. (1969). Precategorical acoustic storage (PAS)[J]. *Perception and Psychophysics, 5,* 365-373.

De Bot, K. (1992). A bilingual production model: Levelt's "speaking" model adapted[J]. *Applied Linguistics, 13,* 1-24.

De Bot, K., Cox, A., Ralston, S., Schaufeli, A., & Weltens, B. (1995). Lexical processing in bilinguals[J]. *Second Language Research, 11,* 1-19.

De Bot, K., & Schreuder, R. (1993). Word production and the bilingual lexicon[A]. In R. Schreuder & B. Weltens (Eds.), *The bilingual lexicon*[C] (pp.191-214). Amsterdam: John Benjamins.

Dell, G. S. (1986). A spreading activation theory of retrieval in sentence production[J]. *Psychological Review, 93,* 283-321.

Deng, Y. C. (邓耀臣), 2007, 中国学习者英语口语中程式化序列特征研究—语料库驱动的方法[D].上海交通大学.

Ding, Y. R., & Qi, Y. (丁言仁, 戚焱), 2005, 词块研究和英语口语和写作水平的相关研究[J]. 解放军外国语学院学报,(3):49-53.

Driscoll, M. P. (2000). *Psychology of learning for instruction*[M]. Needham Heights, MA: Allyn and Bacon.

Friederici, A. D., Meyer, M., & von Cramon, D.Y. (2000). Auditory language comprehension: An event-related fMRI study on the processing of syntactic and lexical information[J]. *Brain and Language, 74,* 289-300.

Eastabrooke, I. V., Mordecai, K., Maki, P., & Ullman, M. T. (2002).

The effect of sex hormones on language processing[J]. *Brain and Language, 83,*143-146.

Eichenbaum, H., & Cohen, N. J. (2001). *From conditioning to conscious recollection: Memory systems of the brain*[M]. New York: Oxford University Press.

Eliasmith, C. (Ed.) (2001). Memory[A]. *Dictionary of philosophy of mind*[C]. Pullman, WA: Washington State University.

Ellis, R. (1991). *Second language acquisition and language pedagogy*[M]. Clevedon: Multilingual Matters.

Ellis, R. (1999). *The study of second language acquisition*[M]. Shanghai: Shanghai Foreign Language Education Press.

Eysenck, M. W., & Keane, M. A. (2005). *Cognitive Psychology: A Student's Handbook*[M]. (5th ed.). Hove & New York: Psychology Press.

Fillmore, C. (1979). On fluency[A]. In C. Fillmore, D. Kempler & W. Wang (Eds.) *Individual differences in language ability and language behavior*[C]. New York: Academic Press.

Fant, G. (1960). *Acoustic theory of speech production*[M]. The Hague: Mouton.

Fant, G. (1986). Glottal flow: Models and interaction[J]. *Journal of Phonetics, 14,* 393-399.

Færch, C., & Kasper, G. (1983). *Strategies in interlanguage communication*[M]. London: Longman Group Limited.

Ferreira, F. (1991). Effects of length and syntactic complexity on initiation times for prepared utterances[J]. *Journal of Memory and Language, 30*(2), 2110-2233.

Fodor, J. A. (1983). *The modularity of mind: An essay in faculty psychology*[M]. Cambridge, MA: MIT Press.

Foster, P., & Skehan, H. (1996). The influence of planning and task type on second language performance[J]. *Studies in Second Language*

Acquisition, *18*, 299-323.

Fredriksson, A. (2000). Maze learning and motor activity deficits in adult mice induced by iron exposure during a critical postnatal period[J]. *Developmental Brain Research, 119*(1), 65-74.

Fromkin, V. (1971). The non-anomalous nature of anomalous utterances[J]. *Language*, 42, 27-52.

Fromkin, V. (1973). *Speech errors as linguistics evidence*[M]. The Hague: Mouton Publishers.

Gallo, D.A., & Roediger, H.L. (2002). Variability among word lists in eliciting memory illusions: Evidence activation and monitoring[J]. *Journal of Memory Language, 47*, 469-497.

Gabrieli, J. D. E. (1998). Cognitive neuroscience of human memory[J]. *Annual Review of Psychology, 49*, 87–115.

Gao, B., Cao, H. & Cao, P.(高兵,曹晖,曹聘), 2006, 句法加工的脑机制[J].心理科学进展, 14(1):32-33.

Gao, S. R.(高素荣), 1993, 失语症[M].北京:北京医科大学中国协和医科大学联合出版.

Garman, M. (2003). *Psycholinguistics*[M]. Peking: Peking University Press.

Garrett, M. F. (1975). The analysis of sentence production[A]. In G. H.Bower (Eds.), *The psychology of learning and motivation*[C] (Vol. 9, pp.133-177). New York: Academic Press.

Gazzaniga, M. S., Ivry, R. B., & Mangun, G. R. (2002). *Cognitive neuroscience: The biology of the mind*[M]. London: W.W Norton & Company.

Giegerich, H. J. (1992). *English phonology: An introduction*[M]. Cambridge: Cambridge University Press.

Gimson, A. C. (1980). *An Introduction to the pronunciation of English* (3rd edition)[M]. London: Edward Arnold.

Graf, P., & Schater, D. L. (1985). Implicit and explicit memory for new associations in normal and amnesic subjects[J]. *Journal of Experimental Psychology: Learning, Memory and Cognition, 11*, 501-518.

Green, D. W. (2000). Control, activation, and resource: A framework and a model for the control of speech in bilinguals[A]. In L. Wei (Ed.), *The bilingualism reader*[C] (pp. 374-385). London; New York: Routledge.

Gui, S. C. (桂诗春), 1991, 实验心理语言学纲要:语言的感知、理解与产生[M]. 长沙:湖南教育出版社.

Guo, X. Y. (郭秀艳), 2004, 内隐学习研究综述[J]. 华东师范大学学报(教育科学版),22(1):50-55.

Halleck, G. B. (1995). Assessing oral proficiency: A comparison of holistic and objective measures[J]. *The Modern Language Journal, 79* (2), 223-234.

Hao, J., & Li, K. C. (郝晶,李坤成), 2002, 脑功能磁共振成像的研究进展[J]. 中国医学影像技术,18 (11) : 1195-1197.

Hartshorne, J. K., & Ullman, M. T. (2006). Why girls say 'holded' more than boys[J]. *Developmental Science*, 9, 21–32.

Hasher, L., & Zacks, R. (1979). Automatic and effort full, processes in memory[J]. *Journal of Experimental Psychology: General, 108,* 356-388.

Hawkins, J. (1990). A parsing theory of word order universals[J]. *Linguistic Inquiry, 21*(2): 223-261.

Hawkins, J. (1994). *A performance theory of order and constituency*[M]. Cambridge University Press.

Hebb, D. O. (1949). *The organization of behavior: A neuropsychological theory*[M]. New York: Wiley.

Hockett, C. F. (1958). *A course in modern linguistics*[M]. New York: Macmillan.

Hormann, Han. (1979). *Psycholinguistics: An introduction to research and theory* (2nd. Ed.)[M]. Trans. H. H. Stern and Peter Leppmann. New York: Springer-Verlag.

Howarth, P. (1998). Phraseology and second language proficiency[J]. *Applied Linguistics*, *19*(1), 24-44.

Hu, Z. L., & Jiang, W.Q. (2003). *Linguistics: An advanced course book*[M]. Beijing: Beijing University Press.

Hudson, R. A. (1980). *Sociolinguistics*[M]. Cambridge: Cambridge University Press.

Hunt, K.W. (1970). Syntactic maturity in school-children and adults[J]. *Monographs of the Society for Research in Child Development*, *35*, 1.

Hymes, D. (1972). On communicative competence[A]. In Pride, J. B. & Holmes, J. (Eds.), *Sociolinguistics: Selected readings*[C]. Harmondsworth: Penguin Books.

Jay, T. B. (2003). *The Psychology of language*[M]. New Jersey: Prentice Hall.

Jensen, E. (2000). *Brain-based learning*[M]. San Diego: Brain Store Incorporated.

Jespersen, O. (1924). *The philosophy of grammar*[M]. Chicago: University of Chicago Press.

Jiang, M.Y.(姜美玉), 2001, 汉语口误研究[D]. 中国社科院研究生院.

Jacoby, L. L., & Witherspoon, D. (1982). Remembering without awareness[J]. *Canadian Journal of Psychology*, *36*, 300-324.

Johnson, N. (1966). On the relationship between sentence structure and the latency in generating the sentence[J]. *Journal of Verbal Learning and Verbal Behavior*, *5*, 375-380.

Jones, D. (1956). *An outline of English phonetics* (8th. ed.)[M]. Cambridge: W. Heffer & Sons Ltd.

Kail, R. V., & Hagen, J. W. (1977). *Perspectives on the development of memory and cognition*[M]. New Jersey: Erlbaum.

Koreman, J. (1996). *Decoding linguistic information in the glottal airflow*[D]. Ph.D. dissertation Nijmegen University.

Krashen, S. (1982). *Principles and practices in second language acquisition*[M]. New York: Prentice-Hall.

Krashen, S. (1988). *Second language acquisition and second language learning*[M]. New York: Prentice-Hall.

Landry, K. L. (2002). Schemata in second language reading[J]. *The Reading Matrix, 2*, 3-20.

Langacker, R. W. (1987). *Foundations of cognitive grammar: Theoretical prerequisites* (vol. 1) [M]. Stanford: Stanford University Press.

Langacker, R. W. (1991). *Foundation of cognitive grammar: Descriptive application* (vol. 2) [M]. Stanford: Stanford University Press.

Lashley, K. (1950). In search of the engram[J]. *Symposia of the Society for Experimental Biology, 4*, 454-482.

Laver, L. (1994). *Principles of phonetics*[M]. Cambridge: Cambridge University Press.

Lennon, P. (1984). Retelling a story in English as a second language[A]. In H.W.Dechert, D.Mohle, and M. Raupach (Eds.), *Second Language Productions*[C] (pp50-68). Tubingen: Gunter Narr.

Lennon, P. (1990). Investigating fluency in EFL: A quantitative approach[J]. *Language Learning,40*, 3,387-417.

Levelt, W. J. M. (1989). *Speaking*[M]. Cambridge, MA: The MIT Press.

Li, B. Q., Xu, Z., & Xu, L.(李毕琴,徐展,徐丽), 2007, 工作记忆中的词长效应 [J]. 心理科学进展,15(5):768-773.

Li, L., & Li, X. X. (李黎,李霄翔), 2006, 功能磁共振(fMRI)与脑语言功能研究综述 [J]. 东南大学学报(哲学社会科学版), (3):116-119.

Li, S. J.(李淑君), 2008, 直接引语和间接引语的教学实践[J]. 考试（教研版）, (11): 66- 67.

Liu, H. P.(刘惠萍), 2004, 计划与口语质量[J]. 广西民族学院学报(哲学社会科学版), (26):146 -149.

Liu, S. L. (刘绍龙), 1996, 背景知识与听力策略—图式理论案例报告[J]. 现代外语, (2): 42-45.

Liu, X.Y., & Liu, G. L.(刘希彦, 刘桂玲), 2004, 心理语言学[M]. 北京: 高等教育出版社.

Logan, G. D. (1980). Attention and automaticity in Stroop and priming tasks: Theory and data[J]. *Cognitive Psychology, 12,* 523-553.

Logan, G. D., & Cowan, W. (1984). On the ability to inhibit thought, and action: A theory of an act of control[J]. *Psychological Review, 91,* 295-327.

Lou, C. F. et al. (楼春芳等), 2006, 第二语言口语评价研究进展[J].外语界, 2006 (3): 66-71.

Lyons, J. (2002). *Linguistic semantics: An introduction*[M]. Cambridge: Cambridge University Press.

MacLeod, C. M. (1991). Half a century of research on the Stroop effects: An integrative review[J]. *Psychological Bulletin, 109*(2),163-203.

McDonald, R. J., & White, N.M. (1993). A triple dissociation of memory systems: Hippocampus, amygdala, and dorsal striatum[J]. *Behavioral Neuroscience, 107,* 3- 22.

McLaughlin, B., Rossman T., & McLeod B. (1983). Second language learning: an information processing perspective[J]. *Language Learning, 33,*135-157.

Mehnert, U. (1998). The effects of different lengths of time for planning on second language performance[J]. *Studies in Second Language Acquisition, 20,* 52-83.

Miller, G. (1956). The magical number seven, plus or minus two[J].

Psychological Review, 63, 81-97.

Milner, B., Corkin, S., & Teuber, H. L. (1968). Further analysis of the hippocampal amnesic syndrome: 14 year follow-up study of H.M[J]. *Neuropsychologia, 6*, 215-234.

Mishkin, M., Malamut, B., & Bachevalier, J. (1984). Memories and habits: Two neural systems[A]. In Lynch, G., McGaugh, J. L., and Weinberger, N.M. (Eds.), *The neurobiology of learning and memory*[C] (pp. 65-88). New York: The Guilford Press.

Mishkin, M., & Petrie, H. L.(1984). Memories and habits: Some implications for the analysis of learning and retention[A]. In Squire, L.R., Butters, N. (Eds.), *Neuropsychology of memory*[C] (pp. 287-296), New York: The Guilford Press.

Moore, B. C. J. (1977). *Introduction to the psychology of hearing*[M]. New York: The MacMillan Press Ltd.

Mortimore, T. (2003). *Dyslexia and learning style*[M]. London: Whurr.

Munro, M. J., & Derwing, T. M. (1995). Processing time, accent and comprehensibility in the perception of foreign-accented speech[J]. *Language and Speech, 38*, 289-306

Murphy, K. R., & Davidshofer, C. O. (2005). *Psychological testing: Principles and applications*[M]. New Jersey: Prentice Hall.

Neisser, U. (1967). *Cognitive psychology*[M]. New York: Appleton-Century-croft.

Nelson, T. O. (1996). Consciousness and metacognition[J]. *American Psychologist, 51* (2), 102-116.

Neumann, O. (1984). Automatic processing: A review of recent findings and a plea for an old theory[A]. In W. Prinz & A. F. Sanders (Eds.), *Cognition and automatic processing*[C] (pp. 255-293). Berlin: Springer-Verlag.

Newman, A. J., Ullman, M. T., Pancheva, R., Waligura, D. L., &

Neville, H. J. (2007). An ERP study of regular and irregular English past tense inflection[J]. *Neuroimage, 34,* 435-445.

Ni, R.[倪蓉], 2004, 图示理论对英语听力教学的启示 [J]. 上海理工大学学报(社科版), 26(4):49-52。

Nolte, J. (1999). *The Human brain: An introduction to its functional anatomy*[M].(4th. ed.). R. Furn, St. Louis.

Oakley, D. A. (1983). The varieties of memory: A phylogenetic approach[A]. In A. Mayes (Eds.), *Memory in animals and humans*[C] *(pp.* 20-82). Cambridge, England: Van Nostrand Reinhold.

O'Connor, J. D. (1973). *Better English pronunciation*[M]. Cambridge: Cambridge University Press.

O'Keefe, D.J., Shepherd, G. J., & Streeter, T. (1982) Role category questionnaire measures of cognitive complexity: Reliability and comparability of alternative forms of central states[J]. *Speech Journal, 33,* 333-338.

O'Malley, J. M., Chamot, A. U., & Walker, C. (1987). Some applications of cognitive theory to second language acquisition[J]. *Studies in Second Language Acquisition, 9,* 287-306.

Ornstein, P. A. (1978). *Memory development in children*[M]. New Jersey: Erlbaum.

Oxford, R. L. (2006).Task-based language teaching and learning: An overview [J]. *Asian EFL Journal, 3* (8), 94-121.

Packard, M. G., Hirsh, R., & White, N. M. (1989). Differential effects of fornix and caudate nucleus lesions on two radial maze tasks: Evidence for multiple memory systems[J]. *Journal* of *Neuroscience, 9,* 1465-1472.

Packard, M.G., & McGaugh, J. L. (1996). Inactivation of hippocampus or caudate nucleus with lidocaine differentially affects expression of place and response learning[J]. *Neurobiology of Learning and Memory, 65,* 65-72.

Pawley, A., & Syder, F. (1983). Two puzzles for linguistic theory: nativelike selection and nativelike fluency[A]. In J. C. Richards and R. Schmidt (Eds.), *Language and communication*[C]. London: Longman.

Pervin, L.A. (1984). *Personality*[M]. New York: Wiley.

Phillips, S. M., & Sherwin, B. B. (1992). Effects of estrogen on memory function in surgically menopausal women[J]. *Psychoneuroendocrinology, 17*(5), 485-495.

Piaget, J. (1945). *Play, dreams, and imitation in childhood*[M]. New York: Norton.

Piaget, J. (1955). *The child's construction of reality*[M]. London: Routledge & Kegan Paul.

Piaget, J. (1985). *The equilibration of cognitive structures*[M]. Chicago: University of Chicago Press.

Pica, T., Kanagy, R., & Falodun, J. (1993). Choosing and using communication tasks for second language instruction[A]. In G. Crookes & S. M. Gass (Eds.), *Tasks and language learning: Integrating theory and practice*[C] (pp.9-34). Clevedon: Multilingual Matters.

Pinker, S. (1999). *Words and rules: the ingredients of language*[M]. New York: Basic Books.

Pinker, S., & Ullman, M. T. (2002). The past and future of the past tense[J]. *Trends in Cognitive Sciences, 6*(11), 456–463.

Poldrack, R. A., & Packard, M. G. (2003). Competition among multiple memory systems: Converging evidence from animal and human brain studies[J]. *Neuropsychologia, 41*(3), 245-251.

Poldrack, R. A., Temple, E., Protopapas, A., Nagarajan, S., Tallal, P., Merzenich, M., & Gabrieli, J. D. E. (2001). Relations between the neural bases of dynamic auditory processing and phonological processing: Evidence from fMRI[J]. *Journal of Cognitive Neuroscience, 13*(5), 687-697.

Posner, M. I. (1978). *Chronometric explorations of mind*[M].

Hillsdale, NJ: Erlbaum.

Prasada, S., & Pinker, S. (1993). Generalizations of regular and irregular morphology[J]. *Language and Cognitive Processes, 8*, 1-56.

Rauterberg, M. (1992). A method of a quantitative measurement of cognitive complexity[A]. In: G. van der Veer, M. Tauber, S. Bagnara, and M. Antalovits (Eds.), *Human-computer interaction: tasks and organization*[C](pp.295-307). Roma: CUD.

Rauterberg, M. (1993). AMME: an automatic mental model evaluation to analyze user behavior traced in a finite, discrete state space[J]. *Ergonomics, 36*(11), 1369-1380.

Reber, A. (1989). Implicit learning and tacit knowledge[J]. *Journal of Experimental Psychology: General, 118*, 219-235.

Rhoades, R.A., & Bell, D.R. (2008). *Medical physiology: Principles for clinical medicine*[M]. Lippincott Williams & Wilkins.

Rickford, J., Denton M., Wasow T., & Espinoza J. (1995). Syntactic variation and change in progress: Loss of the verbal coda in topic-restricting as far as constructions[J]. *Language, 71*(1), 102-131.

Riggenbach, H. (1991). Towards an understanding of fluency: A microanalysis of nonnative speaker conversation[J]. *Discourse Processes, 14*(4): 423-441.

Robinson, P. (1995). Attention, memory and the noticing hypothesis[J]. *Language Learning, 45*(2), 283-331.

Robinson, P. (1997). Generalizability and automaticity of second language learning under implicit, incidental, enhanced, and instructed conditions[J]. *Studies in Second Language Acquisition, 19*, 223-247.

Roediger, H. L. (1980). Memory metaphors in cognitive psychology[J]. *Memory & Cognition, 8*, 231-246.

Rothenberg, M. (1981). Acoustic interaction between the glottal source and the vocal tract[A]. In Stevens K. N. and Hinano M. (Eds.), *Vocal fold physiology*[C], (pp.305–328). Tokyo: University of Tokyo

Press.

Rumelhart, D E. (1980). Schemata: The building blocks of cognition[A]. In R. J. Spiro, B. C. Bruce, & W. F. Brewer (Eds.), *Theoretical issues in reading comprehension*[C](pp. 38-58). Hillsdale, NJ: Erlbaum.

Rumelhart, D. E. (1997). *The architecture of mind: A connectionist approach*[M]. Cambridge, MA: The MIT Press.

Rumelhart, D., & Norman, D. (1978). Accretion, tuning and restructuring: Three modes of learning[A]. In. J.W. Cotton & R. Klatzky (Eds.), *Semantic factors in cognition*[C]. Hillsdale, NJ: Erlbaum.

Ryle, G. (1949). *The concept of mind* [M]. London: Hutchinson.

Sanz, C. (2005). *Mind and context in adult second language acquisition: Methods, theory, and practice*[M]. Washington D.C.: Georgetown University.

Schacter, D. L. (1985). Multiple forms of memory in humans and animals[A]. In N. W. Weinberger, J. L. McGaugh, & G. Lynch (Eds.), *Memory systems of the brain: Animal and human cognitive processes*[C] (pp.351-379). New York: Guilford Press.

Schacter, D. L. (1987). Implicit memory: History and current status[J]. *Journal of Experimental Psychology: Learning, Memory, and Cognition,13*, 501-518.

Schacter, D. L., & Tulving, E. (1982). Memory, amnesia, and the episodic/semantic distinction[A]. In R. L. Isaacson & N. E. Spear (Eds.), *The expression of knowledge*[C] (pp. 33-65). New York: Plenum Press.

Schacter, D. L., & Tulving, E. (1994) (eds.). *Memory systems*[M]. Cambridge, MA: The MIT Press.

Schlaug, G. (2001). The brain of musicians: A model for functional and structural adaptation[J]. *Annals New York Academy of Sciences, 930*(1), 281-299.

Schmidt, R. (1990). The role of consciousness in second language learning[J]. *Applied Linguistics, 11*, 129-158.

Schmidt, R. (1994). Implicit learning and the cognitive unconscious: Of artificial grammars and SLA[A]. In N. Ellis (Eds.), *Implicit and explicit learning of languages* [C] (pp. 165-209). London: Academic Press.

Schneider, W., & Fisk, A. D. (1983). Attentional theory and mechanisms for skilled performance[A]. In R. A. Magill (Eds.), *Memory and control of action*[C] (pp. 119-143). New York: North-Holland Publishing Company.

Schourup, L. C. (1973). A cross-language study of vowel nasalization[J]. *Ohio State University Working Papers in Linguistics, 15*, 190-221.

Schraagen, J. M. C. (1993). How experts solve a novel problem in experimental design[J]. *Cognitive Science, 17*, 285-309.

Schuetze, U. (2002). *Speaking an L2: Second versus foreign language acquisition*[C]. Proceedings of the North West Linguistics Conference.

Shallert, D. L. (1982). The significance of knowledge: A synthesis of research related to schema theory[A]. In W. Otto, & S. White (Eds.), *Reading expository prose*[C] (pp. 13-48). New York: Academic press.

Sherry, D. F., & Schacter, D. L. (1987). The evolution of multiple memory systems[J]. *Psychological Review, 94*(4), 439-454.

Shi, Z. Y. (史正永), 2008, 隐性注意下英语搭配短时记忆效果研究——实验一:句中隐含搭配的短时记忆研究[J].外语研究, (4):46-51.

Shi, Z. Y., & Chen, K. S. (史正永,陈开顺), 2006, 内隐学习及其在外语学习中的作用[J].外语研究, 32-35.

Simon, H. A. (1974). How big is a chunk?[J]. *Science, 183*, 482-488.

Singleton, D. (2002). *The age factor in second language acquisition* (2nd ed.)[M]. Clevedon: Multilingual Matters.

Skehan, P. (1996). A framework for the implementation of task-based instruction [J]. *Applied Linguistics, 17*(1), 38-62.

Skehan, P. (1998). *A cognitive approach to language learning*[M]. New York: Oxford University Press.

Skehan, P., & Foster, P. (1997). Task type and task processing conditions as influences on foreign language performance[J]. *Language Teaching Research, 1*(3), 1-27.

Skehan, P., & Foster, P. (1999). The influence of task structure and processing conditions on narrative retelling[J]. *Language Learning, 49*, 93-120.

Skehan, P., & Foster, P. (2001). Cognition and tasks[A]. In P. Robinson (Ed.), *Cognition and second language instruction*[C] (pp. 183-205). New York: Cambridge University Press.

Solso, R.L., Maclin, M.K., & Maclin, O.H. (2005). *Cognitive psychology* (7th. ed.)[M]. Beijing: Peking University Press.

Song, D.S.(宋德生), 2002, 组块效应及其对外语教学的启示[J]. 外语与外语教学, (9):23-25.

Sorden, S. D (2005) A cognitive approach to instructional design for multimedia learning[J]. *Informing Science Journal,* 8, 263-279.

Sørensen, K. E., & Witter, M. P. (1983). Entorhinal efferents reach the caudato- putamen[J]. *Neuroscience Letters, 35,* 259-264.

Sperling, G. (1960). The information available in brief visual presentations[J]. *Psychological Monographs, 74*(11), 1-19.

Squire, L. R. (1982). The Neuropsychology of human memory[J]. *Annual Review of Neuroscience, 5,* 241-273.

Squire, L. F. (1987). *Memory and brain*[M]. New York: Oxford University Press.

Squire, L. F. (1992). Memory and the hippocampus: a synthesis from findings with rats, monkeys, and humans[J]. *Psychological Review, 99*(2), 195-231.

Squire, L. R. (1994). Declarative and nondeclarative memory: Multiple brain systems support learning and memory[A]. In D. Schacter &E. Tulving (Eds.), *Memory Systems*[C]. Cambridge, MA: MIT Press.

Squire, L.R., & Knowlton, B.J. (2000). The medial temporal lobe, the hippocampus, and the memory systems of the brain[A]. In M. Gazzaniga (Eds.), *The new cognitive neurosciences (2nd ed.)*[C]. Cambridge, MA: The MIT Press.

Stanley, W. B., Mathews, R. C., Buss, R. R., & Kotler-Cope, S. (1989). Insight without awareness: On the interaction of verbalization, instruction, and practice in a simulated process control task[J]. *Quarterly Journal of Experimental Psychology, 41,* 553-577.

Steinberg, D. D., & Sciarini, N.V. (2007). *An introduction to psycholinguistics*[M]. Beijing: World Publishing Corporation.

Stern, H. H. (1983). *Fundamental concepts of language teaching*[M]. New York: Oxford University Press.

Sternberg, R. J. (2006) .*Cognitive psychology*[M]. Beijing: China Light Industry Press.

Stilling, N. A., Weisler, S. E., Chase, C. H., Feubstein, M. H. Garfield, J. L., & Rissland, E. L. (1995). *Cognitive science: An introduction (2nd ed.)*[M]. Cambridge, MA: The MIT Press.

Swain, M. (1985). Communicative competence: some roles of comprehensible input and comprehensible output in its developments[A]. In S. Gass & S. Madden (Eds.), *Input in second language acquisition*[C]. Rowley Mass: Newbury House.

Swain, M. (1995) Three functions of output in second language learning[A]. In G. Cook & B. Seidlhofer (Eds.), *Principles and practice in the study of language*[C]. New York: Oxford University Press.

Tannen, D. (1989). *Talking voices: Repetition, dialogue and imagery in conversational discourse*[M]. Cambridge: Cambridge University Press.

Taylor, I., & Taylor, M. M. (1983). *The psychology of reading*[M]. New York: Academic Press.

Titze, I. R. (1994). *Principles of voice production*[M]. Englewood Cliffs, NJ: Prentice-Hall.

Tarone, E. (1977). Conscious communication strategies in interlanguage: A progress report[A]. In H. D. Brown, C. A. Yorio, & R. C. Crymes (Eds.), *On TESOL ,77* [C] (pp. 194-203). Washington D.C.: TESOL.

Towell, R., Hawkins, R., & Bazergui, N. (1996). The development of fluency in advanced learners of French[J]. *Applied Linguistics, 17*(1), 84-119.

Trudgill, P. (1978). *Sociolinguistic patterns in British English*[M]. London: Edward Arnold.

Tulving, E. (1972). Episodic and semantic memory[A]. In E. Tulving & W. Donaldson (Eds.), *Organization of memory*[C] (pp. 381-403). New York: Academic Press.

Tulving, E. (1983). *Elements of episodic memory*[M]. Oxford, England: Clarendon Press.

Tulving, E. (1984). Precise of elements of episodic memory[J]. *Behavioral and Brain Sciences, 7*, 223-268.

Tulving, E. (1985). How many memory systems are there?[J]. *American Psychologist, 40*, 385-398.

Tulving, E. (1987). Multiple memory systems and consciousness[J]. *Human Neurobiology, 6*, 67-80.

Tulving, E., & Schacter, D.L. (1990). Primary and human memory systems[J]. *Science, 247*, 301-306.

Turban, E., & Aronson, J. (1988). *Decision support systems and intelligent systems*[M]. Upper Saddle River, NJ: Prentice Hall, Inc.

Tzelgov, J. (1997). Specifying the relations between automaticity and consciousness: A theoretical note[J]. *Consciousness and Cognition,*

6, 441-451.

Tzelgov, J. (1999). Automaticity and processing without awareness[J]. *Psyche, 5*(3), 18-23.

Tzelgov, J., Henik, A., & Berger, J. (1992). Controlling Stroop effects by manipulating expectations for color words[J]. *Memory & Cognition, 20*, 727-735.

Ullman, M. T. (2001a). The declarative/procedural model of lexicon and grammar[J]. *Journal of Psycholinguistic Research, 30*(1), 37-69.

Ullman, M. T. (2001b). The neural basis of lexicon and grammar in first and second Language: The declarative/procedural models[J]. *Bilingualism: Language and Cognition, 4*(1), 105-122.

Ullman, M. T. (2001c). A neurocognitive perspective on language: The declarative/procedural model[J]. *Nature Reviews Neuroscience, 2*, 717-726.

Ullman, M. T.(2004).Contributions of neural memory circuits to language: The declarative/procedural model[J]. *Cognition, 92*, 231-270.

Ullman, M. T. (2005). A cognitive neurocognitive perspective on second language acquisition: The declarative/procedural model[A]. In C. Sanz, *Mind and context in adult second language acquisition: Methods, theory and practice*[C] (pp.141-178). Washington D.C.: Georgetown University Press.

Ullman, M. T., Corkin, S., Coppola, M., Hickok, G., Growdon, J. H., Koroshetz, W. J., & Pinker, S.(1997). A Neural dissociation within language: Evidence that the mental dictionary is part of declarative memory, and that grammatical rules are processed by the procedural system[J]. *Journal of Cognitive Neuroscience, 9*(2), 266-276.

Ullman, M. T., Estabrooke, I. V., Steinhauer, K., Brovetto, C., Pancheva, R., Ozawa, K., Mordecai, K., & Maki, P. (2002). Sex differences in the neurocognition of language[J]. *Brain and Language, 83*, 141-143.

Ullman, M. T., & Pierpont, E.I. (2005). Specific language impairment is not specific to language: The procedural deficit hypothesis[J].*Cortex, 41*, 399-433.

VanLehn, K. (1995). Cognitive skill acquisition[A]. In J. Spence, J. Darly & D.J. Foss (Eds.), *Annual review of psychology*[C] (Vol.47). Annual Reviews: Palo Alto, CA.

Vygotsky, L. S. (1961). *Thought and language*[M]. Cambridge, MA: The MIT Press.

Wagner, A.D., Schacter, D.L., Rotte, M., Koutstaal, W., Maril, A., Dale, A.M., Rosen, B. R., & Buckner, R. L. (1998). Building memories: remembering and forgetting of verbal experiences as predicted by brain activity[J]. *Science, 281*, 1188-1191.

Walton, K. D., Lieberman, D., Llinas, A., Begin, M., & Llinas, R. R. (1992). Identification of a critical period for motor development in neonatal rats[J]. *Neuroscience, 51*(4), 763-767.

Wang, D. C. et al. (王德春) 等, 2000, 神经语言学[M]. 上海: 上海外语教育出版社.

Wang, D. J.(王电建), 2008, 中国英语学习者交际策略使用类型的实证研究 [J]. 长春师范学院学报(人文社会科学版), (11):162-166.

Wang, Y.(王宇), 2009, 中国英语学习者自述故事中自我修正的研究 [M]. 苏州: 苏州大学出版社.

Wei, J. H. & Luo, Y. J. (魏景汉, 罗跃嘉), 2002, 认知事件相关脑电位教程[M]. 北京: 经济日报出版社.

Wei, N. X. (卫乃兴), 2004, 中国学习者英语口语语料库初始研究 [J]. 现代外语,(2): 140-149.

Wei, N. X. (卫乃兴), 2007, 中国学生英语口语的短语学特征研究—COLSEC语料库的词块证据分析[J]. 现代外语, (8):280-291.

Wei, N. X., & Wang, X. T. (卫乃兴, 王晓婷), 2005, 中国学生英语口语中的词块特征分析 [A]. 载杨惠中, 卫乃兴. 中国学习者英语口语语料库建设于研究 [C]. 上海: 上海外语教育出版社.

Weinter, R. (1995). The role of formulaic language in second language acquisition: A review[J]. *Applied Linguistics, 16*, 180-205.

Wen, Q. F., & Wang, L.F. (文秋芳, 王立非), 2004, 英语口语研究与测试[M]. 陕西师范大学出版社.

Whitaker, H. A. (1983). Towards a brain model of automatization: A short essay[A]. In R. A. Magill (Eds.), *Memory and control of action*[C] (pp.199-214). New York: North-Holland Publishing Company.

Willingham, D.B. (1998). A neuropsychological theory of motor skill learning[J]. *Psychological Review, 105*, 558-584.

Willingham, D. B., Nissen, M. J., & Bullemer, P. (1989). On the development of procedural knowledge[J]. *Journal of Experimental Psychology: Learning, Memory and Cognition, 15*, 1047-1060.

Winn, W., & Snyder, D. (2001). Mental representation[A]. *The Handbook of Research for Educational Communications and Technology* (Chapter 5)[C]. Bloomington, IN: The Association of Educational Communications and Technology.

Wray, A. (2000). Formulaic sequences in second language teaching: principle and practice[J]. *Applied Linguistics, 21* (4), 463-489.

Wray, A. (2002). *Formulaic language and the lexicon*[M]. Cambridge: Cambridge University Press.

Wray, A., & Perkins, M. (2000). The functions of formulaic language: an integrated model[J]. *Language & Communication, 20*(1), 1-28.

Wu, X. D. (吴旭东), 1999, 外语课堂环境下的口语非语言方面的发展[J]. 现代外语,(1): 1-13.

Wu, X. Q., &Wei, S. L. (吴先强, 韦斯林), 2009, 国外认知负荷理论与有效教学的研究进展及启示[J]. 全球教育展望, (2):28-31.

Xu, S. J.(徐式婧), 2009, 语言能力研究成果浅析[J]. 语文学刊,(4):21-23.

Xu, J. J., & Xu, Z. R. (许家金, 许宗瑞), 2007, 中国大学生英语

口语中的互动话语词块研究[J].外语与外语研究,39(6):437-443.

Yang, H. Z.(杨惠中), 1999, 大学英语口语考试的设计原则[J]. 外语界,(3):48-57.

Yang, H. Z., & Wei, N. X. (杨惠中,卫乃兴), 2005, 中国学习者英语口语语料库建设与研究[C].上海:上海外语教育出版社.

Yang, J., & Chen, H. (杨军,陈桦), 2005, 二语口语产出的韵律——与朗读相关的文献研究[J]. 外语研究,(5):46-50.

Yang, J., & Zhang, Y. X. (杨洁,张亚旭), 2007, 句子产生中的句法启动[J]. 心理科学进展, 15 (2):288-294.

Yang, X. M., & He, M. X. (杨先明,何明霞), 2007, 图示理论与口译记忆能力训练[J].上海翻译, (3): 42-44。

Yang, Z. L. (杨治良), 1991, 内隐记忆的初步实验研究[J]. 心理学报,(2):113-119.

Yong, H. M. (雍和明),1992, 系统功能语法与英语句法研究[J]. 外国语,(1):13-17.

Young, R., & Milanovic, M. (1992). Discourse validation in oral proficiency interviews [J]. *Studies in Second Language Acquisition, 14*, 403-424.

Yuan, P., & Guo, F. R.(原萍,郭粉绒), 2010, 语块与二语口语流利性的相关性研究[J]. 外国语,(1):54-62.

Zhang, H. (张辉), 2003, 熟语及其理解的认知语义学研究[M]. 北京军事谊文出版社.

Zhang H., & Ji, F.(张辉,季锋), 2008, 对熟语语义结构解释模式的探讨[J]. 外语与外语教学,(9):1-7.

Zhang, M. D., & Chen, X. S.(张明岛,陈兴时),1995,脑诱发电位学[M].上海:上海科技教育出版社.

Zhang, P.(张萍), 2009, 中国英语学习者心理词汇联想模式研究[M].南京:东南大学出版社.

Zhang, X. M., & Shu, H.(张学民,舒华), 2004, 实验心理学纲要[M].北京大学出版社.

Zhang, W. Z.(张文忠), 1999a, 第二语言口语流利性发展的理论模式[J]. 现代外语, (2): 202-207.

Zhang, W. Z. (张文忠), 1999b, 国外第二语言口语流利性研究现状[J].外语教学与研究, (2):41-48.

Zhang, W. Z.(张文忠), 2000, 第二语言口语流利性发展定性研究[J]. 现代外语,(3): 273-282.

Zhang, W. Z, & Wu, X. D. (张文忠,吴旭东), 2001, 第二语言口语流利性发展定量研究[J]. 现代外语,24(4):341-351.

Zhang, Y. X., Jiang, X. M., & Huang, Y. J. (张亚旭,蒋晓鸣,黄永静), 2007, 言语工作记忆、句子理解与句法依存关系加工[J].心理科学进展,15 (1): 22-28.

Zhang, Y. Y. (张玉英), 2008, 二语学习者预制词块识别能力与二语水平的关联性研究[J].外语界,(3):62-66.

Zhen, F. C. (甄凤超), 2009, "语块"与外语口语流利度、准确性及恰当性的相关研究---基于COLSEC语料库的实证研究[J].中国外语教育,(11):14-24.

Zhou, A. J. (周爱洁), 2002, 关于4/3/2活动对提高英语口语流利性影响的研究[J].外语教学,(5):72-83.

Zhou, A. J., & Zhang, C. (周爱洁,张弛), 2006, COOL EDIT PRO 软件在英语口语流利性测量中的应用[J]. 外语电化教学,(4): 67-70.

Zhou, D. D.(周丹丹), 2006, 输入与输出的频率效应研究[J],现代外语,(2):154-162.

Zhou, Y. (周艳), 2007, 正确认识语块促进英语教学[J].成都大学学报(教育科学), (1): 74-76.

Zhou, R. L., Guo, X. Y., &Ye, M. L. (周仁来,郭秀艳,叶茂林), 2008, 记忆的认知神经科学导论[M].北京师范大学出版社.

Zhou, X. (周侠), 2003, 大学英语学生口语障碍及教学对策研究[D].西北师范大学.

Zipf, G. K. (1972). *Human behavior and the principle of least effort: an introduction to human ecology*[M]. New York: Hafner.

Zhu, L., & Yang, Z. L. (朱磊, 杨治良), 2003, 多种记忆分类之研究[J]. 心理科学, 26(4): 694-697.

Zhu, Y. (朱滢), 2000, 实验心理学[M]. 北京大学出版社.

Zhu, F. Y., & Zhang, H. (朱风云, 张辉), 2007, 熟语语义的加工模式与其影响因素[J]. 外语研究, (4):8-15.

Zi, W. L. (訾韦力), 2004, 近年国内图式理论应用研究述评[J]. 中国农业大学学报, (3): 77-80.

Websites available:

http://www.answers.com

http://en.wikipedia.org/wiki

http://books.google.com.hk

http://www.memory-key.com/EverydayMemory/procfailures.htm

http://www.ageworks.com/course_demo/520/module3/module3.htm#padm

APPENDICES

Appendix 1   An Oral Task

Part 1   A greeting between the examiner and the examinee (2 minutes)

> Good afternoon, everybody. Could you please tell me your name and the number of your seat? Your name, please. And the number of your seat? ···Thank you.

> Now would you please briefly introduce yourself to me?

Part 2   Questions and answers (3 minutes)

> OK, now that we know each other we can do some group work. First of all, I'd like to ask you to say something about living in Nanjing.
> 1) Do you like living in Nanjing? Why or why not?
> 2) What do you think is the most serious challenge of living in Nanjing?
> 3) Where would you like to find a job after graduation, in a big city like Nanjing or Shanghai or in a small town? Why?

Part 3 Oral presentation (3 minutes)

Examiner: Now let's move on to something more specific. The topic for our discussion today is "**The Advantages and Disadvantages of the Internet**". You'll have 5 words/phrases listed in the following box. I'd like you to use the 5 given words/phrases in your presentation. You'll have one minute to prepare and two minutes to talk about the topic. Don't worry if I interrupt you at the end of the time limit.

[1 minute later] Now, would you please start?

The 5 given words/phrases are listed in the following box:

>   surf the internet
>   resources
>   be addicted to
>   time-consuming
>   in conclusion

Now, that's the end of the test. Thank you.

Appendix 2　全国大学英语四六口语考试（CET-SET）大纲

一、评分标准：

A．准确性：指考生的语音、语调以及所使用的语法和词汇的准确程度。

B．语言范围：指考生使用的词汇和语法结构的复杂程度和范围。

C．话语的长短：指考生对整个考试中的交际所作的贡献、讲话的多少。

D．连贯性：指考生有能力进行较长时间的、语言连贯性的发言。

E. 灵活性：指考生应付不同情景和话题的能力。
F. 适切性：指考生根据不同场合选用适当确切的语言的能力。

二、语言功能：

CET-SET考试要求考生参与不同形式的口头交际，其语言能力将根据其在考试中的表现予以测量。考生需掌握的语言功能和意念在《大学英语教学大纲》中已明确列出，如：友好往来（问候、介绍、告别、祝愿、感谢、道歉、提议、邀请、应答），相互交流（开始交谈、继续交谈、改变话题、停止交谈），态度（愿意、希望、意向、决心、责任、能力、允许、禁止、同意、否定、喜欢、偏爱、抱怨、判断），劝说（命令、建议、承诺、提醒），感情（焦虑、惊奇、兴趣），存在与否，空间描述（位置、方向、距离、运动），时间（时刻、时段、时间关系、频度、时序），发表意见和看法，争辩。

三、考试形式：

第一部分是考生和CET授权的主考进行交谈，采用问答的形式，约5分钟。

第二部分包括1.5分钟的考生个人发言和4.5分钟的小组讨论，约10分钟。

第三部分由主考再次提问以进一步确定考生的口头交际能力，约5分钟。

四、信息输入：

画面提示、文字提示。

五、标准描述：

5分：语法和词汇基本正确，表达中词汇丰富、语法结构较为复杂，允许有母语口音；能进行较长时间的、语言连贯的发言，允许偶尔的停顿；能自然、积极地参与讨论，总体上与语境、功能和目的相适应。

4分：语法和词汇有一定错误但不严重影响交际，词汇较丰富，发音尚可；发言连贯性但较短，组织思维和词语时频繁停顿，有时会影响交际；能积极参与讨论但有时不切题或不能与同组成员直接交流，总体基本适应语境、功能和目的。

3分：语法和词汇有错误，词汇不够丰富，语法结构较为简单，发音有缺陷；发言简短，经常出现停顿影响交际，但能基本完成任务；不能积极参与讨论，有时无法适应新话题或讨论内容的改变。

2分：上述各项均较差。

六、能力等级标准：

A+（14.5-15分）A（13.5-14.4分）能用英语就熟悉的题材进行口头交际，基本上没有困难。

B+（12.5-13.4分）B（11-12.4分）能用英语就熟悉的题材进行口头交际，虽有些困难，但不影响交际。

C+（9.5-10.9分）C（8-9.4分）能用英语就熟悉的题材进行简单的口头交际。

D（7.9分以下）尚不具有英语口头交际能力。

Appendix 3　Multiple Choices

Directions: Change the sentences into indirect speech and choose the best one.

1. "Let's go dancing," he said.
   A. He said let's go dancing.
   B. He said to let us go dancing.

C. He told us to go dancing.
D. He suggested going dancing.

2. He said to Kate, "How is your sister now?"
A. He said to Kate how her sister was then.
B. He asked Kate how is her sister now.
C. He asked Kate how her sister was now.
D. He asked Kate how her sister was then.

3. She asked me, "When do they have their dinner?"
A. She asked me when they had their dinner.
B. She asked me when do they have their dinner.
C. She asked me when did they have their dinner.
D. She asked me when they have their dinner.

4. "Practice makes perfect," the teacher told me.
A. The teacher told me practice made perfect.
B. The teacher told me practice makes perfect.
C. The teacher told me practice make perfect.
D. The teacher told me practice had made perfect.

5. "Where shall I buy the ticket?". he asked her.
A. He asked her where he shall the ticket.
B. He asked her where she would buy the ticket.
C. He asked her where he would buy the ticket.
D. He asked her where he should buy the ticket.

6. Jack said, "I'm going to London with my father."
A. Jack said that I'm going to London with my father.
B. Jack said that I was going to London with his father.

C. Jack said that he was going to London with my father.
D. Jack said that he was going to London with his father.

7. "How long have you been in China?" I asked George.
A. I asked George how long has he been in China.
B. I asked George how long had he been in China.
C. I asked George how long he has been in China.
D. I asked George how long he had been in China.

8. He said, "Mother, the boy is very naughty."
A. He said his mother that the boy was very naughty.
B. He said to his mother that the boy is very naughty.
C. He suggested his mother that the boy was very naughty.
D. He asked his mother that the boy was very naughty.

9. "You have submitted your paper, haven't you?" Helen asked Jim.
A. Helen asked Jim you has submitted your paper.
B. Helen asked Jim if he has submitted his paper.
C. Helen asked Jim if he submitted his paper.
D. Helen asked Jim if he had submitted his paper.

10. "Don't play football on the street, Tom," the teacher said.
A. The teacher told Tom not to play football on the street.
B. The teacher didn't say to Tom to play football on the street.
C. The teacher didn't tell Tom to play football on the street.
D. The teacher said to Tom to play football on the street not.

11. "Was your car stolen last week?" Xiao Ming asked Alice.
A. Xiao Ming asked Alice whether his car was stolen last week.
B. Xiao Ming asked Alice whether her car was stolen last week.

C. Xiao Ming asked Alice whether her car stole the week before.

D. Xiao Ming asked Alice whether her car had been stolen the week before.

12. "Clean the classroom after class today, Tom," said the monitor.
    A. The monitor said that Tom cleaned the classroom after class that day.
    B. The monitor told Tom to clean the classroom after class that day.
    C. The monitor said to Tom he clean the classroom after class that day.
    D. The monitor told Tom to clean the classroom after class today

13. "Will you go to the concert with me this evening?" Mary asked me.
    A. Mary asked me if I will go to the concert with her this evening.
    B. Mary asked me if I would go to the concert with her this evening.
    C. Mary asked me if she would go to the concert with me that evening.
    D. Mary asked me if I would go to the concert with her that evening.

14. "Are you sorry for what you have done?" the mother asked the naughty boy.
    A. The mother asked the naughty boy if he's sorry for what you have done.
    B. The mother asked the naughty boy if he was sorry for what you had done.
    C. The mother asked the naughty boy if he is sorry for what he has done.

D. The mother asked the naughty boy if he was sorry for what he had done.

15. "Do you remember what your aunt told you last night?" Jack's father asked him.
   A. Jack's father asked him if he remembered what his aunt had told him the night before.
   B. Jack's father asked him if he remembered what his aunt told him the night before.
   C. Jack's father asked him if he remembers what his aunt had told him last night.
   D. Jack's father asked him if he remembered what had his aunt told him the night before.

Appendix 4　CBE I: Listen, Judge and Speak & Listen and Repeat

Group A: Listen, Judge and Speak

Directions: Listen to the 20 sentences first. Then utter the revised sentence immediately if there are some mistakes in the sentence you heard OR repeat the sentence immediately if there are no mistakes in the sentence you heard.

1. She said why Jacky would be busy with his study.
2. *She asked him to bring her a cup of tea.*
3. His mother asked him what had he done the day before.
4. He suggested if they should go to see the film.
5. He asked me whether did I leave this book there.
6. *He began to think about what he should do.*

7. Tom asked me how long had I been in Nanjing.
8. *I've received the letter you sent to me three days ago.*
9. My father said the earth runs around the sun.
10. Jack asked John where is he going when he met him.

(Pause)

1. *He showed me the room where he drew his pictures.*
2. He told his mother that these books are his.
3. *I'd like to know when they will let him out.*
4. He told me whether my bike was stolen the night before.
5. *He invited Helen to attend their meeting yesterday afternoon.*
6. Peter said what I had better go there that day.
17. The geography teacher asked us to help him with that task.
18. His father told him to concentrate to Chinese calligraphy.
19. He said he had achieved the first place in the mathematics competition.
20. He asked whether had studied I geometry since I was a boy.

(**Note:** The sentences in italics are not about indirect speech. CBE I: Cognitive Behavioral Experiment One; **Keys:** See the scripts of Group Two: Listen and Repeat.).

Group Two: Listen and Repeat

Direction: Repeat the sentence you heard immediately.
1. She said Jacky would be busy with his study.
2. *She asked him to bring her a cup of tea.*
3. His mother asked him what he had done the day before.
4. He suggested that they should go to see the film.
5. He asked me whether I had left that book there.
6. *He began to think about what he should do.*

7. Tom asked me how long I had been in Nanjing.
8. *I've received the letter you sent to me three days ago.*
9. My teacher said the earth runs around the sun.
10. Jack asked John where he was going when he met him.

Pause

1. *He showed me the room where he drew his pictures.*
2. He told his mother that those books were his.
3. *I'd like to know when they will let him out.*
4. He asked me whether my bike was stolen the night before.
5. *He invited Helen to attend their meeting yesterday afternoon.*
6. Peter said that I had better go there that day.
7. The geography teacher asked *us to help him with that task.*
8. *His father told him to concentrate on Chinese calligraphy.*
9. He said he had achieved the first place in the mathematics competition.
10. He asked whether I had studied geometry since I was a boy.

(**Note:** The sentences in italics are not about indirect speech.)

Appendix 5　CBE II: Questions and Answers

Directions: Listen to the dialogues made in Chinese first. Then answer the questions you heard in English.

Dialogue 1:
M: 小明和小芳还没有来呢。
W: 他们今天上午不可能到达国际展览中心了。
Q: What did the woman say to the man?

Dialogue 2:
M: 这本书很有趣。
W: 汤姆,我明天在什么地方能买到这本书啊?
Q: What did the woman ask the man?

Dialogue 3:
M: 我现在没什么事可做。
W: Tom,你昨天就完成作业了,是不是啊?
Q: What did the woman ask the man?

Dialogue 4:
M: 我家住在新街口。
W: 你骑自行车还是乘公交车上学啊?
Q: What did the woman ask the man?

Dialogue 5:
M: 我觉得有点不舒服。
W: 赶紧去医院看病吧!
Q: What did the woman suggest the man?

Dialogue 6:
M: 我是1990年大学毕业的。
W: 我是1996年大学毕业的。
Q: What did the woman say to the man?

Possible Keys:
(1) The woman said that they couldn't arrive at/reach/get to the International Exhibition Center.

(2) The woman asked the man where she would buy that book the

next day.

(3) The woman asked the man whether he had finished his homework the day before.

(4) The woman asked the man whether he went to school by bike or by bus.

(5) The woman suggested the man going to see the doctor.

(6) The woman said to the man that she graduated in 1996.

(**Note**: CBE II: Cognitive Behavioral Experiment Two)

Appendix 6　Questionnaire

实验反馈及英语口语水平调查问卷

2010年1月9日

同学：你好！

　　本调查问卷是为更好地了解你刚刚完成的实验任务及英语口语水平状况，其反馈数据仅用于研究。你的回答将直接影响本调查所收集数据的可靠性。为此，我们真诚地希望你能如实填写/回答。该问卷不记名，答案不公开。我们对你的合作表示衷心的感谢！

　　请你在各题中选择符合/最接近自己情况的选项，并把每道题目的所选选项字母写下来。

Part One: Personal Information

　　1. 你的性别：_____
　　2. 你的年龄：_____
　　3. 你的专业：_____
　　4. 你学习英语的时间：_____
　　5. 你每天进行口语练习或交流的时间有：_____

Part Two: Attitudes towards English Speaking

6. 在当今社会中，你认为英语听、说、读、写这四个基本技能中，它们的重要程度依次为：

请按你认同的程度排列顺序（其中1为你认为最为重要的基本技能，2为你次重要的基本技能，依次类推）

1	2	3	4

A）听　　B）说　　C）读　　D）写

Part Three: Problems and Their Causes in Oral English

7. 你的口语产出中存在哪些方面的主要问题？（可以多选）

A) 发音的熟练度和准确度

B) 词汇和固定搭配的熟练度和准确度

C) 句法运用（如词序、时态、语态、句型变化等）熟练度和准确度

D) 交际策略得体性

8. 你认为以下几个语言单位相关的因素对你的口语产出影响的程度如何？并请按你认同的程度排列顺序（其中1为你最为认同的观点，2为你次认同的观点，依次类推）

1	2	3	4

A) 发音

B) 词汇

C) 固定搭配，语块，熟语等

D) 句法(如词序、时态、语态、结构、句型变化等)

9. 你认为影响英语口语提高的原因有哪些？并请按你认同的程度排列顺序（其中1为你最为认同的观点，2为你次认同的观点，依次类推）

1	2	3	4

　　A) 自身存在的问题。如羞于开口或惧怕出错的心理；练习口语不得法、主动性不强；对交际中的文化冲突束手无策
　　B) 语言环境不利。除了在英语课堂上，其他使用英语口语的环境非常少，因而学生很难有大量的'真枪实弹'的口语演练
　　C) 师资力量薄弱。主要表现在：口语教师人数较少，不能满足日益增加的研究生训练口语的要求；口语教师口语教学理论和实践水平缺乏
　　D) 学校重视程度不够。如口语课的课时量较少等

Part Four: Approaches to Improving Oral English

　　10. 你觉得如何加强某个语法现象（如本课题中的间接引语中宾语从句结构）的口语产出水平呢？并请按你认同的程度排列顺序（其中1为你最为认同的观点，2为你次认同的观点，依次类推）。

1	2	3	4

　　A) 重复练习，直到完全流利
　　B) 背诵词汇、语法、习惯用法、文章的段落等
　　C) 寻找并创造口语交流的机会，增加交流的次数
　　D) 观看或收听英语视频、音频节目，并模仿本族语人的口语

　　11. 请列举其他提高口语水平的有效途径。

Appendix 7 The E-prime Experiment: The Change of Sentence Patterns

Directions: Change the sentence patterns according to the requirements in the brackets.

1. Her mother bought her a book. (⟶ Passive voice)
2. He found his bike last night. (⟶ Passive voice)
3. My classmates gave me many good suggestions on the paper.
(⟶ Passive voice)
4. They are repairing my piano at the moment.
(⟶ Passive voice)
5. "We're going to study in Australia next month," they said.
(⟶ Indirect speech)
6. "I'm checking your home work now," his mother said.
(⟶ Indirect speech)
7. "Can you tell me how to get to the nearest restaurant?" the man asked the policeman. (⟶ Indirect speech)
8. "Where shall I get off to change to a No.3 bus?" he asked the conductor. (⟶ Indirect speech)
9. "How many factories have been built in your city?" he asked me.
(⟶ Indirect speech)
10. "What did Edison do to help the doctor operate on his mother?" The teacher asked. (⟶ Indirect speech)
11. "Go to the front at once!" the officer said to the soldiers.
(⟶ Indirect speech)
12. "Do you remember what your father told you last night?" She asked him. (⟶ Indirect speech)
13. "Let's go shopping." he said. (⟶ Indirect speech)
14. "How will you do this experiment tomorrow?" he asked.

15. "Where does your English teacher live, Mike?" he asked.
(⟶ Indirect speech)
16. "You have finished your homework, haven't you, George?" she asked. (⟶ Indirect speech)
17. The window of his room was brokeh by the boy.
(⟶ Active voice)
18. His advice was accepted by his teacher. (⟶ Active voice)
19. The task will be finished next week. (⟶ Active voice)
20. She has been invited to the party by them. (⟶ Active voice)

Appendix 8　The Tests and Training Plans for Jun

Items involved	Tasks involved
Test 1	1. An Interview. 2. The first oral test of Question and Answers followed by a retrospective interview. 3. The first oral test of The Change of Sentence Patterns followed by a retrospective interview.
The 8-week training plan	1. To spend at least one hour reading the 20 sentences used in Listen and Repeat. 2. To listen carefully to the MP3 sound file in which the 20 sentences used in Listen and Repeat could be heard and repeat each sentence. 3. To spend at least one hour practising reading the 20 sentences used in Listen and Repeat by changing the subjects, verbs, adverbials of each sentence. For example. The original sentence is "She said Jacky would be busy with his study." The subject should practice like: He said Jacky would be busy with his study. He said Mary would be busy with her study.

continued

Items involved	Tasks involved
The 8-week training plan	Mom said Jacky would be busy with his study. …… 4. To pay attention to the words or phrases that the subject has difficulties in pronouncing. If he is not certain about the pronunciations, he may ask the researcher for help. 5. To remember grammatical knowledge about indirect speech. 6. To report the training progress to the researcher regularly.
Test 2	1. The second oral test of Questions and Answers followed by a retrospective interview. 2. The second E-prime experiment with Change the Sentence Patterns followed by a retrospective interview.
The 4-week training plan	The researcher did not arrange any training plan for Jun.
Test 3	1. The third oral test of Question and Answers followed by a retrospective interview. 2. The third E-prime experiment with Change the Sentence Patterns followed by a retrospective interview.